## About this book

This collection of essays by leading feminist thinkers from the North and the South constitutes a major new attempt to reposition feminism within development studies.

Feminism's emphasis on social transformation makes it fundamental to development studies. Yet the relationship between the two disciplines has frequently been a troubled one. At present, the way in which many development institutions function often undermines feminist intent through bureaucratic structures and unequal power quotients. Moreover, the seeming intractability of inequalities and injustice in developing countries has presented feminists with some enormous challenges. Here, emphasizing the importance of a plurality of approaches, the authors argue for the importance of what 'feminisms' have to say to development.

Confronting the enormous challenges for feminisms in development studies, this book provides real hope for dialogue and exchange between feminisms and development.

## About the editors

*Andrea Cornwall* is Fellow of the Institute of Development Studies at the University of Sussex. Her work on gender includes ethnographic research and writing on gender identities and relationships, on men and masculinities, and on gender and participatory development. She is co-editor of *Dislocating Masculinity: Comparative Ethnographies* (with Nancy Lindisfarne, Routledge, 1994), *Realizing Rights: Transforming Sexual and Reproductive Wellbeing* (with Alice Welbourn, Zed Books, 2002) and editor of *Readings in Gender in Africa* (James Currey/Indiana University Press, 2004).

*Ann Whitehead* is Professor of Anthropology at the University of Sussex. A contributor to foundational debates on feminist engagement with development and on theorising gender, she has had a wide engagement with national and international feminist politics. She was co-founder of the first UK Masters course on Gender and Development at IDS and the University of Sussex in 1985. Building on research on agrarian transformation and changes in rural social and gender relations in Northern Ghana, her work addresses changing gender relations under the impact of economic processes and development policy discourses on gender and economic change.

*Elizabeth Harrison* is a Senior Lecturer in Anthropology at the University of Sussex. She has undertaken research in Southern Africa, Ethiopia, Sri Lanka and Bangladesh. Her research has focused on the anthropology of development, with a particular interest in understandings of gender and development from different positions in the development process. She has been co-director of the MA in Gender and Development at the University of Sussex over several years and is the co-author of *Whose Development? An Ethnography of Aid* (with Emma Crewe, Zed Books, 1998).

ANDREA CORNWALL, ELIZABETH HARRISON
& ANN WHITEHEAD | editors

# Feminisms in development

Contradictions, contestations and challenges

Zed Books

LONDON | NEW YORK

*Feminisms in development: contradictions, contestations and challenges* was first published in 2007 by Zed Books Ltd, 7 Cynthia Street, London N1 9JF, UK and Room 400, 175 Fifth Avenue, New York, NY 10010, USA

<www.zedbooks.co.uk>

Cover designed by Andrew Corbett
Set in Arnhem and Futura Bold by Ewan Smith, London
Index: <ed.emery@britishlibrary.net>
Printed and bound in Malta by Gutenberg Press Ltd

Distributed in the USA exclusively by Palgrave Macmillan, a division of St Martin's Press, LLC, 175 Fifth Avenue, New York, NY 10010.

A catalogue record for this book is available from the British Library.
US CIP data are available from the Library of Congress.

ISBN  1 84277 818 8 | 978 1 84277 818 0  hb
ISBN  1 84277 819 6 | 978 1 84277 819 7  pb

# Contents

## Part two: Institutionalizing gender in development

## Part three: Looking to the future: challenges for feminist engagement

# Acknowledgements

This book has its origins in a workshop entitled 'Gender Myths and Feminist Fables: Repositioning Gender in Development Policy and Practice' held at the Institute of Development Studies in Brighton, as part of a joint IDS and University of Sussex initiative, in July 2003. We would like to thank the Swedish Ministry of Foreign Affairs, the Swedish development cooperation agency Sida and the UK government's Department for International Development for funding this workshop and for supporting the publication of this book.

We incurred many debts in producing this book. We are very grateful to Julia Brown, Jenny Edwards and Kirsty Milward who worked tirelessly to organize the workshop on which it is based, and provided editorial support for the production of this volume. An initial collection of papers from the workshop was published in a special issue of the *IDS Bulletin* (Vol. 35, no. 4, 2004). We are grateful to the *IDS Bulletin* for permission to reprint a selection of articles, most of which have been extended and updated for publication in this collection. Lastly, we would like to thank our colleagues at IDS and the University of Sussex, for all their support.

# 1 | Introduction: feminisms in development: contradictions, contestations and challenges

ANDREA CORNWALL, ELIZABETH HARRISON
AND ANN WHITEHEAD

This book explores the contested relationship between feminisms and development and the challenges for reasserting feminist engagement with development as a political project. Its starting point is pluralist – there are feminisms, not feminism, and 'development' covers a multitude of theoretical and political stances and a wide diversity of practices. Our contributors represent some of this diversity. They include those who have been involved with key conceptual and political advances in analysis and policy, feminist 'champions' from within development organizations, and researchers and practitioners engaged in critical reflection on gender generalizations and their implications for policy and practice.

Most of the chapters in the book derive from a workshop held at the Institute of Development Studies, University of Sussex, in July 2003. Entitled 'Gender Myths and Feminist Fables: Repositioning Gender in Development Policy and Practice', this workshop was designed to encourage reflection and taking stock. It drew together people from across diverse sites of thinking and practice that constitute contemporary engagement with questions of gender in development. One widely shared perspective was the sobering recognition of the enormous gap between feminists' aspirations for social transformation and the limited, though important, gains that have been made.

Gender inequality has proven to be much more intractable than anticipated. In several arenas women's capabilities and quality of life have worsened, not improved; legislative reform is not matched by changes in political and economic realities to enable women to use new laws; gains in one sphere have produced new, detrimental forms of gender inequality; women everywhere are having to fight to get their voices heard, despite new emphases on democracy, voice and participation. At the same time, arguments made by feminist researchers have become denatured and depoliticized when taken up by development institutions. For many, what were once critical insights, the results of detailed research, have now become 'gender myths': essentialisms and generalizations, simplifying frameworks and simplistic slogans.

This introduction sets out three interconnected themes that our contributors explore to illuminate these disappointments. These are also reflected in the structure of the book. First, we highlight the struggle for interpretive power as a core element of feminist engagement with development. Moves from 'women' to 'gender' and the creation and critique of specific gender myths signal what has been a continual battle over interpretation – a battle that is embedded in a politics of engagement in which the initial power quotients are unequal. Second, we scrutinize how the way that development institutions function undermines feminist intent. Bureaucratic resistance plays a major role here, but the ways in which this takes place are complex, reflecting power both inside and outside of institutions. Lastly, we explore a major challenge in the project of repoliticizing feminism in gender and development; that of how to achieve solidarity across difference, because there is no simple 'us' in feminism, let alone a single diagnosis of either problems or their solutions. This is especially demanding in a context of shifting development policy preoccupations, changing aid modalities and ever more polarized geo-politics.

Thirty years of feminist engagement with development has led to the distinctive and plural field of inquiry and practice of gender and development. This field includes an institutionalized set of practices and discourses within development institutions which goes under the acronym GAD, but it is not confined to this. The wider field of gender and development also refers to the innovations in research, analysis and political strategies brought about by very diversely located researchers and activists. There has been no shortage of reflexive engagement within gender and development research, writing and activism (Kabeer 1994; Goetz 1997; Miller and Razavi 1998). The collection edited by Cecile Jackson and Ruth Pearson (1998), *Feminist Visions of Development*, critically reflected on changing orthodoxies, and on issues of positionality and representation. And a growing and increasingly sophisticated literature exists on the experience of gender mainstreaming (for example, Macdonald 2003; Rai 2003; Kabeer 2003; Prügl and Lustgarten 2005). This book engages with these debates through a particular lens, that of the narratives that gender and development has done much to popularize. It is situated firmly in the changing global context, in which new myths and struggles for interpretive power are emerging.

Feminists work towards social transformation and in doing so create new political spaces. The influence of forums such as DAWN (Development Alternatives with Women for a New Era) and AWID (Association for Women's Rights in Development), and the many international networks of researchers and activists, has been vitally important in stimulating debate and engagement on the challenges of redressing gender inequalities. The contributors to this collection provide several examples of critical struggles for voice, representation and resources through forums such as these. As new forms of political space, they have succeeded in lending visibility to demands for change, creating constituencies that span diverse contexts, and alliances between those working at different sites of development policy and practice. It is through them that many real gains have been made.

The project of social transformation demands not only activism but also engagement with the content and processes of international development policy – not least because, despite the failure of most states to meet the target of 0.7 per cent of Gross Domestic Product (GDP) for their aid budgets, spending in aid and loans has been rising in the last twenty-five years. For many very poor countries this now constitutes a major source of government revenue. A central element of that engagement has been the development and proliferation of the concept of 'gender mainstreaming', discussed in several chapters in this book.

Officially first adopted by the UN at the 1995 World Conference on Women in Beijing, gender mainstreaming was seen by many feminists as a response to the need more fully to 'integrate women' in development policy and practice. However, once adopted within development institutions, the practice of gender mainstreaming has led to further disappointments – as Gouws puts it: 'While the driving force around gender activism used to be women's experience, mainstreaming turns it into a technocratic category for redress that also suppresses the differences between women' (2005: 78). Arguably, the ready adoption of gender mainstreaming by development institutions may itself reflect the fact that working with a technocratic category may be a more attractive proposition than achieving gender justice.

Reflecting these themes, the book is structured as follows. Chapters in the first section explore the origins and status of some of the gender orthodoxies that have become embedded in gender and development advocacy and programming. Some interrogate particular axioms, locating them within struggles for interpretative power that shape policy processes and politics. Others explore how policy fields have been constructed in specific ways in particular places. They address the making and shaping of the language of 'gender' in development.

Part two turns its focus more directly on development institutions. Contributors examine the ways in which changing constructions of 'gender' have framed the objects of development and set the parameters for debate and intervention. Speaking from different locations within development organizations, contributors analyse the institutional dimensions of efforts

3

at gender transformation. Several look closely at how gender mainstreaming has affected progress towards gender equality and the power of the gender agenda within development institutions. Lastly, Part three moves beyond the often insular world of development institutions and debates to the social and political contexts in which development interventions are located. We consider issues emerging from the new frames through which development has come to be 'read' – such as the efflorescence of talk of 'rights', 'citizenship', 'inclusion' and 'democratization' in recent years. Contributors set feminist engagement with development on a broader geo-political terrain, capturing dilemmas, struggles and conquests, as well as new ambivalences and uncertainties.

## The struggle for interpretive power

The adoption of the language of 'gender' and of phrases associated with feminist activism to address women's subordination and gender inequality within gender and development policy and practice is a not entirely palatable fruit of a long-run struggle. In the course of it, lessons learnt from particular places have been turned into sloganized generalities: 'women are the poorest of the poor', 'women do most of the work in African agriculture', 'educating girls leads to economic development', and so on. Simplification, sloganization even, have been understood as necessary to get gender on to the development agenda. Some of these gender myths have provided extremely useful Trojan Horses to lever open debates and to mobilize support. Others have been deployed as a kind of catchy shorthand to capture the policy limelight, generating in their wake popular preconceptions that gain an axiomatic quality that becomes difficult to dislodge. Women appear in these slogans, fables and myths both as abject victims, the passive subjects of development's rescue, and as splendid heroines, whose unsung virtues and whose contributions to development need to be heeded.

The word 'myth' is often used as a synonym for 'not true'. In development writing, articles about 'myths' are often concerned with busting them, showing their falsity, enlightening readers to the 'facts'. Myths may be bolstered by what economists call 'stylized facts'; they may be nurtured with selective statistics, with case studies, with quotes, with vignettes. In using the term 'myth' here, our intention is not to join in the 'myth busting'. It is, rather, to inquire into how the stories about 'gender' have drawn on feminist research in ways that may be dissonant with the original intentions of the authors, or with the realities they describe. These stories are not necessarily based on untruth, nor on faulty data. They might well extrapolate from one setting to another, use partial and cautious findings to make incautious claims. But they may also be based on the soundest of fieldwork, the most scrupulously rigorous research design. This in itself has little bearing on whether or not they make suitable material for myth-making. What makes them 'myths' has nothing to do with what they tell us about the world. It is the *way* in which they encode the ways of that world in a form that resonates with the things that people would like to believe, that gives them the power to affect action (Sorel 1999).

Narratives advocating GAD have done a great deal within development institutions. They have facilitated the dedication of resources, the produc-tion of policy spaces, the creation of a cadre of professionals and a body of organizations of various kinds whose work is to deal with issues of gender. 'Discourse coalitions' (Hajer 1995) constructed around particular feminist insights (for example, that households are sites of conflict as well as cooperation; that women face a double burden of productive and reproductive work) have involved those working inside development insti-tutions and feminist activists and lobbyists, grassroots practitioners and feminist academics who do not. 'Gender' has been foundational, both as an organizing principle and a rallying call, for these discourse coalitions. This concept has been put to myriad uses in attempts to redefine and reshape development intervention. Researchers have used it to generate insights into the relational dimensions of planned intervention that development policy and practice had ignored. Activists and advocates have used it to frame a set of demands and to challenge, and reframe, assumptions.

In many ways, the generalizations that are now part of the currency of GAD therefore represent a success story. Originating in the discourses of a minority of politically motivated advocates, they are now taken for granted and espoused by people occupying many different spaces in a multitude of development institutions. But the extent of change in women's lives does not match this discursive landslide. The equation of women and poverty does not seem to have had much effect on reducing women's poverty. And all but the most stoic defenders of 'gender mainstreaming' would admit that for all the effort that has been poured into trying to make mainstream-ing work, many agencies would be hard pressed to boast much in the way of effects in terms of institutional policies and practices.

There has been an increasing sense among many involved in the femin-ist struggle to put 'gender' on the agenda in development institutions that the term itself has been effectively eviscerated of any of its original political intent. Represented to technocrats and policy-makers in the form of tools, frameworks and mechanisms, 'gender' became a buzzword in development frameworks in the 1990s. In more recent times, it has fallen from favour and has a jaded, dated feel to it. Diluted, denatured, depoliticized, included everywhere as an afterthought, 'gender' may have become something everyone who works for an aid organization knows that they are supposed to do something about. But quite what, and what would happen if they carried on ignoring it, is rarely pungent or urgent enough to distract the attention of many development bureaucrats and practitioners from business as usual. An aid bureaucrat from a bilateral agency considered by many to be one of the most progressive summed it up: 'when it comes to "gender", everyone sighs' (Cornwall, fieldnotes).

The term 'gender' initially offered sufficient scope, despite the potentially disparate meanings that different actors might give to it in practice, to bring them together in a transformative project to which all were able to subscribe. But despite tangible, material positive effects, when taken up and used by development institutions, 'gender' has clearly proved to be a double-edged sword. Why is this so? Making sense of these dynamics calls for a closer look at the ways in which development institutions make use of research, and at the politics of the policy process itself.

Development agencies are continually in search of clearly put, policy-friendly stories that tell them what the problem is and how it might be solved. Analysis of policy processes has recently focused on the 'framing, naming, numbering and coding' (Apthorpe 1996: 16) that underlies development policy, and on the way particular narratives come to be produced and reproduced in the process, sometimes in the face of glaringly contradictory evidence (Keeley and Scoones 2003; Mosse 2005). What this rich body of work highlights is the extent to which the use of particular representations of those whom development seeks to assist are worked into 'story-lines' that come not only to frame, but also to legitimize particular kinds of intervention and forms of knowledge (Hajer 1995; Keeley and Scoones 2003). Emery Roe's (1991) analysis of development policies as narratives offers important insights into this process. By framing development dilemmas in ways that invoke heroic interventions that rescue those in need and provide the means to a happy ending, policies imbue particular pathways for action with moral purpose. Yet while these narratives encode particular meanings of concepts like 'gender' or 'participation', other meanings come into play as policies are translated into practice; they may frame, but never completely contain, alternative interpretations.

The struggle over meaning occurs and has occurred in a constantly changing discursive landscape. Cecília Sardenberg's chapter provides a detailed analysis of the debates among feminists in different geographical contexts that gave rise to the adoption of 'gender'. The use of particular terminology may represent either depoliticization or repoliticization – which in turn has implications for policy. In Brazil, the concept of gender has been used in ways that fit the perspectives of competing institutions and individuals. This has often had the result of erasing its more radical implications and making women's interests less visible. Sardenberg argues that redefining and reclaiming the category women 'may be not only desirable and feasible, but also fundamental to granting greater visibility both to women as well as to the relevance of a gender perspective in development' (Sardenberg, this volume, p. 49).

Some of the most contested discursive terrain in today's development discourse is around 'women's empowerment'. As associations with collective action and more radical transformative agendas are sloughed away to make the notion palatable to the mainstream, 'empowerment' has been reduced from a complex process of self-realization, self-actualization and mobilization to demand change, to a simple act of transformation bestowed by a transfer of money and/or information. Srilatha Batliwala and Deepa Dhanraj's chapter shows the troubling convergence between certain ways of thinking and doing 'gender', and pervasive neo-liberal policy narratives that reduce the complex social and political processes that constitute empowerment to individualized 'choices'. They take the example of self-help groups in India, favoured for their association with 'empowerment', and suggest that they may not only have deepened the immiseration of poorer women, but that they have also deflected their energies away from other forms of engagement, not least the political.

Sylvia Chant offers another powerful example of the use of simple slogans to frame development intervention, analysing the widespread association of female-headed households with poverty. The story-line of the brave, suffering, female household head as poorest of the poor gains its mythical appeal for its capacity to galvanize action, precisely because her image is of someone who exists in a state of lack that development can remedy: lack of a man to look after her, of money to feed her children, of the possibility of a life beyond the everyday struggle to care for her family. As Chant shows, this association is based on some grain of truth: female household heads *may well be* poor. But the reasons for their poverty may less often be those contingently associated with the myth of the impoverished female head: that they have to cope without the male breadwinner who is the person responsible for the relative affluence of male-headed households – as if, of course, all male heads are breadwinners and that it takes a man to be a breadwinner of any substance. Chant argues that the myth of female-headed households as the poorest of the poor may not necessarily do women in this position a disservice: even if not *all* female heads are poor, there may be some net benefit to be gained from their pervasive representation as the poorest of the poor – not least

7

being the target of certain kinds of benefits. The myth of the female head in development narratives is relatively benign, after all: the very image of poverty, in soft focus, in stark contrast to the image of the feckless 'single mother' in northern policy narratives.

Where this analysis takes us is in highlighting the extent to which the struggle for interpretive power is waged through the juxtaposition of words and images in the production of these story-lines. Rosalind Eyben's chapter explores precisely this. It describes the period when the UK government's Overseas Development Administration (ODA, now Department for International Development, DFID) had just embarked upon producing what was to become a series of booklets about women in development. Her analysis charts how particular images and phrases came to be inserted in these booklets, and how they came to reflect incremental shifts in the framing of 'gender' and its salience within the development debates of the moment. In the process, she shows, certain ways of representing women came to be naturalized through the choice of photographs and emphases; shifting policy frames were encoded in iconic images that captured what advocates within the organization saw as the most salient entry points for change.

Other chapters contain less benign examples, telling cautionary tales about instrumentalism and the ambivalent benefits of alignment with discursive framings of mainstream development. If the struggle for interpretive power is one in which mythical images come to be deployed alongside other narrative devices to create room for manoeuvre or to open policy space from within development institutions and discourses, or enable those outside them to insert the thin end of the wedge to lever open such space, what happens when this struggle gives way to the wholesale stereotyping of gendered power relations? This is powerfully evoked in Everjoice Win's account of the use and abuse of the stereotype of the African woman, whose discursive position as perpetually poor, powerless and pregnant works to place African women in general as illiterate victims of national systems of resource distribution and disadvantage. They are, as a result, reduced to such abject positions, so lacking in agency and in such political and economic deficit, that only development can rescue them. Powerlessness described in this way by outsiders simply serves to reinforce it.

Yet, as Nandinee Bandyopadhyay's chapter shows, mobilizing to reclaim identities as agents from the most damning of stereotypes offers not only scope for change, but for hope. The coalition of Indian sex workers described by Bandyopadhyay succeeded in undermining deeply entrenched stereotypes about both sex work and trafficking in novel and challenging ways. This work involved providing channels for women's own ability to gain control both over their lives and over others' perceptions of them, particularly to move away from the situation in which sex workers are stigmatized and vilified. For them, carving out a space in the public arena is an important part of presenting alternative perspectives. They remind us that feminisms' struggles for interpretive power have changed language, have altered perceptions and have created new popular and analytical landscapes of meaning.

## Working within development institutions

Several contributors to this collection are preoccupied by the question of how 'doing gender' became something different from 'doing feminism', as Sardenberg puts it. One recurring theme is that of the ways in which the political project of gender and development has been reduced to a 'technical' fix: something that is ahistorical, apolitical and decontextualized and 'which leaves the prevailing and unequal power relations intact' (Mukhopadhyay, this volume, pp. 135–6). But how did the essentially political – and at the same time, deeply personal – issues of gender get rendered technical in ways that narrow, rather than widen, the scope for transformation? The chapters in Part two of the book focus particularly on the politics of institutional location – of what kind of institutions one is working in or for – and on the dilemmas of institutionalization. Among our contributors are several who reflect on their work within powerful international agencies, for example within bilateral donors or UN organizations that interface with multilateral donors. As feminists they have sought to make a place for new ideas and objectives in institutions whose organization, resource distribution, cultures and power relations are not of their own making. Together with other chapters, these accounts provide powerful reflections on the complex processes of making policy, and provide highly nuanced accounts of becoming a player at powerful tables. Running throughout this section of the book is a consciousness of the contradictions involved in seeking to bring about radical social change by engaging with those who hold the power and resources in international and national arenas.

Hilary Standing's chapter takes this as one of its main themes, and argues for the need to understand the mandates of different kinds of development institutions and actors in order to assess whether they should be held responsible for the social transformatory goals of feminism. She points out that the policy objectives of government ministries are centred on the services they are charged with delivering, such as health and education. Standing's chapter is an account of the perils of decontextualized and top–down gender mainstreaming. She poses a clear question: Why do we expect sectoral ministries to be the sites of the policy objectives of gender transformation? She suggests that many feminists have remained naïve about the nature of policy processes and institutional change.

Certainly, a linear approach to policy-making has tended to inform explicit attempts to change policies. Yet there is also a broad recognition, as Goetz (1997) pointed out, that what policy-makers and bureaucrats *want* to know will make for a very selective uptake of insights produced by feminist researchers or lobbied for by feminist advocates. In Standing's account, the slippage occurs when donors take a top-down approach to their partners and insist on gender mainstreaming, gender training and gender goals as part of the establishment of externally demanded gender commitments and gender credentials. Standing argues that gender interventions associated with externally imposed mainstreaming have become a stick with which to beat government bureaucrats.

Where 'gender' comes to be represented in the guise of approaches, tools, frameworks and mechanisms, these instruments become a substitute for deeper changes in objectives and outcomes. The fit between the worlds they describe and any actually existing relationships between women and men is often partial. This emerges in Prudence Woodford-Berger's powerful account of the ways in which particular readings of 'gender' come to form part of the representations of donor agencies, no matter how little their Eurocentric perspectives fit with the realities of women's and men's lived experiences and relationships in other cultural contexts. Maitrayee Mukhopadhyay and Ramya Subrahmanian describe the disjunctures and dissonances that have accompanied the mainstreaming agenda as it has taken shape. Mukhopadhyay asks how possible it is to enforce gender equity commitments if institutions do not have the promotion of gender rights or gender justice as their objective. Drawing on the instructive example of gender in education policy in Australia, Subrahmanian argues that it is necessary to get things right in many different political arenas to create the kind of synergy that will enable feminists working within government bureaucracies to be successful.

Gender and development has become another technical fix simultaneously with its professionalization and institutionalization. These processes of embedding loosen the link with feminism, at the same time as providing feminists with livelihoods, work and, indeed, identities. Commonplace aspects of feminists' experience of their working lives, such as insecure conditions of employment, dwindling research funding and barriers to promotion, all produce pressures for complicity with bureaucratic norms. These need to be acknowledged more openly. 'Complicity' may also arise from the understandable desire to get resources for progressive work and projects, when it is often essential to accept some of the objectives and framings of those who hold the purse strings. Making sense within or to these institutions, as well as to the multiple actors on whose cooperation the success of projects or other innovations depends, may, as Sardenberg suggests, involve recourse to the very notions that one might otherwise be at pains to avoid (see also Porter and Judd 1999). Yet it *is* still possible to find ways to work with gender that are congruent with transformational agendas. The chapters giving detailed accounts of how feminists have worked in different institutional sites contain some pointers as to how this can be done.

Anne-Marie Goetz and Joanne Sandler consider how bureaucracies respond to changing mandates through reflection on their work as gender equality advocates within UNIFEM, the UN fund for women. Their argument is a sobering one; that the problems facing UNIFEM in effecting change, and indeed in *even being listened to*, are a product of the fact that, 'When it comes to gender equality and women's rights, both the threat and the opportunities are low' (Goetz and Sandler, this volume, p. 166). Goetz and Sandler argue forcefully that, in accepting 'mainstreaming' as the way to address the challenges of women's rights, feminists have made an important error. They have underestimated both the ways in which bureaucratic logic disarms threats, and the fact that there is much more to being an advocate for gender equality than merely becoming a 'gender focal point'.

Feminists engaging with development in different parts of the world have very different experiences, which come from the ways in which their nations and regions are positioned, materially, politically and discursively. This is a point made particularly effectively by Amina Mama. Her chapter describes the difficult conditions in which feminists work on gender at the under-resourced universities of Africa. The largest department of gender/women's studies in the continent, the Gender and Women's Studies Department at Makerere University in Uganda, struggles with demands from competing constituencies; donors looking for training and quick-fix consultancies, the need to develop academic research, and the pressures of teaching over a thousand students.

In a powerful indictment of the development industry, Everjoice Win shows how difficult it is to exercise agency as an educated African feminist working as a policy advocate when the only African woman portrayed as having legitimate 'voice' is a grassroots woman, who is all too often represented in stereotypical ways as 'poor, powerless and pregnant'. Win's message is softened with humour but, together with that from Mama, these are telling accounts. They reveal the alienating and limited social, political and research identities available to African women in a world dominated

11

by development institutions and development discourses. Feeling fawned upon by the ways in which development actors and initiatives want them, and ignored because they are seen through distorting and rigid stereotypes, their accounts remind us of the power of labelling and the continuing importance of geo-political position.

'Gender' comes, with this, to be located in a broader terrain of contestation over the framing of development priorities and the politics of intervention by foreign governments and development agencies. This point is raised explicitly by Islah Jad, who explores the multilateral agencies' support for Arab women's non-governmental organizations (NGOs) within the context of the US- and UK-backed war of words, weapons and resources unleashed against particular Arab nations. This funding is touted as part of a broader project of support to 'bottom-up' democracy, but is also a form of increasing dependency on the West, which Jad argues is changing the character of women's mobilization. She accepts that the proliferating Arab women's NGOs may have a role to play: in advocating Arab rights in the international arena, providing services for certain groups, and developing policy and information bases. Her research suggests, however, that many of these NGOs have limited objectives, low membership and unaccountable directors. She contrasts them with local women's social movements whose mobilization in pursuit of gender justice roots the impetus for change in forms of engagement that go beyond projectized interventions and offer the prospect for more meaningful and lasting change.

## International feminism in troubling times

Gender and development originated in a particular era of feminist thinking that was embedded in the politics of the time. Revisiting feminist agendas and their relationship with development calls not only for taking stock of what has happened with gender in development, but also for a broader view that takes in the much-changed global setting. New global economic relations underpin several of the chapters. Maxine Molyneux's account of child-centred anti-poverty programmes in Brazil and Mexico explores the new politics of social policy in these changing times. In the programmes Molyneux describes, cash is paid to mothers on condition that they both ensure their children attend school and health clinics and fulfil other obligations, such as cleaning schools and clinics and promoting the programme. The net effect, she argues, may do little to trouble existing gender inequalities, serving to further entrench a division of labour that loads women with additional responsibilities.

Ruth Pearson's chapter places today's GAD debates about the relation between empowerment and work for women within an empirical context in which 'Being exploited by capital is the fate of virtually all women in today's global economy' (Pearson, this volume, p. 211). Arguing that increases in wages will not on their own make women either less poor or more powerful, Pearson urges minimum income, labour regulation and proper social policy as key feminist expectations from states, which should resource the collective provision of services and recognize women's reproductive responsibilities. However, this is in a context where increased formalization of the labour market, in both North and South, makes such provision doubly problematic. This informal employment is not a transitional phenomenon; Pearson argues that there is considerable statistical, empirical and analytical evidence to indicate its increased consolidation, both driven and supported by patterns of economic globalization.

Rethinking feminist engagement with development is, it becomes clear from the analyses in this volume, not simply a matter of thinking anew what 'gender' is, and of finding new ways to engage with development institutions. There is a more urgent need to explore a feminist response to the dark international political climate of the new millennium that could both respect and bridge difference. Deniz Kandiyoti's reflections on 'democratization' in Afghanistan and Iraq illustrate just how narrow the political space for international feminist solidarity work might be and the need for highly nuanced and contextual responses to support national and local women activists. The geo-political context she identifies is that of the new politics of armed democratization and regime change within in-aptly named failed states – those that are war torn, lack governance and whose political economies are based on illegal trade in drugs, arms or high-value commodities.

Along with Jad, Kandiyoti questions the effects of the good governance, democratization and women's rights 'trinity' at the core of international development policy for the new US-dominated regimes. Emphasizing that prospects for Afghani and Iraqi women depend on the outcomes at the national level of struggles over constitutional and citizenship rights, she suggests that 'the promise of democratic consolidation is itself compromised in contexts where security remains the key issue. An expansion of women's formal rights cannot be expected to translate into actual gains in the absence of security and the rule of law' (Kandiyoti, this volume, p. 197).

Echoing themes raised in Batliwala and Dhanraj's chapter, Molyneux also reflects on the troubling state of feminism in the context of a resurgence of ideologies, meta-narratives and the exercise of power from the right. She affirms a stronger sense of the value of feminisms in today's political climate, suggesting that excessive soul-searching about the value

13

of feminism as ideology, vision and form of organizing may be misplacing vital energy. Her assessment is based on a balanced and cautionary assessment of the 'data' on women's progress over the last half-century. Despite positive signs according to many standard indicators (education, access to political life, health), Molyneux notes important qualifications. Importantly, change in the private sphere remains slow, with the gender division of labour scarcely changing. Income gaps are still significant, and violence against women is apparently on the increase. As Goetz and Sandler note, though, the fact that up to 6 million women die of gender-related violence every three years still fails to generate the outrage that it deserves.

As Dzodzi Tsikata points out, when economic decisions are increasingly taken outside the effective control of the nation-state, it may be a strategic error to identify the state as the primary site of accountability that can deliver on rights. Tsikata's chapter records her profound misgivings concerning the adoption of rights language by UN agencies and international donors and lenders. She remarks on two coincidences: first, that the requirement by international agents that Southern governments guarantee more rights for their citizens coincides with their promotion of economic policies which restrict access to basic services; and second, that these requirements are being made at the same time as US and UK governments have denied their responsibility to international law to pursue the so-called 'war on terror' and are eroding their own citizens' civil and political rights and some women's rights.

Without understating the importance of rights and rights talk for feminists, Tsikata suggests that there is little reason to believe that top-down rights approaches will be any more likely to deliver gender justice than previous top-down approaches, especially given the great difficulty the majority of women have in accessing any forms of justice at all. A particularly important variable here is what scope for sovereign decisions is left after the effects of 'democratization' enforced by either arms or heavy aid dependency.

For others, however, rights-based approaches represent a considerable advance. As Mukhopadhyay argues, talking about rights privileges women's identities as *citizens*, rather than simply as mothers, wives and daughters (Lister 2003; Meer with Sever 2003). The language of rights lays claim to public space for women. After all, as Molyneux reminds us, women's movements in a number of continents have used the instruments of human rights as a basis for their struggles, countering a 'thin' utilitarian version of rights with a wider ethic of socio-economic justice to provide a new normative and analytic framework for fighting discrimination and injustice. For Win, rights talk has further implications: it requires a critical shift that 'would see us moving beyond our favourite African woman, to strategic engagements with those other women who not only need support, but who can be strategic allies and leaders in development' (Win, this volume, p. 85).

What would it take to make the kind of 'strategic engagements' that Everjoice Win calls for possible? Perhaps the most pressing task for feminist engagement with development in these troubling times, Kandiyoti reflects, is that of finding an 'appropriate politics of solidarity' (this volume, p. 192). Feminist engagement with development, we suggest here, has required the embrace of simplifications, in order to make strategic alliances and some inroads in the intensely political arena of policy-making. Reflecting years of effort to achieve gender justice and get new ways of working taken on by development agencies, contributors advance a diversity of critiques of how such simplified gender ideas have been understood and policies implemented, and provide different understandings of the way in which institutions influence outcomes, as well as different views of the pitfalls and compromises of political engagement. As Woodford-Berger argues, alliances are always made at some cost, because they are made with those who share some, but not all, political goals; and while many can agree on the need for such alliances, it is much more difficult to agree on the point at which compromise becomes defeat.

When do 'some costs' become costs that are just too great? Molyneux's chapter points to several commentaries that suggest that the transformative agenda has been 'neutralized where not excised', not because of technification or bureaucratization, but from 'a theoretical position that sees integration into or even negotiation with governments and international institutions as, *in itself*, an abandonment of the broader, "critical" and, at least implicitly, revolutionary goals of much second-wave feminism' (Molyneux, this volume, pp. 232–3). This book attempts to put clear water between GAD, as a particular form of gender and development practice and rhetoric, and the many different kinds of practices and discourses which make up the multiple field of feminist practice in gender and development. We argue that this is an essential move to repoliticize radical, feminist engagement with development.

The utility of certain ways of thinking about women's disprivilege – and the associated gender myths, feminist fables and stylized facts that have been used in different institutional and discursive contexts to promote or defend them – has become much clearer through the mixed successes and failures of feminisms in the last twenty years. Inevitably, the history of that period is also a history of debates, disputes and dialogues within feminism and between feminists. The struggle for interpretive power is not simply a struggle *against* and a struggle *for*, it is also a struggle *within*. By this we mean that the myths, stories and fables are also part of the discursive work feminists do to make sense of the world. Discourses are not just tactical, but are powerful forms of interpretation for ourselves as well as others. They enable feminists to act. The final lesson of this collection is that these feminist discourses and feminist actions are above all diverse, differentiated and themselves sites of contestation. We have shifted and changed our discourse and analysis in response to the histories of our own engagements with development and with each other and in plural sites and changing times. While we have learnt much from the experience of acting tactically in different discursive and policy arenas, we have also learned from trying to make sense of our own political and personal commitments, not only in the contested arenas of development institutions but also in the contested arenas of multiple and diverse feminisms. Forging appropriate forms of solidarity across difference has never been more important than in the precarious geo-political realities of today's world.

The meaning of 'gender' and the content of gender analysis and political and policy objectives *must* remain contested within feminism, at the same time that they *will* continue to be particular objects of contestation when applied and advocated within bureaucracies. Working within them, feminists are constantly frustrated when they come up against barriers to any exercise of power. The links that can be made with other feminists, locally, nationally and internationally, become vitally important. Advances in technology mean new forms of connectedness, from fast and independent communication with local political actors, to access to knowledge about movements and practices around the globe. The difference this has made for feminist engagement, from within and outside development institutions, is significant. For these strategic engagements to flourish, new forms of partnership are needed that are sensitive to the differences that have divided us and the dangers of the polarities that the very notion of development constructs. It is through finding new ways of working with difference, expanding the possibilities for building appropriate forms of solidarity to create new alliances for influence and action that bridge old divides, that feminist engagement with development can begin to meet some of the formidable challenges that we all now face.

## References

Apthorpe, R. (1996) 'Reading Development Policy and Policy Analysis: On Framing, Naming, Numbering and Coding', in R. Apthorpe and D. Gasper (eds), *Arguing Development Policy: Frames and Discourses* (London: Frank Cass), pp. 16–35.

Goetz, A. M. (1997) *Getting Institutions Right for Women in Development* (London: Zed Books).

Gouws, A. (2005) 'Shaping Women's Citizenship: Contesting the Boundaries of State and Discourse', in *(Un)thinking Citizenship: Feminist Debates in Contemporary South Africa* (Cape Town and Aldershot: UCT Press and Ashgate), pp. 71–90.

Hajer, M. (1995), *The Politics of Environmental Discourse: Ecological Modernization and the Policy Process* (Oxford: Clarendon Press).

Jackson, C. and R. Pearson (eds) (1998) *Feminist Visions of Development: Gender Analysis and Policy* (London: Routledge).

Kabeer, N. (2003) *Gender Mainstreaming in Poverty Eradication and the Millennium Development Goals: A Handbook for Policy-Makers and Other Stakeholders* (London: Commonwealth Secretariat and International Development Research Centre).

— (1994) *Reversed Realities: Gender Hierarchies in Development Thought* (London: Verso).

Keeley J. and I. Scoones (2003) *Understanding Environmental Policy Processses: Cases from Africa* (London: Earthscan).

Lister, R. (2003) *Citizenship: Feminist Perspectives* (Basingstoke: Palgrave Macmillan).

Macdonald, M. (2003) 'Gender Equality and Mainstreaming in the Policy and Practice of the UK Department For International Development (DFID): A Briefing from the UK Gender and Development Network' (London: UK Gender and Development Network).

Meer, S. with C. Sever (2003) 'Gender and Citizenship: Overview Report', *Gender and Citizenship Cutting Edge Pack* (Brighton: BRIDGE, Institute of Development Studies).

Miller, C. and S. Razavi (eds) (1998) *Missionaries and Mandarins: Feminist Engagement with Development Institutions* (London: Intermediate Technology Publications in association with United Nations Research Institute for Social Development).

Mosse, D. (2005) *Cultivating Development: An Ethnography of Aid Policy and Practice* (London: Pluto Press).

Porter, M. and E. Judd (1999) *Feminists Doing Development: A Practical Critique* (London: Zed Books).

Prügl, E. and A. Lustgarten (2005) 'Mainstreaming Gender in International Organizations', in J. Jaquette and G. Summerfield (eds), *Gender Equity in Development Theory and Practice: Institutions, Resources, and Mobilization* (Durham, NC and London: Duke University Press), pp. 53–70.

Rai, S. (2003) *Mainstreaming Gender, Democratizing the State? Institutional Mechanisms for the Advancement of Women* (Manchester: Manchester University Press).

Roe, E. (1991) 'Development Narratives, or Making the Best of Blueprint Development', *World Development*, Vol. 19, no. 4: 287–300.

Sorel, G. (1999) *Reflections on Violence* (1908) (Cambridge: Cambridge University Press).

ONE | **The struggle over interpretation**

(b) The struggle over interpretation

## 2 | Gender myths that instrumentalize women: a view from the Indian front line

SRILATHA BATLIWALA AND DEEPA DHANRAJ

Religious fundamentalism and neo-liberal economic reforms are converting poor grassroots women in India into both agents and instruments in a process of their own disempowerment. Though these forces are not necessarily acting in concert, they are none the less reconstructing both gender and other social power relations. While we have analysed this dynamic elsewhere (Dhanraj et al. 2002), in this chapter we examine certain gender myths[1] – or rather, myth complexes – that are being used to convert poor women into instruments of both neo-liberal and fundamentalist agendas in India. The operation of these myths is analysed in the context of a government-initiated rural poverty alleviation programme in southern India and the constitutionally-mandated reservation of seats for women in *panchayats* (local elected councils).

At the outset, we wish to emphasize that we do not offer this critical analysis as academic observers, or deny our own participation in these processes. Indeed, the choice of examples is guided, at least partly, by our own involvement, and that of many close colleagues. We have both been complicit, through our past roles in grassroots activism, feminist training and advocacy, in promoting various gender myths and feminist fables that we have only recently begun to recognize as such. Thus, it is not our intention to point fingers or place blame. This analysis has emerged from critical examination of our own as well as others' past assumptions and interventions. We believe this is an historic moment when all feminists – whether activists, policy advocates or researchers – must interrogate past assumptions and strategies, or risk becoming completely marginalized and/or instrumentalized by the forces of resurgent patriarchy, religious fundamentalism and unregulated neo-liberalism.

### Gender myth complex I

*Giving poor women access to economic resources – such as credit – leads to their overall empowerment* This myth arose out of successful feminist efforts to shift economic resources into women's hands, gain recognition for women's roles in household economies and support women's leadership in local development. Feminist efforts were rooted in empirical data and an understanding that economic power and access to productive resources would weaken traditional gender and social roles and empower poor women to demand further change. But as these strategies began to demonstrate the wisdom of investing in women's entrepreneurship, they were quickly converted into a new development mantra: poor women became a sound economic and political investment. At the international level, the World Bank, USAID, the UK Department for International Development (DFID) and other bilateral and private donors have embraced and enthusiastically promoted the new formula. At the national level, both central and state governments and rural banks have begun actively to promote self-help groups and women's savings and credit programmes through schemes such as the Development of Women and Childen in Rural Areas (DWCRA), the Indira Mahila Yojana and Swayamsidha. The creation of special directors for micro-credit within many provincial DWCRAs tells its own story.

The conceptual legerdemain achieved here is neatly summed up by Mary John. She observes that a nationwide study like Shramshakti (National Commission on Self-Employed Women and Women in the Informal Sector 1988) recorded an enormous amount of evidence of the incredible work burdens stoically borne by poor self-employed and informal-sector working women in India; but in the hands of neo-liberal advocates, 'these findings are no longer arguments about *exploitation* so much as proofs of *efficiency*' (John 2004: 247, emphasis in original). Poor women were gradually seen as harder working, easier to mobilize, more honest and better credit risks. They would selflessly work for the betterment of their entire families and communities, and were thus great poverty alleviation agents. Politically, they were soon imagined as loyal voters and excellent anti-corruption vigilantes. Obviously, many of these stereotypes were basically true. But the myth-making arose when qualities born out of women's struggle for survival were turned to political and economic ends, rather than the feminist commitment to their empowerment.

In India, one of the most high-profile propagators of this myth was the former Chief Minister of Andhra Pradesh state, Chandrababu Naidu. His affinity for hi-tech corporate management systems had earned him the epithet 'The CEO of Andhra Pradesh'. From 1999, his regime launched an economic restructuring project, and Naidu decided to use rural women as key instruments in his political strategy for staying in power. The restructuring project included a major poverty alleviation component to appease the mass of poorer rural voters, who were unlikely to benefit from the deregulation, improved investment incentives and removal of bureaucratic hurdles that facilitated the urban affluent classes. Naidu's *modus operandi* was to create government-owned NGOs (amusingly called 'GONGOs' in some quarters), administered by elite Indian civil servants. Naidu made it clear to both his party cadres and government functionaries that implementation of the anti-poverty programme would be *solely* through grassroots women's groups. In the Indian *realpolitik*, this signalled that the only political constituency he was interested in building was women, and he conflated women with 'poor', 'rural' and 'community'.

Thus it was that the largest poverty alleviation programme in the state focused entirely on rural women: the World Bank-funded District Poverty Initiatives Project (DPIP), with a budget of 26,000 million Indian rupees (US $553 million; UK £333 million) in twenty districts of the state. Headed by hand-picked officers of the elite Indian Administrative Service, the project began with the identification of all formations of women at the village level (self-help groups, *Mahila Mandals*, *Bhajan Mandalis*).[2] Simultaneously, NGOs were asked to conduct training for the women's groups in gender issues, income-generation activities, and financial skills such as accounting and bookkeeping.

Although the project was initially designed to enable the women's groups to determine and create local projects based on their own priorities (including building community assets such as drinking water pumps), it was rapidly reduced to distributing loans to individual women for income-generating activities. Very poor women soon fell through the net because they could not pay the weekly contribution required to retain membership of the self-help group. In a short while, only women with some stable earning capacity remained in the groups. The project also tried to improve women's access to and relations with markets. For instance, women who gathered and sold tamarind were often being swindled by middlemen who drove down purchase rates and used falsified weights and scales. An internet-based system was therefore introduced to check market rates on a daily basis, in order to give women more bargaining power. But many women could not exercise that power since they were heavily indebted to the buyers. The self-help group was simply not a powerful enough structure from which to challenge weights and measures or purchase prices, as a cooperative or trade union might have been – particularly since rights awareness and strengthening the capacity for collective struggle were not part of the organizing strategy for such groups.

The project's community organizers also began to press women to take multiple production loans; and the number of hours they were working increased dramatically – there was no other way to keep pace with their mounting debt. Older daughters had to pick up the slack by leaving school in order to perform the domestic subsistence tasks their mothers could no longer do. But if one converted their profits from all these enterprises into wages, not one of them was netting an income above the minimum daily wage. At a workshop on 'Rethinking Micro-Credit', held at the recent World Social Forum in Bombay, rural women from different parts of the country spoke passionately about their multiple debt burdens and how repayment had increased their workloads to inhumane levels. Yet, such projects continually cite these women as models of entrepreneurship – not surprising since the only indicator they use is monthly cash turnover. Meanwhile, men in project villages became sullen and resentful. Women handling so much money had become a source of humiliation; they neither understood nor acknowledged the women's onerous workload, or the debt trap. Thus, apart from being overworked and anxious about mounting interest and repayments, women had to deal with this growing hostility (and possibly violence) from men.

Far more problematic, however, was the assumption behind the project's strategy: that once money was handed over to women in the form of loans, they were responsible for improving their lot, and the state's role had ended. At the same time, this munificence would earn the ruling party rural women's allegiance, and secure its political future. The women's political agency has been reduced to the privilege of being agents, consumers and beneficiaries of state-controlled credit and micro-enterprise programmes, with no other resources for improving the condition of their daily lives. There are no investments, for example, in providing cooking fuel, water close to the home, or daycare for younger children, so that older daughters can go to school. Women are so preoccupied with earning income to repay loans that they have little time or energy to participate in other public affairs, or organize to address other issues.

Ironically, this is the same region of India that once saw massive participation by poor women in large-scale political movements (such as the armed struggle in Telengana, see Sanghatana 1989; Sen 2000: 24) for land, for minimum wages, in protests against the rise in prices of basic commodities, and against the sale of country liquor that beggared families while filling state coffers with revenue. How ironic that the women of this same region were converted into passive instruments of the regime's single-point anti-poverty programme, with little or no capacity to negotiate for a different agenda or approach.

It is no wonder, then, that Naidu's Telugu Desam party suffered a humiliating rout in the May 2004 state elections in Andhra Pradesh. Electoral data showed that both men and women from rural areas had voted almost *en masse* against his party, demonstrating a vehement rejection of his political strategy and policies. Clearly, the poor women of the region had reclaimed their political agency through the ballot box. Since then, the

DPIP continues to function, but in a very low-key way. The message sent by women (and men) has not been lost on other political parties, including Naidu's successors.

This kind of narrow approach is not unusual in credit-focused strategies. A decade ago, staff of BRAC, a Bangladeshi NGO famous for its very large-scale women-focused poverty alleviation programme, acknowledged the same in a review of the gender impact of their work:

> The evidence suggested that participation in BRAC's programs had strengthened women's economic roles and, to some extent, increased women's empowerment measured in terms of mobility, economic security, legal awareness, decision making and freedom from violence within the family. However, widely acknowledged among BRAC staff was the fact that the imperatives of credit delivery were eclipsing the objectives of social change. (Rao et al. 1999: 43)

Programmes to alleviate poverty are obviously rooted in ideological frameworks. The DPIP and the oppressive manner in which it was implemented demonstrate the heavy influence of the neo-liberal paradigm. It ensured that people (for which read women) participated in their economic upliftment in the most apolitical and disempowering way imaginable. As Lucy Taylor argues, the neo-liberal agenda requires the state to keep those 'who have not forgotten their politicised past ... busy and out of harm's way, distracted from wider political considerations and submerged within the minutiae of issues in their own backyard' (1996: 785).

The neo-liberal agenda, Taylor suggests, requires citizens to accept the reformed identity of the state as facilitator, not key agent, of social and individual betterment. It also demands the twin identities of citizen and individual – i.e. the active, socially responsible citizen and the active, socially responsible individual who is in charge of her own destiny. The neo-liberal rules for the new woman citizen, as evidenced in the Andhra Pradesh project, were quite clear: improve your household's economic condition, participate in local community development (if you have the time), help build and run local (apolitical) institutions like the self-help group; by then, you should have no political or physical energy left to challenge this paradigm. These rules sustain a sort of depoliticized activism at the local level – one that inherently does not build upward momentum. It is a matter for celebration that the women of Andhra Pradesh refused to be so diminished and instrumentalized.

Readers may wonder why we are so concerned about this attempt at depoliticizing poor women. Isn't it a good thing if poor women gain greater access to productive resources? The answer lies a few hundred kilometres away. It is the experience of Gujarat state, with some of the oldest and largest networks of women's credit and income-generation groups, that challenges such complaisance. It is here that totalitarian, fundamentalist, anti-poor ideologies and their Hindu cadres, largely undisturbed and unchallenged, have waged their violent politics at the grassroots level, culminating in the horrifying and organized carnage against the Muslim minority (the worst since the partition of India in 1947, with Muslim women being particularly targeted) of early 2002.

Despite extensive grassroots-level women's economic empowerment programmes, mostly operated by NGOs who claimed to promote a tolerant, unifying value system, neither Muslim nor Hindu members of these networks seem to have been aware of the approaching carnage, or brought up for discussion the vicious hate campaigns that had been afoot for at least a year before the pogroms (Khan 2002). In the very neighbourhoods in which these women lived, the aggressively fundamentalist Vishwa Hindu Parishad had been actively mobilizing other women into *Durga Vahinis* (women's militias), and providing arms training (to defend themselves against the insatiable sexual appetite of minority men). It seems incredible that none of this came to the attention of women in the micro-enterprise or self-employed groups that dot the state, or to the NGOs who organize them. Was this because, as in the BRAC case, they were so narrowly absorbed in their economic activities that they never sensed the political winds blowing through their very villages and neighbourhoods? Or was it because the discussion of larger politics was never included on weekly or monthly women's group meeting agendas?

What we are seeing is a troubling picture. On the one hand, the state and its international allies are promoting not just narrowly-conceived self-help programmes for poor rural and urban women, but a model of citizenship and participation that is highly instrumentalist, dissipating women's political agency. On the other, fundamentalist organizations and political parties are actively mobilizing women of all classes to advance their agendas. It is frightening indeed to contemplate the fact that, in India, the only force currently interested in empowering poor women as political actors is the Hindu fundamentalist movement.

### Gender myth complex II

*If women gain access to political power, they will opt for politics and policies that promote social and gender equality, peace and sustainable development. Thus, quotas or other methods of ensuring high proportions of women in elected bodies will transform these institutions. Women will alter the character of political culture and the practice of public power. It* is not hard to understand how this fable came into being (at some time in the 1970s, we think). Male domination of public power and politics had led to the destruction of life, humanity and the earth itself. Even in so-called 'liberal democracies', the notion of democracy itself had been reduced, as the late Claude Ake pointed out, to a minimalist version, where the main privilege enjoyed by citizens is that of some protection from state power (Ake 1996). As feminists from the North and South began to expand and deepen their understanding of the roots of gender discrimination, they argued that women's access to power and decision-making authority in the public realm was as critical to achieving gender equality as changing power relations in the private sphere of households (UN Beijing Declaration and Platform for Action, Strategic Objectives G.1 and G.2). Looking back, and again having been part of this process, we believe there were several implicit and explicit assumptions underlying this analysis, including:

- that the transformation of both the *position* and *condition* of women (Young 1988) – i.e. meeting both their practical and strategic needs – could only be achieved and sustained in macro terms through political change (facilitating policies, legislation and the protection and enforcement of women's rights)
- that women representatives in local, national and global political bodies would advance the cause of gender equality and women's rights and sustain the momentum for such change over time
- that a critical mass of women in political institutions would also initiate policies of development and international relations that would advance social and economic justice and peace, by fostering and promoting non-violent conflict resolution, sustainable and socially just development, access to and protection of the full body of human rights, and placing people and the environment above profits
- that a critical mass of women in political institutions would transform the very *nature of power* and the *practice of politics* through values of cooperation and collaboration, holding power in trusteeship (power on behalf of, not over) and acting with greater transparency, honesty and public accountability; in other words, there was a belief that women would *play politics* differently and *exercise power* accountably.

With the wisdom of hindsight, we can see how these assumptions reflected our then limited understanding of citizenship, and of how citizenship was constructed in not just gendered ways, but through other categories of social power. We assumed that citizenship was a fixed and bounded terrain, rather than that 'like power relations, citizenship rights are not fixed, but are objects of struggle to be defended, reinterpreted and extended' (Meer with Sever 2004: 2). We believed that once women had access to political power, they would act for greater justice and equity.

The push for getting women into politics became strong and visible in many parts of the developed and developing world by the mid-1970s. By the 1990s, several European countries, the USA, and developing countries such as India, the Philippines, South Africa, Uganda, Brazil, Chile, Mexico and many others had large numbers of women in their political parties and governing institutions at various levels. In some contexts – notably India and South Africa – 'pull' factors such as quota systems were used; in others, such as the USA and some parts of Western Europe, 'push' strategies (mainly pressure from women's movements) worked effectively to increase the number of women elected as representatives. Over time, feminist struggles to promote women's greater representation and participation in politics were picked up and encapsulated into modules and templates by international donor agencies and other institutions that began to promote the new 'good governance' agenda, particularly in the South.

It would be a grave disservice to thousands of courageous women to say that all the assumptions about their impact on public policy, politics and power have been belied. But the experience of the last two decades forces us to confront some troubling realities and recast our vision for transformation through political power. The most worrying phenomenon at the present time is that the expanding space for women in politics has been seized far more effectively by right-wing, conservative and fundamentalist parties and agendas. In the USA, for instance, while the Democrats boasted of having fielded the largest number of women candidates for both Congress and Senate, Republicans are rapidly closing the gap. Although American women have been more progressive voters (the 'gender gap' in US parlance), tending to vote for more liberal and progressive candidates and parties, this trend is gradually shifting. Christian fundamentalist groups, with their close affiliation to conservative political agendas, have successfully mobilized poor and middle-class grassroots American women voters in the Bible-belt and 'middle America', not the progressive movements or parties. In the 2004 US elections, in fact, fewer women voted for progressive John Kerry than had voted for Al Gore in the 2000 election. Conservative forces have polarized women and the general public by reshaping issues such as abortion rights, and focusing on the 'average' grassroots women the progressives have neglected or taken for granted.[3]

In South Asia, the mass mobilization of women by religious fundamentalists, including the fielding of women political candidates, is nothing short of frightening. In India, the extremist Vishwa Hindu Parishad has launched special training camps for young Hindu women to act as 'Protectors of the Faith', including training in the use of swords and other weapons. Muslim fundamentalists in neighbouring Pakistan and Bangladesh use very similar rhetoric to muster women's support. The Tamil Tigers in Sri Lanka had rallied Tamil women to their cause and even constructed an image of the *'Pudumai Pen'* or 'new woman', who would raise militant children and selflessly dedicate them to fight for the cause.

Let's look more closely at the Indian case to see how it challenges this gender myth. Fundamentalist organizing of women first became evident in the late 1980s when the media flashed images of thousands of Hindu women across the country joining the marches and the symbolic carrying of construction material to the Babri Masjid. This was the ancient mosque that was eventually destroyed by Hindu fundamentalist mobs in 1992, purportedly to rebuild the Ram temple that was allegedly destroyed when the mosque was built. The images of women's participation became more aggressive during the anti-Muslim riots in Bombay in 1993: hundreds of Hindu women made petrol bombs that their men then hurled on Muslim shanties. The pinnacle, however, was reached before, during and after the anti-Muslim pogroms in Gujarat state in early 2002, when thousands of Hindu women, both poor and middle class, actively supported the attackers, joined in the looting of Muslim shops, and marched in massive numbers in the political rallies and processions that were held in support of the state's fundamentalist regime. Before the 2004 Indian general elections, there were four women Chief Ministers of various Indian state governments, the highest number since Independence – and *all* of them were members of the ruling Hindu nationalist party, or its close allies.

To dismiss these phenomena simply as a result of false consciousness, or the instrumentalization of passive women by shrewd and sinister leaders, is a grave mistake. The defeat of the Hindu nationalist regime in the 2004 general elections was not by a wide margin, and should not cause complacency. Seen from close up, women's participation in these movements is far from passive or blind, but very much through their active agency. As we have argued elsewhere (Dhanraj et al. 2002), the fact is that fundamentalist movements have created a genuine *political space and role* for women. They have given them the possibility of being real political actors, an active sense of being architects of a momentous social and political project. Regrettably, this is something which none of the so-called 'progressive' forces has done on the same scale or with the same deadly sense of purpose – neither other political parties, nor the labour movement, nor radical social movements (including feminist women's movements). It is unfortunate but true that, currently, Hindu fundamentalists are the most effective and deliberate in deploying mass mobilization strategies, and have the most conscious programme of women's mobilization within them. And progressives, rather than waking up to this fact, continue to instrumentalize women as convenient, passive tools whenever a mass protest or event requires their presence!

Meanwhile, India boasts of over one million elected women in its village and town councils, about a quarter of whom are from the poorest communities. This is thanks to the passing of the 73rd Amendment to the Constitution of India – in which, incidentally, Indian feminists had little role. The amendment made it mandatory for 33 per cent of all positions in local councils to be reserved for women. There were also reservations for Dalit (scheduled/untouchable caste) and tribal people. This was brought about by well-intentioned Gandhian advocates and bureaucrats who envisaged a form of local governance and decentralization that would transform rural India, a social revolution that could redress centuries of marginalization for both Dalits and women, orchestrated by the state.

The discourse on the impact of this unprecedented structural change, the largest-scale experiment of its kind anywhere in the world, is banal at best. It is also quite polarized, between gloomy stories of women representatives' subordination, cooption or subversion on the one side, and cheering protagonists on the other, who dismiss criticism or any analysis that is less than laudatory. Both positions are often derived from anecdotal evidence and ideological positions, rather than a serious inquiry into what is happening on the ground. There are, of course, some large-scale and highly quantitative studies, but these fail to capture many of the complexities and nuances of the reality. They tell us little about what this change has meant for elected women and men from poor castes and communities, how they are negotiating their new roles, or about the nature of grassroots political culture and dynamics.

What we have witnessed on the ground – as documented in Dhanraj's film *Taking Office* – is a complex picture, where both patriarchal and feudal/semi-feudal gender and social power relations are being simultaneously challenged, changed, accommodated and modified. A landless Dalit woman labourer is elected to and becomes the chairperson of a village council in which her upper-caste landlord (or his wife) is also an elected member. Dalit, tribal, other oppressed caste and minority women and men elected representatives have to negotiate a vast and dangerous minefield of religion, class and caste politics, patronage networks and affiliations, while the social and economic bases of their lives outside the *panchayat* remain unchanged. We know of elected women who have been placed under virtual house arrest for attempting to challenge budget allocations;

they have been beaten up, threatened, bribed and cajoled into supporting dominant caste or class agendas in the councils.

On the other hand, we know many hundreds of women who have triumphed amazingly over these odds and managed to deliver needed resources to their constituency. Indeed, most of the elected women with whom we have interacted are far from passive puppets. They show remarkable resilience in repeatedly trying to exercise their agency, to fulfil their responsibilities, to flex their political muscles, or simply to function autonomously. The problem, we find, is that since most women have entered these institutions without any kind of political or ideological training, skills or experience – they have not been members of a political party or cadre, for example, or have only the limited apolitical experience of their participation in a village self-help group – they are forced to learn and acquire these skills in the most arduous ways and at great cost. We have seen women devote all their time and energy simply to learn how to steer through the maze. But far too many fall victim to their inexperience and the pressure to become corrupt or expedient.

A major handicap is that these women struggle in the absence of any alternative models of power. As Anne-Marie Goetz (2003: 3, 5–6) points out, their images of leadership and experience of the exercise of power are gained within the family/household, from the feudal and caste-based social and economic structures they live in, and the few state and non-state institutions they have interacted with in their lives: schools, local government officers, and maybe rural NGOs and development organizations. None of these is exactly a model of alternative politics, much less an innovative practitioner of power. Feminist activists have attempted to create these alternatives in a few locations – but more often, women's groups are quick to stigmatize these elected leaders for becoming coopted or corrupted by the dominant political culture, rather than supporting them to create an alternative. Apart from celebrated examples – Indira Gandhi, Benazir Bhutto, Margaret Thatcher, Jayalalitha – there are growing numbers of 'Women with Moustaches', as Latin American feminists have called them, in politics at all levels today: hard-nosed, tough, aggressive and sometimes corrupt women politicians. We believe it is much too simplistic to dismiss this as the result of male consciousness masquerading in female bodies. Nevertheless, in a country like India, there are very few successful elected women to serve as mentors or models.

## Conclusion

The above analysis of the operation of two major gender myths seems to suggest that a larger project is at work in India – one that is constructing and then utilizing women as particular types of social, economic and political citizens.

On the economic front, the myth of women as the most effective anti-poverty agents and the mass-scale creation of women's self-help groups seems to be nurturing a form of depoliticized collective action that is completely non-threatening to the power structure and political order. These groups, forced to focus all their energies on their productive activities, their loan repayments and the survival of their collective, seem to be rendered oblivious to the ideological/political mobilizations going on under their very noses. Lucy Taylor's analysis of the reinterpretation of civil society and citizenship in Chile in the dictatorship and post-dictatorship years, where the 'twin strategies of incorporation and marginalization' (1996: 780) were used, demonstrates not only how self-help groups were the policy instruments of this agenda, but that this strategy is not unique to India.

We are not suggesting that economic empowerment programmes for women are either disempowering or unmitigated failures. The successes of micro-credit for women are well documented (see ILO 1998) and there is little purpose in raising yet another paean to them here. Our purpose, rather, is to highlight the manner in which such interventions are being designed and delivered in increasingly disempowering ways, instrumentalizing poor women, and being distorted to serve other agendas.

On the political front, far from women transforming politics, evidence of the reverse is mounting. Particularly disturbing is the way in which fundamentalist parties have fostered women's political participation to advance their agenda. At the grassroots level, we are witnessing both this kind of instrumentalization and the marginalization of women elected representatives in multiple ways, in a manner very similar to what is happening in other parts of the world (Goetz and Hassim 2003). As one analysis puts it, 'the system of representation that gives women "*authority*" through holding an elective post has not transformed into actual "*power*"' (Vijaylakshmi and Chandrasekhar 2001).

What is clear, however, is that the myths regarding women's capacity to transform both politics and public power have been central to all these processes. We clearly underestimated the power of existing modes of power and politics to corrupt, coopt, or marginalize women, or how it would compel or manipulate them to compromise their goals for narrow party interests. And we failed to address the possibility that women would be proponents of reactionary, sexist, racist, elitist or fundamentalist ideologies.

Thus, if we combine the mobilizations of women by the fundamentalist agenda, the depoliticized forms of collective action promoted by state-sponsored micro-credit programmes, and the subversion of the agency of elected women in *panchayats*, what emerges is a deeply problematic and bounded construct of women's citizenship – a construct that must be seriously analysed, challenged and reframed.

But this is also a serious learning moment for feminists. We are clearly at an historic juncture where the marginalization of feminist critiques and corporatization of feminist strategies forces us to recast our analyses and approaches. This cannot be achieved without looking closely at what is happening to women on the ground. Using the lens of gender myths helps us unearth the deeper, more fundamental processes of restructuring power and politics that are afoot – the ways in which resurgent patriarchy, neo-liberal economics and fundamentalism are combining to construct a new kind of female citizen. The challenge now is to move towards more nuanced and contextualized approaches that can, it is hoped, begin to confront and contain these formidable forces.

## Notes

1 For the purpose of this chapter, we are treating gender myths as the 'feminist insights [that] become mythologised as they become development orthodoxy', and feminist fables as assumptions and analyses that informed strategies advanced by feminists themselves. Some of the most problematic of today's gender myths are not single ideas but a web of interlinking beliefs and views.

2 These are women's clubs and the equivalent of Western choral societies.

3 It was interesting to note, for example, that African American women were the single largest constituency opposed to the war on Iraq, yet have never been significantly mobilized by any progressive movement in the USA after the civil rights era.

## References

Ake, C. (1996) 'Mistaken Identities: How Misconceptions of Relations Between Democracy, Civil Society and Governance Devalue Democracy', keynote paper for the International Workshop on Government, Getulio Vargas Institute, São Paolo, Brazil, November.

Center for American Women in Politics (2004) *Advisory, the Gender Gap and the 2004 Women's Vote: Setting the Record Straight* (New Brunswick, NJ: Center for American Women in Politics, Rutgers University), <www.cawp.rutgers.edu/Facts/Elections/GenderGapAdvisory04.pdf>, accessed 29 January 2006.

Dhanraj, D., G. Misra and S. Batliwala (2002) 'The Future of Women's Rights: An Action Framework for South Asia', in J. Kerr et al. (eds), *The Future of Women's Rights – Global Visions and Strategies* (London: Zed Books), pp. 80–96.

Goetz, A. M. (2003) 'Political Cleaners: How Women are the New Anti-

Corruption Force', paper presented at the conference 'Gender Myths and Feminist Fables: Repositioning Gender in Development Policy and Practice', Institute of Development Studies, Brighton, 2–4 July.

Goetz, A. M. and S. Hassim (2003) *No Shortcuts to Power: African Women in Politics and Policy Making* (London: Zed Books).

ILO (1998) 'Women in the Informal Sector and Their Access to Microfinance', paper prepared by ILO for the Inter-Parliamentary Union (IPU) Annual Conference, Windhoek, Namibia, 2–11 April.

John, M. (2004) 'Gender and Development in India, 1970–90s', in M. Chaudhuri (ed.), *Feminism in India* (New Delhi: Kali for Women and Women Unlimited).

Khan, Z.-I. (2002) 'New Evidence that Gujarat Pogroms were Preplanned', <www.milligate.com/Archives/01112002/0111200291.htm>, accessed 13 November 2003.

Meer, S. with C. Sever (2004) 'Gender and Citizenship: Overview Report', *Bridge Pack on Gender and Citizenship* (Brighton: Institute of Development Studies).

National Commission on Self-Employed Women and Women in the Informal Sector (1988) *Shramshakti* (Delhi: Government of India, Ministry of Human Resource Development).

Rao, A., R. Stuart and D. Kelleher (1999) 'Building Gender Capital at BRAC: A Case Study', in A. Rao, R. Stuart and D. Kelleher (eds), *Gender at Work – Organizational Change for Equality* (Connecticut: Kumarian Press).

Sanghatana, S. (1989) *We were Making History – Life Stories of Women in the Telengana Struggle* (New Delhi: Kali for Women).

Sen, S. (2000) 'Toward a Feminist Politics? The Indian Women's Movement in Historical Perspective', *World Bank Policy Research Report on Gender and Development, Working Paper Series* 9 (Washington, DC: World Bank).

Taylor, L. (1996) 'Civilising Civil Society: Distracting Popular Participation from Politics Itself', in *Contemporary Political Studies*, Proceedings of the Annual Conference, University of Glasgow, Political Studies Association, pp. 778–85. <www.psa.ac.uk/cps/1996.htm>, accessed 7 November 2003.

Vijaylakshmi, V. and B. K. Chandrasekhar (2001) *Authority, Powerlessness and Dependence: Women and Local Governance in Karnataka* (Bangalore: Institute of Social and Economic Change).

Young, K. (1988) *Gender and Development: A Relational View* (Oxford: Oxford University Press).

# 3 | Dangerous equations? How female-headed households became the poorest of the poor: causes, consequences and cautions

SYLVIA CHANT

The idea that women bear a disproportionate and growing burden of poverty at a global scale, often encapsulated in the concept of a 'feminization of poverty', has become a virtual orthodoxy in recent decades, despite the dearth of reliable data on poverty, let alone its gender dimensions (Moghadam 1997). Yet this has not dissuaded a large segment of the development community, including international agencies, from asserting that 60–70 per cent of the world's poor are female, and that tendencies to greater poverty among women are deepening. In broader work on poverty, and especially in policy circles, the poverty of female-headed households has effectively become a proxy for women's poverty, if not poverty in general, a set of 'dangerous equations' which have been increasingly challenged (Chant 1997, 2003; Jackson 1996; Kabeer 1996).

The fact that female-headed households are a 'visible and readily identifiable group in income poverty statistics' (Kabeer 1996: 14) provides fuel for a range of political agendas. In one respect, it serves neo-liberal enthusiasm for efficiency-driven targeting of poverty reduction measures to 'exceptionally' disaffected parties. In another vein, highlighting the disadvantage of female-headed households has also catered to Gender and Development (GAD) interests by providing an apparently robust tactical peg on which to hang justification for allocating resources to women (Chant 2003; Jackson 1996).

This chapter explores some of the tensions emanating from growing equivocation over the links between female household headship and poverty. Setting out the principal reasons why women-headed households have traditionally been regarded (and portrayed) as the 'poorest of the poor', the chapter examines evidence that has been used to support or challenge this orthodoxy. It then proceeds to focus on social and policy implications, from the problems of targeting to the need to maintain high visibility of gender in the face of shrinking resources for development and/or social assistance. The chapter concludes with reflection on the potential outcomes of surrendering a conventional wisdom that has undoubtedly helped to harness resources for women.

## How women-headed households became the 'poorest of the poor'

*Key rationales* In the last ten to fifteen years, pronouncements about women-headed households being the 'poorest of the poor' have proliferated in writings on gender (see Chant 2003 for examples). Often made without direct reference to empirical data, the assumption in such statements that women-headed households face an above-average risk of poverty is by no means groundless. Indeed, there are persuasive reasons why we might expect a group disadvantaged by their gender to be further disadvantaged by allegedly 'incomplete' or 'under-resourced' household arrangements. This is especially so, given the assumption that female household headship is prone to arise in situations of economic privation and insecurity.

The factors responsible for the 'feminization of poverty' have been linked with gender disparities in rights, entitlements and capabilities, the gender-differentiated impacts of neo-liberal restructuring, the informalization and feminization of labour, and the erosion of kin-based support networks through migration, conflict and so on. However, a primary tenet has been the mounting incidence of female household headship, and in some circles the 'culture of single motherhood' has been designated the 'New Poverty Paradigm' (Thomas 1994). The links so frequently drawn between the 'feminization of poverty' and household headship derive from the idea that women-headed households constitute a disproportionate number of the poor, and that they experience greater extremes of poverty than male-headed units. An additional element, commonly referred to as an 'intergenerational transmission of disadvantage', is that the privation of female household heads is passed on to their children (Chant 1997), purportedly because female heads cannot 'properly support their families or ensure their well-being' (Mehra et al. 2000: 7).

Moghadam's (1997) extensive review of the 'feminization of poverty' identifies three main reasons which, *prima facie*, are likely to make women poorer than men. These are, first, women's poverty-inducing disadvantage in respect of entitlements and capabilities; second, their heavier work burdens and lower earnings; and, third, constraints on socio-economic mobility due to cultural, legal and labour market barriers. Lone mother units are often assumed to be worse off than two-parent households because in lacking a 'breadwinning' partner they are not only deprived of an adult male's earnings, but have relatively more dependants to support. On the one hand, female heads are conjectured to have less time and energy to conserve resources, such as by shopping around for the cheapest foodstuffs. On the other, women's 'reproduction tax' (Palmer 1992) cuts heavily into economic productivity, with lone mothers often confined to part-time, flexible and/or home-based occupations. This is compounded by women's disadvantage in respect of education and training, their lower average earnings, gender discrimination in the workplace, and the fact that social and labour policies rarely provide more than minimal support for parenting.

In most parts of the South, there is little or no compensation for earnings shortfalls through 'transfer payments' from external parties such as the state, or 'absent fathers'. As Bibars notes in relation to non-contributory poverty alleviation programmes in Egypt: 'The state has not provided women with an institutional alternative to the male provider' (Bibars 2001: 86). While in many places legislation governing maintenance payments has now extended to cover children born to couples in consensual unions, levels of 'paternal responsibility' are notoriously low and men are seldom penalized for non-compliance (Budowski and Rosero-Bixby 2003; Chant 2003). Men may be unable, but also unwilling, to pay. In Costa Rica, for example, men tend to regard 'family' as applying only to women and children with whom they are currently involved, and distance themselves from offspring of previous relationships (Chant 1997).

Another reason offered to account for their poverty is that female heads have smaller social networks, because they lack ties with ex-partners' relatives, or because they 'keep themselves to themselves' in the face of hostility or mistrust on the part of their own family networks or others in their communities. Indeed, lone mothers may deliberately distance themselves from kin as a means of deflecting the 'shame' or 'dishonour' attached to out-of-wedlock birth and/or marriage failure, not to mention, in some instances, stigmatized types of employment such as sex work. Some female heads are unable to spare time to actively cultivate social links and/or may eschew seeking help from others because they cannot reciprocate (ibid.). Yet, as discussed in more detail later, we cannot necessarily assume that women heads lack transfers from external parties, that women's individual disadvantage maps directly on to the households they head, or that living with men automatically mitigates women's risks of poverty.

### Challenges to the construction of women-headed households as the 'poorest of the poor'

Challenges to 'poorest of the poor' stereotyping have gathered increasing momentum on a number of grounds.

*Lack of 'fit' with quantitative data* There are actually very few 'hard data' – even on the basis of aggregate household incomes – that reveal consistent links between female household headship and poverty. More critically, perhaps, there does not appear to be any notable relationship between trends in poverty and in the incidence of female headship over time. Although in some countries, such as Costa Rica, poverty among women heads is on the rise, Arriagada asserts for Latin America as a whole that: 'the majority of households with a female head are not poor and are those which have increased most in recent decades' (Arriagada 1998: 91). Research in this and other regions also indicates that children in female-headed households can actually be better off than their counterparts in male-headed units (see Chant 2003 for discussion and references).

Such findings clearly need to be balanced against research indicating that women-headed households are likely to be poorer than male-headed units. One of the most ambitious comparative reviews to date, based on over sixty studies from Latin America, Africa and Asia, concluded that in two-thirds of cases, households headed by women were poorer than those headed by men (Buvinic and Gupta 1997). Nevertheless, given conflicting and often tenuous evidence for any systematic relationship between female household headship and poverty, blanket generalizations are unhelpful. In fact, given widespread economic inequalities between women and men, it is perhaps more important to ask how substantial numbers of female heads succeed in *evading* the status of 'poorest of the poor'.

*Heterogeneity of female-headed households* That links between female household headship and poverty may not be as definitive as suggested by 'feminization of poverty' orthodoxy owes in part to the heterogeneity of women-headed units. This heterogeneity, which can have important mediating effects on poverty, hinges on variations in women's routes into headship – for example, by 'choice' or involuntarily, and/or through marriage, separation, widowhood and so on. Other axes of diversity include rural versus urban residence, household composition, stage in the life course (including age and relative dependency of offspring) and access to resources from beyond the household. While female heads as individuals may have to contend with discrimination, above-average work burdens and time constraints, their personal disadvantage as women may be compensated for by contributions from other co-resident individuals as well as migrant family members. One strategy is to invite co-residence by extended kin, which can increase productive and reproductive labour supply, bolster earning capacity and reduce vulnerability (Chant 2003). As Wartenburg (1999) notes for Colombia, the manner in which female-headed households organize themselves can help to neutralize the negative effects of gender bias.

*Intra-household resource distribution* Feminist research has revealed that households are sites of competing claims, rights, power, interests and resources, with negotiations frequently shaped by differences according to age, gender, position in the family hierarchy and so on. Popularized most widely in the shape of Amartya Sen's 'cooperative conflict' model, this perspective requires abandoning the notion that households are intrinsically cohesive, internally undifferentiated entities governed by 'natural' proclivities to benevolence, consensus and joint welfare maximization.

Acknowledging the need to avoid essentializing constructions of 'female altruism' and 'male egoism', a remarkable number of studies have found that women devote the bulk (if not all) of their earnings to household expenditure, often with positive effects on other members' nutritional intake, healthcare and education. Men, on the other hand, are prone to retain more of their earnings for discretionary personal expenditure. In some instances, men's privileged bargaining position allows them to command an even larger share of resources than they actually bring to the household (Folbre 1991). Along with reducing the resources available to other household members, irregularity in financial contributions can lead to serious vulnerability and 'secondary poverty' among women and children.

Even if female heads have lower incomes than their male counterparts, then, relative disadvantage may be mediated by the extent and manner in which income and assets are converted (or not) into consumption (and investments) which benefit the household as a whole. In this light, the absence or loss of a male head may not precipitate destitution so much as enhance the economic security and well-being of other household members. Many women in Mexico, Costa Rica and the Philippines, for example, stress that they feel more secure financially without men, even when their own earnings are low and/or prone to fluctuation. They also claim to be better able to cope with hardship when they are not at the mercy of male diktat and are freer to make their own decisions (Chant 1997). Critically, therefore, even if women are poorer in *income* terms as heads of their own household, they may *feel* they are better off and, importantly, less vulnerable. As Davids and van Driel put it, 'a lower income may even be preferred over a position of dependence and domination' (2001: 164).

*Poverty as a multidimensional and subjective concept* That *command* over resources may be deemed more important than *level* of resources in determining gendered experiences of poverty is further highlighted by 'social deprivation' thinking about poverty which calls for holistic, multidimensional conceptualizations which incorporate people's subjectivities (Razavi 1999). Taking on board the multidimensionality of poverty provides important inroads into explaining why some low-income women make 'trade-offs' between different forms of privation which, at face value, may seem prejudicial to their well-being. One such case is where female heads refuse offers of financial support from absent fathers in order to evade ongoing contact and/or sexual relations. Another instance is where women forfeit assets such as their homes or neighbourhood networks in order to exit abusive relationships.

It is also significant that while financial pressures may force some women to search for new partners following conjugal breakdown, others choose to remain alone rather than return to ex-partners or to form new relationships. As noted by Fonseca for Brazil, women who live without partners often do so not through lack of opportunity, but by choice. In many cases these are older (post-menopausal) women, who, 'having gained a moment of respite in the battlefield of the sexes' (Fonseca 1991: 157), prefer to rely upon sons than spouses. Recognizing that not all female heads have access to financial help from sons or other male kin, and that a 'high price' may have to be paid for independence (Jackson 1996), benefits in other dimensions of their lives may be adjudged to outweigh the costs.

Female headship is far from being a 'panacea for poverty' (Feijoó 1999: 162). It is clear that some women's individual endowments and household characteristics make them more vulnerable than others. Recognizing that poverty is multi-causal and multifaceted, and that, in some ways and in some cases, female household headship can be positive and empowering, is no justification for lack of assistance from state agencies and other institutional providers. How female heads might be best aided, however, needs serious consideration.

### Implications of competing constructions of female household headship and the links with poverty

There is little doubt that the 'feminization of poverty' thesis has been powerful in pushing gender to the centre-stage of international forums on poverty and social development, with women's economic empowerment now widely seen as crucial not only in achieving gender equality but in eliminating poverty. Indeed, seeking to alleviate poverty *through* women seems to have become one of the most favoured routes to ensuring all-round developmental benefits: 'Economic progression and improvements in the quality of life for all people is more rapidly achieved where women's status is higher. This is not simply a focus on a single individual, but because of women's communal role positive effects will be seen in the family, home, environment, children, elderly and whole communities and nations' (Finne 2001: 9).

While notions of 'returns' or 'pay-offs' from investing in women can clearly serve to secure resources for women, such naked instrumentalism leaves much to be desired. Moreover, whether linking poverty and female household headship is an appropriate part of the equation is another question. As Moore argues: 'The straightforward assumption that poverty is always associated with female-headed households is dangerous, because it leaves the causes and nature of poverty unexamined and because it rests on the prior implication that children will be consistently worse-off in such households because they represent incomplete families' (Moore 1994: 61).

## Female-headed households as the 'poorest of the poor'

Over and above the little substantive evidence that exists to suggest that women-headed households are the 'poorest of the poor', a number of undesirable (if unintended) consequences result from seeing them as such. One is the suggestion that poverty is confined to female heads alone, which thereby overlooks the situation of the bulk of women in general (Jackson 1996). Davids and van Driel note: 'The question that is not asked … is whether women are better-off in male-headed households. By making male-headed households the norm, important contradictions vanish within these households, and so too does the possibly unbalanced economical [sic] and social position of women compared to men' (Davids and van Driel 2001: 162).

Lack of attention to intra-household inequalities in resource allocation, as we have seen, can also draw a veil over the 'secondary poverty' often experienced by women in male-headed units (Chant 1997; González de la Rocha and Grinspun 2001), as well as wider structures of gender and socio-economic inequality.

Persistent portrayals of the economic disadvantage of female-headed units not only misrepresent and devalue the enormous efforts made by female heads to overcome the problems they face on account of their gender, but also obliterate the meanings of female headship for women. As Davids and van Driel assert: 'Female-headed households appear as an objective category of households in which the subject position of the female head vanishes completely as does the socio-cultural and psychological meaning that their status has for them personally' (Davids and van Driel 2001: 166).

Last, but not least, the tendency for static and universalizing assumptions of the 'feminization of poverty' thesis to produce policy interventions that either target women in isolation or focus mainly on those who head their own households can neglect vital relational aspects of gender which are likely to play a large part in accounting for gender bias within and beyond the home (Buvinic and Gupta 1997; Jackson 1996). Some of these issues are discussed below in relation to the pros and cons of targeted programmes for female-headed households.

*Consequences and cautions of de-linking female household headship from poverty* While there are many persuasive reasons to de-link female household headship from poverty, this can undermine the case for policy attention. Denying that households headed by women are the 'poorest of the poor' potentially deprives them of resources which could enable them to overcome some of the inequities faced by women in general, and lone mothers in particular. Is this wise in a situation of diminishing public funds for social expenditure and increasing market-driven economic pressure on households, especially given that many female-headed households have struggled under the auspices of a 'survival model' requiring high degrees of self-exploitation, that now looks to be exhausting its possibilities (González de la Rocha 2001)?

The answer here is probably no, but *how* female-headed households should be assisted merits more dedicated attention. One response to date has been to target such households in poverty programmes, as has occurred in various forms in Singapore, Cambodia, Iran, Bangladesh, India, Honduras, Puerto Rico, Chile, Colombia and Costa Rica. Although targeted initiatives remain relatively rare, they have grown in number in the last two decades. This is not only because of the momentum built up by 'poorest of the poor' stereotyping, but because neo-liberal 'efficiency' strategies have favoured streamlining as a means of reducing public expenditure on universal social programmes.

*Pros and cons of targeted programmes for female-headed households living in poverty* Recognizing the empirical limitations of few 'test cases', Buvinic and Gupta's (1997) review of the potential benefits and drawbacks of dedicated initiatives for female heads of household identifies three major arguments in favour of targeting. The first is that in situations where data on poverty are unreliable, isolating households headed by women is likely to capture a significant share of the population 'in need', especially where there are substantial gaps in male and female earnings and where subsidized childcare facilities are limited. Second, targeting assistance to lone mothers may be effective in improving child welfare given widespread evidence that children fare better where women have resources at their own disposal. A third potential benefit is greater equity in development spending between men and women.

Arguments against targeting include the fact that female-headed households may become male-headed over time through remarriage or cohabitation, thereby resulting in a leakage of benefits to male-headed households (Buvinic and Gupta 1997). Another potential slippage of benefits is to non-poor households given that not all female-headed households have low incomes, and some may receive support, albeit periodically, from men. Further problems arise from difficulties inherent in screening processes whereby some female-headed households may not be classified as such due to cultural norms of naming men as heads of household, even if they are largely or permanently absent, or make little contribution to family life and welfare. Tactics for determining which types of female heads are most in need may also be problematic.

On top of this, many women may not want to be identified as lone mothers given the stigma attached to the status. They may also feel that taking public money will increase antagonism against them. In Egypt, for example, Bibars (2001) notes that whereas the predominantly male beneficiaries of mainstream contributory aid and welfare schemes are perceived as having 'rights', the recipients of non-contributory programmes (who are mainly female), are regarded in the disparaging light of 'charity cases', especially given the build-up of a 'distrustful, punitive and contemptuous attitude towards female-headed households and the poor in general' in recent years. Buvinic and Gupta (1997) further highlight how targeting can alienate male household heads, especially where female heads are beneficiaries of assistance not perceived as 'female-specific' such as housing subsidies and food coupons.

Another argument against targeting, particularly common among government bodies, is that it may produce so-called 'perverse incentives' and encourage more households to opt for female headship. Fear of this has been so pronounced in Costa Rica that when the Social Welfare Ministry established its first programme for female household heads in 1997, a specific declaration was made in the supporting documentation that there was no intention to promote increases in lone motherhood. Moreover, subsequent programmes of a related nature, such as *Amor Jóven* for adolescent mothers, have been oriented as much to preventing rises in lone parenthood as assisting the client group (Chant 2003). Bibars comments for Egypt that free and unconditional assistance is thought not only to increase the numbers of female-headed households, but to encourage them 'to relax and not work' (Bibars 2001: 67).

Finally, we have to acknowledge the limited impacts of targeted schemes for female household heads when the resources allocated are small and/or where broader structures of gender inequality remain intact. It is instructive that in Cuba, where although Castro's government has resisted providing special welfare benefits to female heads, policies favouring greater gender equality in general, high levels of female labour force participation and the availability of support services such as daycare, have all made it easier for women to raise children alone (Safa 1995).

*Alternative strategies to address the 'feminization of poverty'* Targeted approaches recognize barriers to well-being in female-headed households and should not on this count be abandoned. Efforts to address the putative 'feminization of poverty' could, however, be more effective if they were to acknowledge that women in male-headed households also suffer poverty. As Bradshaw suggests, women's poverty is not only multidimensional, it is also 'multisectoral', namely, 'women's poverty is experienced in different ways, at different times and in different "spaces"' (Bradshaw 2002: 12). One of the main differences between women in female- and male-headed units is that the former tend to face problems of a limited asset base, while the latter's main challenge may be restricted access to and control over household assets (Bradshaw 2002). Accordingly, gender inequality needs to be addressed *within* as well as *beyond* the boundaries of household units.

Interventions to reduce women's poverty, whether as heads of household or otherwise, have taken a number of forms. These include investing in women's capabilities, through education, health, vocational training and so on, and/or enhancing their access to assets such as employment, credit and housing. While such interventions potentially go some way to narrowing gender gaps in well-being, and have arguably moved into a new gear given increasing experimentation with 'gender budgets' at national and local levels, the 'private' sphere of home and family is often left out of the frame. This relative neglect of 'family matters' is surprising given the common argument that it is families who benefit from reductions in women's poverty.

### Conclusion

It is paradoxical that, despite three decades of rhetoric and intervention to reduce gender inequality, women's poverty is said to be rising. Yet, while to talk of the 'feminization of poverty' as an ongoing and/or inevitable process, and as intrinsically linked with the feminization of household headship, is arguably overdrawn, this should not detract from the fact that the 'social relations of gender predict greater vulnerability among women' (Moghadam 1997: 41). Williams and Lee-Smith argue: 'The "feminization of poverty" is more than a slogan: it is a marching call that impels us to question our assumptions about poverty itself by examining how it is caused, manifested and reduced, and to do this from a gender perspective' (Williams and Lee-Smith 2000: 1).

While consensus on different tenets of the 'feminization of poverty' thesis remains elusive, debates have drawn attention to the problems of generalizing about women's poverty, and of engaging in superficial dualistic comparisons between male- and female-headed households. Even if it continues to be impossible to pin down exactly how many women are poor, which women are poor, and how they become and/or remain poor, unpacking the 'feminization of poverty', and problematizing some of its core assumptions, broadens prospects for change. This not only signifies interventions to redress gender inequalities in different spaces, such as the labour market, legal institutions and the home, but those which confront different dimensions of poverty and inequality in ways which are personally, as well as pragmatically, meaningful to women.

## Note

This chapter draws from research conducted under the auspices of a Leverhulme Major Research Fellowship, 2003–06 (Award no. F07004R). Thanks also go to Sarah Bradshaw, Monica Budowksi, Andrea Cornwall, María del Carmen Feijoó, Brian Linneker, Cathy McIlwaine, Maxine Molyneux, Silvia Posocco and Ramya Subrahmanian for their helpful advice and comments. A longer and fully referenced version of this paper is published as an *LSE Gender Institute Working Paper* (Chant 2003).

## References

Arriagada, I. (1998) 'Latin American Families: Convergences and Divergences in Models and Policies', *CEPAL Review*, Vol. 65: 85–102.

Bibars, I. (2001) *Victims and Heroines: Women, Welfare and the Egyptian State* (London: Zed Books).

Bradshaw, S. (2002) *Gendered Poverties and Power Relations: Looking Inside Communities and Households* (Managua: ICD, Embajada de Holanda, Puntos de Encuentro).

Budowski, M. and L. Rosero-Bixby (2003) 'Fatherless Costa Rica? Child Acknowledgement and Support Among Lone Mothers', *Journal of Comparative Family Studies*, Vol. 34, no. 2: 229–54.

Buvinic, M. and G. Gupta (1997) 'Female-headed Households and Female-maintained Families: Are They Worth Targeting to Reduce Poverty in Developing Countries?', *Economic Development and Cultural Change*, Vol. 45, No. 2: 259–80.

Chant, S. (2003) 'Female Household Headship and the Feminization of Poverty: Facts, Fictions and Forward Strategies', *New Working Paper Series*, no. 9 (London: LSE Gender Institute), <www.lse.ac.uk/Depts/GENDER/publications.htm#chant/>.

— (1997) 'Women-headed Households: Poorest of the Poor? Perspectives from Mexico, Costa Rica and the Philippines', *IDS Bulletin*, Vol. 28, no. 3: 26–48.

Davids, T. and F. van Driel (2001) 'Globalisation and Gender: Beyond Dichotomies', in F. J. Schuurman (ed.), *Globalisation and Development Studies Challenges for the 21st Century* (London: Sage), pp. 153–75.

Feijoó, M. del C. (1999) 'De pobres mujeres a mujeres pobres', in M. González de la Rocha (ed.), *Divergencias del Modelo Tradicional: Hogares de Jefatura Femenina en América Latina* (México DF: Centro de Investigaciones y Estudios Superiores en Antropología Social), pp. 155–62.

Finne, G. (2001) *Feminization of Poverty* (Geneva: World Alliance of YMCAs, Global Programmes and Issues), <www.ywca.int/programs>.

Folbre, N. (1991) 'Women on Their Own: Global Patterns of Female Headship', in R. S. Gallin and A. Ferguson (eds), *The Women and International Development Annual,* Vol. 2 (Boulder, CO: Westview Press), pp. 69–126.

Fonseca, C. (1991) 'Spouses, Siblings and Sex-linked Bonding: A Look at Kinship Organisation in a Brazilian Slum', in E. Jelin (ed.), *Family, Household and Gender Relations in Latin America* (London and Paris: Kegan Paul International and Paris: UNESCO), pp. 133–60.

González de la Rocha, M. (2001) 'From the Resources of Poverty to the Poverty of Resources: The Erosion of a Survival Model', *Latin American Perspectives*, Vol. 28, no. 4: 72–100.

González de la Rocha, M. and A. Grinspun (2001) 'Private Adjustments: Households, Crisis and Work', in A. Grinspun (ed.), *Choices for the Poor: Lessons from National Poverty Strategies* (New York: UNDP), pp. 55–87.

Jackson, C. (1996) 'Rescuing Gender from the Poverty Trap', *World Development*, Vol. 24, no. 3: 489–504.

Kabeer, N. (1996) 'Agency, Well-being and Inequality: Reflections on the Gender Dimensions of Poverty', *IDS Bulletin*, Vol. 27, no. 1: 11–21.

Mehra, R., S. Esim and M. Simms (2000) *Fulfilling the Beijing Commitment: Reducing Poverty, Enhancing Women's Economic Options* (Washington, DC: International Center for Research on Women).

Moghadam, V. (1997) 'The Feminization of Poverty: Notes on a Concept and Trend', *Women's Studies Occasional Paper 2* (Normal: Illinois State University).

Moore, H. (1994) 'Is There a Crisis in the Family?', *Occasional Paper 3* (Geneva: World Summit for Social Development).

Palmer, I. (1992) 'Gender, Equity and Economic Efficiency in Adjustment Programmes', in H. Afshar and C. Dennis (eds), *Women and Adjustment Policies in the Third World* (Basingstoke: Macmillan), pp. 69–83.

Razavi, S. (1999) 'Gendered Poverty and Well-being: Introduction', *Development and Change*, Vol. 30, no. 3: 409–33.

Safa, H. (1995) *The Myth of the Male Breadwinner: Women and Industrialisation in the Caribbean* (Boulder, CO: Westview Press).

Thomas, S. (1994) 'From the Culture of Poverty the the Culture of Single Motherhood: The New Poverty Paradigm', *Women and Politics*, Vol. 14, no. 2: 65–97.

Wartenburg, L. (1999) 'Vulnerabilidad y Jefatura en los Hogares Urbanos Colombianos', in M. González de la Rocha (ed.), *Divergencias del Modelo Tradicional: Hogares de Jefatura Femenina en América Latina* (México DF: Centro de Investigaciones y Estudios Superiores en Antropología Social/ Plaza y Valdés Editores), pp. 77–96.

Williams, C. and D. Lee-Smith (2000) 'Feminization of Poverty: Re-thinking Poverty Reduction from a Gender Perspective', *Habitat Debate*, Vol. 6, no. 4: 1–5, <www.unhabitat.org/HD>.

# 4 | Back to women? Translations, resignifications and myths of gender in policy and practice in Brazil

CECÍLIA M. B. SARDENBERG

Travelling theories have always experienced bumpy rides on their journeys, be they across territorial borders, disciplinary traditions or institutions (Clifford 1989; Thayer 2001). Although they have the power to transform the contexts into which they are imported, they are also prey to semantic slippages – if not thorough resignification – as they are translated into different institutional, disciplinary and cultural contexts (Barrett 1992; Hillis Miller 1996; Costa 2000). As Claudia de Lima Costa notes: 'in their migration, these theories face epistemological, institutional, and political coercion, such that they end up passing through imperfect terrains, taking sudden detours, and running into occasional snares' (Costa 2000: 45, my translation).

In the case of the detours taken by gender and development frameworks as 'travelling theories', the problem arises from the fact that neither the meanings of gender nor of development are fixed, but rather 'defined differently by development institutions, gender and development experts, and multiply positioned women and men around the world' (Radcliffe et al. 2004: 388). As a consequence, gender has become a 'contentious' concept and, in some cases, it 'has been used to side-step a focus on "women" and the radical policy implications of overcoming their disprivilege' (Razavi and Miller 1995: 41). As Lilian Celiberti observes:

> The inclusion of the concept of gender in the international conferences and in the mandates of bilateral cooperation agencies is, first of all, the result of a multiple and rich experience of women's movements and has signified an advance in the visibilization of power relations and subordination between men and women. However, the popularization of the term 'gender' is contributing to its vulgarization and simplification. (Celiberti 1996: 96, my translation)

In this chapter, I identify and reflect upon some of these redefinitions and the consequent detours and distortions that have marked the translation of gender theory to policy and planning in Brazil. I argue that the adoption of a gender approach in Brazil has faced considerable resistance on the part of planners and practitioners. As such, the concept of gender has been subjected to much bending and stretching in order to fit the needs and interests of contending institutions and actors. This has often led to the smoothing out of its more radical undertones, turning women's interests invisible once again. More importantly, the consequent resignification of the concept of gender has resulted in interpretations in which 'doing gender' is no longer a part of what 'doing feminism' is all about (Sardenberg et al. 1999: 20; Costa and Sardenberg 1994; Alvarez 1998). No wonder feminist scholars and activists alike have called for a return to the category 'women' in feminist practice, albeit not without reconceptualizing it first (Nicholson 2000; Costa 2002, 1998; Piscitelli 2002).

It pays, I argue here, to reflect upon what they are proposing, and consider instances and domains in which redefining and reclaiming the category 'women' may be not only desirable and feasible, but also fundamental to granting greater visibility both to women as well as to the relevance of a gender perspective in development. In considering these issues in what follows, I will draw from my own experience as an academic feminist and activist in women's movements, and as a practitioner involved in translating theory into policy and policy into practice. Here, then, I will be speaking not only as someone situated in distinct and, sometimes, even conflicting locations in the field of gender and development, but also facing all the epistemological and ethical problems that arise when we attempt to analyse a praxis in which we ourselves are involved (Durham 1986).

## From 'women' to 'gender' in feminist theory

Despite their common origins and goals, feminist scholarship and political activism are distinct practices. They stand on different bases, advance in different rhythms and, as such, are not necessarily harmonious – far from it. There is a tense, ambivalent, relationship between them. This tension also exists in relation to the practice of feminisms in the intermediary space of so-called NGOs, as well as in relation to feminists in state agencies (or as consultants to them), where theories are usually translated into action (Alvarez 1998). These tensions have intensified with the construction of the concept of gender and its adoption as the theoretical object of feminist scholarship.

Rare is the book, paper, or even workshop manual on gender and development that does not include a chapter or section discussing the passage from Women in Development (WID) to Gender and Development (GAD), often taking a comparative approach that favours the GAD perspective. Such accounts tend to over-simplify the differences between the two approaches, as well as smooth out the process whereby one has come to substitute the other.[1] They also tend to pass over debates among feminist theorists that have led to the adoption of 'gender' as its central analytical category. In opposing 'women' to 'gender', these accounts lead to the misconception that they are categories of the same order, that is to say, that one can substitute the other or that they are mutually exclusive. As I hope will become clear throughout this chapter, they are not. But, for the moment, let us just observe that 'gender' refers to a more encompassing phenomenon – that of the social construction of the sexes – whereas 'women' is but a category of gender, a social construction in itself. It follows that there can be no 'opposition, exclusion or substitution' of one for the other because one ('women') is a class or category *within* the other ('gender') (Kofes 1993: 29). The question remains: When is it proper to use one instead of the other?

Like gender, 'women' is a slippery concept, marked by tensions and ambiguity in its meanings. On the one hand, the term refers to a construction – to women as representation – whereas, on the other, it refers to 'real' people and to a social category – to women as historical beings, subjects of social relations. There is a gap between the two meanings and slippages occur between one and the other; these slippages occur not only in uses of the concept, but also in our lives. As Teresa de Lauretis (1994: 217–18) points out, as 'real' beings, we, as women, are both inside and outside of 'gender', both within and outside of 'women' as representation. This entails an irreconcilable contradiction. It is precisely in this gap 'between the constructions and our actual lives as sexed creatures' (Cornell 1995: 86) that feminism is rooted; it is this complex, even contradictory, interplay between 'fantasies of Woman and the material oppression of women' (Cornell 1995: 76), in this 'constant rifting' between them, that feminist politics is grounded. Donna Haraway (1991) captures this in her observation that a feminist is someone who fights for women as a class and for the eradication of this class.

Not surprisingly, feminist politics has emerged and thrived as identity politics, founded on claims for and by women; there could be no feminism without 'women' (Alcoff 1994). Likewise, as a political practice rooted in the feminist movement, feminist scholarship was established by and for women, having as its major goal to transform women's lives through the production and dissemination of knowledge. Though this exercise focused initially on finding the sources of women's subordination in society, it was also a means of denouncing the exclusion of women both as subjects as well as objects of science, revealing that women have been not only underrepresented but also misrepresented in the construction of knowledge, over a wide range of disciplines. Here, then, rested the basis for the development of a field of 'women's studies' – with the anthropology of women, sociology of women, history of women, and so forth – an exercise which has revealed the diversity of women's experiences throughout history (Sardenberg 2002b).

These initiatives, then, not only provided the much-needed greater visibility to women, filling the existing gaps in knowledge, but, more importantly, they also revealed the perverse and pervasive workings of the androcentric bias in Western thought, paving the way for the emergence of feminist epistemologies (Sardenberg 2002b). Furthermore, the accumulated knowledge on the diversity of women's experiences, coupled with the increasing sophistication in feminist theorizing, revealed shortcomings in feminist thinking as well, leading, in time, to a shift of focus and terrain in feminist scholarship (Piscitelli 2002).

Michelle Barrett and Anne Phillips (1992) have argued that this shift denotes a considerable difference between feminist theorizing in the 1970s and that of the 1990s. They point out that despite the plurality of approaches that characterized feminism up until the late 1970s – i.e. liberal, socialist and radical – there were some important points held in common among them, even if they embraced significantly distinctive, if not actually irreconcilable, traditions of thought in social theory. There were acute differences in the political projects of these different feminisms; liberal feminists focused on removing discrimination through education and legislative reforms, while socialist and radical feminists focused on the need for deep structural changes. But they too disagreed profoundly: which structure was the determining one – production or reproduction; and who benefited the most from the exploitation of women – capitalists or men?

By the 1980s, the earlier consensus was broken. A significant contributory factor was the critique of non-white feminists of the racist and ethnocentric assumptions of mainstream (Western and white) feminisms. The distinct gender experiences, desires and needs that differences of class, race, age, sexual orientation as well as ethnic and national identities produced demanded new theorizing as well as a redefinition of feminism as a political project. This coincided with the formulation of a new problematic with gender as the object of feminist analysis (Scott 1988; Flax 1990). Barrett and Phillips highlight increasing 'uneasiness' about the distinctions between 'sex' (as a biological given) and 'gender' (as a cultural and psychological construct) and the theoretical problems involved in drawing sharp divides between biology and social constructions. For some, although sexual difference was to be seen as more intransigent, it was also regarded in a more positive manner – as witnessed in eco-feminist-inspired eulogies of difference, a countermove to the notion of gender. For others these profound 'destabilizations' within feminist thinking itself (Benhabib et al. 1995) arose from the 'appropriation and development by feminists of post-structuralist and post-modernist ideas' (Barrett and Phillips 1992: 5) – a process which, we may add, depended fundamentally on feminist notions of gender.

The paradigmatic change in this shift of terrain from 'women' to 'gender' 'emerged at a moment of great epistemological turmoil' (Scott 1988: 41) when all these elements combined to bring gender to the centre of feminist theorizing. With gender, feminisms (as thought as well as practice) finally had an instrument for denaturalizing social inequalities based on sex differentiation. A gender perspective not only 'stressed the relational character of normative definitions of femininity' (Scott 1988: 29), but also provided the means for the deconstruction of women and men as essentialist categories, and for re-presenting them as gender categories as well as historical beings, immersed in historically determined social relations. Gender is but one component of these social relations; yet, it transverses all the different social planes and other social determinants – such as class, race, ethnicity, age and sexual orientation, for instance – which together contribute to the construction of social identity. A gender perspective makes it possible to reconcile singularity and commonality; gender makes sense of the substantiality of women and men cross-culturally and throughout history.

'Gender' is also a fundamental tool with which to analyse the impact of ideologies in the structuring of the social and intellectual world, far beyond the events and bodies of women and men. Gender is also a central constituting element of the self, of a person's sense of being, as well as a classificatory principle for ordering the universe. It is a category of thought and thus of the construction of knowledge, which means that 'traditional concepts of epistemology must be re-valuated and redefined', so as to make possible analyses of the 'effects of gender on and about knowledge' (Flax 1990). Here, then, rests the stepping stone for the construction of feminist epistemologies and for a feminist critique of modern science (Sardenberg 2002b). No wonder the formulation of a new problematic with gender as object of feminist analysis would in time displace the terms of the debates that carried feminisms through the 1970s.

All of this explains why 'gender' was embraced with great enthusiasm among feminist scholars; they saw (and most still see) in it a significant theoretical advancement, offering greater analytical and political possibilities. However, the wide appropriation of the term has not necessarily implied common understandings and uses of the concept behind it. On the contrary, in some instances, in fact, 'gender' has merely replaced 'women', discarded as something *passé*, or worse, as too closely identified with feminism – that is, too much politically charged, and thus not 'scientific' enough. 'Gender studies' sounds much more aseptic, less contaminated (more 'objective'?) than women's studies or feminist studies, the change in terms making it easier for some to conquer space within the academic canon instead of challenging it. Indeed, the use of gender instead of women gave more status to the researcher, in so far as it was (and remains) identified with greater theoretical sophistication, and permitted an escape from the women's studies ghetto (Costa and Sardenberg 1994; Heilborn 1992). More recently, however, particularly since its adoption by the international conferences and development cooperation agencies, gender has fallen into common use. The very fact that the term is now used by feminists of all different walks and talks – and by non-feminists and even anti-feminists alike – should caution us as to its slippery nature.

### Translations and (mis)uses of gender in Brazil

It is worth recalling that, originally, the term *gender* was appropriated by English-speaking feminists in opposition to *sex* (and not necessarily to 'women'), as a means of combating biological determinism. But this distinction was not necessarily a feminist creation. According to Nellie Oudshoorn (1994), in fact, the term *gender* had been around in psychology since the 1930s, when it was used to distinguish psychological from physiological characteristics. It was Robert Stoller (also a psychologist), in his book *Sex and Gender*, first published in 1968, who came out with the sex/gender distinction as a biological/social distinction. This same distinction was made by Anne Oakley in *Sex, Gender and Society* (1972), perhaps the first feminist publication to apply the concept against biological determinism, as per her definition: '"Sex" is a word that refers to the biological differences between male and female: the visible difference in genitalia, the related difference in procreative function. "Gender" however is a matter of culture: it refers to the social classification into "masculine" and "feminine"' (Oakley 1972: 16).

As Donna Haraway (1991) points out, whereas in English-speaking countries the term *gender* had for long been included in dictionaries, carrying a sexual difference connotation, this was not true of most other languages. Indeed, *gender* does not translate easily. In romance languages, for instance, the term has many different meanings, none with the same connotation as in English, thus opening the way to much confusion in its usage. As Marta Lamas (1996: 328, my translation) well observes: 'To say in English "let's study *gender*" has the implicit meaning that one will deal with a question related to the sexes; to say the same in Spanish remains unclear to the non initiated: what *gender* will one be studying, a literary style, a musical genre, or a painting?' (Lamas 1996: 328, my translation). No wonder French feminists did not incorporate the term *gender* ('*genre*') until recently, nor, for that matter, *gender relations* – preferring instead the expression *rapport social des sexes* (social relations of sex). True enough, this preference has relied, to a great extent, on the notion that *sex* itself should not remain in the biological realm since it is also an object of social elaboration (Ferrand 1988; Saffioti 1992). But the multiple meanings of *genre* have certainly contributed significantly to a reluctance on the part of French feminists to adopt it fully.

Though equally characterized by the ambiguities of multiple and diverse meanings in Portuguese, the term *gênero* (gender) has found greater and more immediate acceptance in Brazil. By the mid-1980s, it was already figuring in the parlance and works of Brazilian feminist scholars.[2] A good indication of this is to be found in the names of the women's studies centres being created in the country at that time. Whereas up to 1985, they were usually named *núcleos de estudos da mulher* (nucleus of women's studies), afterwards, the terms *gênero* or *relações de gênero* (gender relations) began to appear in the names of nearly all newly created centres (Costa and Sardenberg 1994).[3] The presence of the term *gender* does not, of course, guarantee that the 'original' concept comes behind the label (Bahovec and Hemmings 2004).

As elsewhere, so too in Brazil the emergence of the field of 'women's studies' was intrinsically linked to the emergence of local feminist and women's movements. Indeed, many of the women who were activists, involved in the movement and integrated in feminist groups, were precisely the same women who formed women's studies groups and dedicated themselves to carrying out research and theoretical reflections on women's issues.[4] These first academic efforts centred on women had a militant, activist tone. So-called 'second wave' feminism did not emerge in Brazil until the mid-1970s, delayed by the repressive military regime that came into power in 1964 (Sardenberg 2004; Sardenberg and Costa 1994).[5] Despite the publication of pioneering works in the 1960s, 'women's studies' in Brazil only came into being at around the same time that 'gender studies' were gaining momentum in the 'North'.

One of the immediate consequences was the tendency to incorporate the term 'gender' (a novelty) in substitution for 'women', without the necessary theoretical/epistemological shift of one problematic to the other. Thus, analysing the works produced in the *Antropologia da Mulher no Brasil* (Anthropology of Women in Brazil) during the 1980s, Maria Luisa Heilborn noted that from studying 'women in all places and from the most different angles', everybody turned to 'gender':

From sex they have gone to gender, but the category is being used without the perception of being imbricated in a relational system that it should have, and without the perception that, if it maintains any link with any anatomical basis, its main utility is to point to and explore the social dimension which, in last instance, is what is important when we do anthropology. (Heilborn 1992: 94, my translation)

Suely Kofes (1993) argues that where 'gender' is an *analytical category*, 'women' is an *empirical* one. She further stresses, as noted earlier, that 'women' is a category of gender, thus the theoretical relevance of using both of these categories.

This seems to be a point of convergence in current feminist thinking in Brazil (Prá and Carvalho 2004). However, among Brazilian feminist scholars, whether gender should be regarded as an analytical or historical category is still debated; or as both, as professed by Heleieth Saffioti (1992). Indeed, to date, beyond a loose consensus that gender refers to the phenomenon of the social construction of sexual differences, there is little agreement among Brazilian scholars as to the proper uses of the concept.

According to Claudia de Lima Costa, it is possible to identify at least five different approaches to gender at use, as follows:

- gender as a *binary variable*, in which sexual difference is regarded as being determinant in the construction of Woman and Man, and, as such, they become static, a-historical categories;
- gender as *dichotomised roles,* an approach which emphasises sexual divisions and the imposition of feminine and masculine roles, but does not deal much with how these roles come into being, nor regard the issue of power relations among the sexes;
- gender as a *psychological variable,* which focuses on gender identity in terms of degrees of masculinity and femininity, but not as relational categories;
- gender as a *translation of cultural systems,* in which men and women are seen to live in separate worlds, emphasising differences which are created with the socialisation process; and
- gender as a *relational category,* breaking with the dualism of conceptualising gender in terms of a system of social relations, opting instead for dynamic and historically situated notions of masculinity and femininity and an emphasis on power relations. (Costa 1994)

In Brazil, it is the last approach which has gained greater purchase among feminist academics and activists: the gender approach that feminist practitioners had in mind when advocating for the shift from WID to GAD (Razavi and Miller 1995).

## Gender in development policy and planning in Brazil

Although gender and development discourse has yet to find great receptivity or a wide audience in Brazil, a gender and development framework has been adopted in public policy and planning. New spaces 'more sensitive to practices of citizenship' (Valente 2003: 1) have opened up in recent years, including the creation of specific arenas for participation and control of women's and gender equity programmes in the state apparatus (Prá and Carvalho 2004).

The dissemination of the uses of gender beyond the academy has not been primarily the work of academics.[6] Rather, this task has been taken up by feminists active in the numerous NGOs which have proliferated in the region within the last decade (Alvarez 2004). In Brazil, the 1992 translation of Joan Scott's (1988) article, 'Gender: A Useful Category of Historical Analysis', by SOS Corpo – a feminist NGO based in Recife – played a pivotal role (Thayer 2001). Though this translation was intended mainly to make it possible for more members of the group to participate in the collective reading and discussion of the text, copies of the translation were soon circulating among different feminist circles around the country, including women's studies centres.

Based on this translation, SOS Corpo prepared a booklet (*cartilha*) that was to be used in gender-sensitive training courses and among poor women in Pernambuco (Camurça and Gouveia 1995). Thus it was that a twice-translated version of Joan Scott's article began to be read and discussed by poor rural women in the hinterlands of the Brazilian Northeast (Thayer 2001). Soon after, other feminist NGOs around the country also began to make use of the concept and prepare similar booklets, such that, by 1995, even before the Beijing conference took place and the gender perspective was endorsed by most participating countries, gender was already in the process of being incorporated widely into feminist discourse in Brazil. Of course, this does not mean that practice has followed discourse. That is to say, although the concept of gender has gained greater acceptance, it is always necessary to verify the meaning at play behind it (Simião 2002), and what approach to the concept does in fact get implemented. In practice, a range of simplifications arise, for pragmatic reasons as much as through the inevitable resignifications required to translate the language of the academic into the worlds of policy and practice.

*Gender as 'man and woman': the 'happy family'* I must confess that although I defend the so-called *relational approach*, in thinking of gender relations as power relations, and have consistently criticized the *sex has to do with biology, gender is about culture*, as well as the *gender as dichotomized roles* approaches in my Feminist Theories classes at the Federal University of Bahia and in writing (Sardenberg 2002a), I have at times relied on them during gender-sensitive training seminars geared to participants who are not familiar with the sophistications of theoretical abstractions, and particularly so in the countryside.

I am not alone in following this course of action; these approaches seem to be the ones most commonly adopted by NGOs in Brazil, as they are more easily understood by non-academic audiences (Simião 2002). However, they can just as easily lead to passing on the notion of male and female roles as being complementary and, as such, precisely to the 'family model' that gender-sensitizing should aim to deconstruct. Not surprisingly, the *complementary gender roles* approach is often the one found in operation in rural development projects. In point of fact, this is the approach employed by MST (the Landless People's Movement), the major social movement in contemporary Brazil, even though much lip service is paid to the relational approach in their booklets.

The simplification of the concept of gender generally depicted in many gender-sensitizing training kits and manuals – i.e. the 'sex is not equal to gender', 'gender is not equal to women', 'gender has to do with men and women' drills – and often used in gender-sensitizing workshops, can lead to an equally conservative notion of gender. Such was the notion held by the chief agronomist in a rural development programme in Bahia, Brazil, where I worked as part of a gender advisory group. After attending a gender awareness workshop held by project co-sponsors IFAD, where such drills were in order, he began to oppose the creation of the women's production groups we proposed, arguing that since gender had to do with 'men and women', we could not work with women alone. Unfortunately, he had no regard to the unequal power relations at play between the sexes, remaining oblivious to the *relational* character of gender throughout my participation in the said project (Sardenberg et al. 1999).

*Gender as 'women'* Interestingly enough, the head coordinator of that same project fell on the other extreme. For her, 'doing gender' meant working with women: more specifically, creating income-generating programmes for women. She also maintained this notion throughout the period I worked in the project – she could never find enough time to participate in the gender-sensitizing workshops we held – and was overheard while engaged in the following conversation with the director of the agency implementing the project:

DIRECTOR: What is this stuff about gender? Are they talking about *gêneros alimentícios* [foodstuff]?

57

COORDINATOR: No, this gender thing is about women.

DIRECTOR: What?

COORDINATOR: Gender is like women.

DIRECTOR: Then it is the same thing as *gêneros alimentícios*, it is a food item.[7]

In another rural development project in Bahia, the director told us 'not to bother to talk about gender'; why complicate matters if it was all about women, anyway? No wonder he found it 'amazing' when we proposed to have workshops for the men of the participating communities as well.

It should be emphasized that the notion that 'gender has to do with women' (and women only) is not necessarily one held by rural project directors alone. Even within the academic world it is common to find researchers and scholars who propound such a view, or even worse: that gender is but a feminist catchword to make women's studies look more respectable, as one of my male colleagues once told me.

Of course, it cannot be forgotten that the construction of the gender problematic as an object of feminist scholarship is, in fact, a feminist creation. Nor can it be denied that gender was originally employed by some feminists precisely as an attempt at legitimizing women's studies by dissociating it from the political stance of feminism (Scott 1988). In the world of Latin American development planners and practitioners, this dissociation seems to be well established by now; indeed, 'doing gender' is now commonly opposed to what 'doing feminism' is all about (Sardenberg et al. 1999; Alvarez 2004).

*Doing gender vs doing feminism* The change from the WID to the GAD framework in development policy resulted from the recognition that development needed to deal with the structures of women's subordination in society and, as such, with the existing power relations between women and men. This represented a challenge not only to the dominant models of development and forms of intervention, but also to local cultural values regarding those relations. Not surprisingly, there is usually much resistance against the GAD approach, leading to attempts to redefine it, freeing it of its more political overtones.

In the different projects I have had the opportunity to work with in rural Bahia, I have observed that it is acceptable to work with 'gender', so long as one deals primarily with the *practical gender needs* of women and with raising their self-esteem; for example, with helping them realize the significance of their contribution to the family or talking about women's constitutional rights. This is all right, this is 'doing gender'. However, when one attempts to work on issues of *power* relations, such as those regarding domestic violence, then it is seen as 'doing feminism', that is, as taking a 'radical' approach and 'threatening to destroy families', as we were accused of doing in one project. Indeed, we were dropped out of that project for being 'feminists' (Sardenberg et al. 1999; Sardenberg 2000).

Unfortunately, this is not specific to Brazil. Sonia Alvarez (2004) reports a similar attitude on the part of government officials in Colombia. As one of them told her: 'Now things have changed, it is no longer that radical feminism of the 1970's, now it's policies with a gender perspective' (2004: 132). Perhaps the greatest problem lies in the fact that such an attitude seems to be taking hold among practitioners who deem themselves to be 'gender experts' or 'technicians', as the woman director of an NGO in Chile explained to Alvarez (2004: 132): 'our work is as technical as possible ... and there is a great deal of work to be done in the operational side of gender'.

*Gender hiding women* In Brazil, whether in pursuit of this 'non-political technicality', or perhaps trying to be 'politically correct', more and more practitioners, NGOs, government agents and the like have been adopting the term 'gender', using it even when the correct term would be 'sex' (such as in population statistics) or, more commonly, in substitution for 'women', when, in fact, it is often precisely 'women' that they should be talking about.

Indeed, we find that affirmative action programmes that should be clearly addressed to women, the excluded or whichever marginalized segment the action aims to redress, are often referred to as 'affirmative action programme for gender', or 'public policy for gender', whatever that may mean, turning women invisible once again (Costa 1998; Costa and Sardenberg 1994). This is particularly so in the case of labour unions who have come to speak of the 'Gender Department', in lieu of their former Departamento Feminino ('Feminine Department'), or of social movements, such as MST (Landless People's Movement), which now has a 'Gender Sector'. We must then agree with Grau, Olea and Pérz, when they argue that 'when the State, unions, etc., absorb and resignify feminist discourses, we need to be more and more careful so as not to speak only within the hegemonic discourse about "gender"' (in Alvarez 1998: 279).

## Back to women?

Let us remember that the feminist critique of WID challenged both the notion of 'development' and an essentialist and universal category of 'women' (Jackson and Pearson 1998). However, it is clear that in many instances, particularly in terms of advocating legislation, policies, and of representational politics in general, we must 'make claims in the name of women' (Butler 1995: 49) – even if 'the category "women" that is constructed via those claims is necessarily subject to continual deconstruction' (Fraser 1995: 69). At the same time, we must be aware that no matter our various attempts at 'refining' the concept of gender, and independent of our constant struggle to politicize it, translations and retranslations of the term may always 'water it down' or incur some other form of 'corruption' of the meaning we strive to assert (Scott 2001).

It seems clear that, whatever we do, there will always be 'tensions ... between a feminist critique of social structures and more utilitarian uses of a "gender" focus in development' (Radcliffe et al. 2004: 02). As Lewis Carroll observed long ago in *Through the Looking Glass*:

'When *I* use a word,' Humpty Dumpty said in a rather scornful tone, 'it means just what I choose it to mean – neither more nor less.'

'The question is,' said Alice, 'whether you *can* make words mean so many different things.'

'The question is,' said Humpty Dumpty, 'which is to be master – that's what the question is.'

## Notes

Paper prepared for presentation at the workshop 'Feminist Fables and Gender Myths: Repositioning Gender in Development Policy and Practice', IDS, University of Sussex, Falmer, 2–4 July 2003.

1 For an exception to this, see the excellent work of Razavi and and Miller (1995) and Kabeer (1994).

2 See, for example, the works of Elizabeth Souza-Lobo (1991), many dating from the mid-1980s.

3 For example, created in 1983, our group, the Nucleus of Interdisciplinary Women's Studies (NEIM) of the Federal University of Bahia (UFBA), did not have *gênero* in its name, whereas the Nucleus of Women and Gender Studies (NEMGE) of the University of São Paulo (USP), created in 1986, did.

4 For instance, many of the women in the steering group that created NEIM at UFBA (including myself) came from Brasil Mulher, an autonomous feminist reflection and action group in Bahia.

5 It should be noted as well that it was not until the 1970s that the participation of women in the Brazilian labour force began rapidly rising.

6 In fact, within the last decade, the gap between academic production and that of other feminists seems to have widened (Sardenberg 2002a).

7 This was actually a sexist comment on the part of the director: in Brazilian Portuguese, to refer to women as 'food' means that they are to be 'eaten', that is, used as sex objects.

# References

Alcoff, L. (1994) 'Cultural Feminism versus Poststructuralism: The Identity Crisis in Feminist Theory', in N. Tuana and R. Tong (eds), *Feminism and Philosophy: Essential Readings in Theory, Reinterpretation and Application* (Boulder, CO: Westview Press).

Alvarez, S. E. (2004) 'Advocating Feminism. The Latin American Feminist NGO "Boom"', in L. Ricciutelli, A. Miles and M. H. McFadden (eds), *Feminist Politics. Activism & Vision: Local and Global Challenges* (Toronto and London: Inana and Zed Books), pp. 122–48.

— (1998) 'Feminismos Latinoamericanos', *Revista de Estudos Feministas*, no. 2: 265–84.

Bahovec, E. D. and C. Hemmings (2004) 'Teaching Travelling Concepts in Europe', *Feminist Theory*, Vol. 5, no. 3: 333–42.

Barrett, M. (1992) 'Words and Things: Materialism and Method in Contemporary Feminist Analysis', in M. Barrett and A. Phillips (eds), *Destabilizing Theory: Contemporary Feminist Debates* (Stanford, CA: Stanford University Press), pp. 201–19.

Barrett, M. and A. Phillips (1992) 'Introduction', in M. Barrett and A. Phillips (eds), *Destabilizing Theory: Contemporary Feminist Debates* (Stanford, CA: Stanford University Press).

Benhabib, J., J. Butler, D. Cornell, N. Fraser and L. Nicholson (1995) *Feminist Contentions: A Philosophical Exchange* (New York: Routledge).

Butler, J. (1995) 'Contingent Foundations: Feminism and the Question of Postmodernism', in S. Benhabib, J. Butler, D. Cornell, N. Fraser and L. Nicholson, *Feminist Contentions: A Philosophical Exchange* (New York: Routledge), pp. 35–58.

Camurça, S. and T. Gouveia (2000) *O que é gênero* (Recife: Cadernos SOS Corpo).

Celiberti, L. (1996) 'Reflexiones acerca de la perspectiva de género en las experiencias de educación no formal com mujeres', in T. Büttner (ed.), *Hacia una Pedagogia de Género. Experiencias y Concpetos Innovativas* (Bonn: Centro de Educación, Ciencia y Documentación).

Clifford, J. (1989) 'Notes on Travel and Theory', in J. Clifford and V. Dhareshwar (eds), 'Traveling Theories, Traveling Theorists', *Inscriptions*, Vol. 5: 177–88.

Cornell, D. (1995) 'What is Ethical Feminism?', in S. Benhabib, J. Butler, D. Cornell, N. Fraser, L. Nicholson, *Feminist Contentions: A Philosophical Exchange* (New York: Routledge), pp. 75–106.

Costa, A. A. and C. M. B. Sardenberg (1994) 'Teoria e praxis feministas nas ciências e na academia: Os núcleos da mulher nas Universidades Brasileiras', *Revista Estudos Feministas* (Rio de Janeiro: CIEC/ECO/UFRJ), special issue: Anais do Simpósio Internacional, Formação, Pesquisa e Edição Feministas nas Universidades.

Costa, C. de Lima (2002) 'O sujeito no feminismo: revisitando os debates', *Cadernos Pagu*, Vol. 19: 59–90.

— (2000) 'As teorias feministas nas Américas e a política transnacional da tradução', *Revista Estudos Feministas*, Vol. 8, no. 2: 43–8.

— (1998) 'O tráfico do Gênero', *Cadernos Pagu*, Vol. 11: 127–40.

— (1994) 'O leito do procusto: Gênero, linguagem e as teorias feministas', *Cadernos Pagu*, Vol. 2: 141–74.

de Lauretis, T. (1994) 'A Tecnologia do Gênero', in H. Buarque de Hollanda (ed.), *Tendências e Impasses: O Feminismo como Crítica da Cultura* (Rio de Janeiro: Rocco), pp. 206–42.

Durham, E. (1986) 'A pesquisa antropológica com populações urbanas: problemas e perspectivas', in R. Cardoso (ed.), *A Aventura Antropológica* (Rio de Janeiro: Paz e Terra).

Ferrand, M. (1988) 'Reflexões metodológicas sobre uma abordagem em termos de relações sociais de sexo', paper presented at the GT Mulher na Força de Trabalho, 13th Encontro Anual da ANPOCS, Caxambu.

Flax, J. (1990) *Thinking Fragments. Psychoanalysis, Feminism, and Postmodernism in the Contemporary West* (Berkeley: University of California Press).

Fraser, N. (1995) 'Pragmatism, Feminism, and the Linguistic Turn', in L. Nicholson (ed.), *Feminist Contentions: A Philosophical Exchange* (New York: Routledge).

Haraway, D. (1991) 'Gender for a Marxist Dictionary: The Sexual Politics of a Word', in D. Haraway, *Simians, Cyborgs, and Women* (New York: Routledge).

Heilborn, M. L. (1992) 'Fazendo Gênero? A Antropologia da Mulher no Brasil', in A. O. Costa and C. Bruschini (eds), *Uma Questão de Gênero* (Rio de Janeiro and São Paulo: Rosa dos Tempos and Fund. Carlos Chagas), pp. 93–126.

— (1991) 'Gênero e Condição Feminina: uma abordagem antropológica', in A. M. Brasileiro (ed.), *Mulher e Políticas Públicas* (Rio de Janeiro: IBAM/ UNICEF).

Hillis Miller, J. (1996), 'Border Crossings: Translating Theory', in S. Budick and W. Iser (eds), *The Translatability of Cultures: Figurations of the Space Between* (Stanford, CA: Stanford University Press) pp. 207–339.

Jackson, C. and R. Pearson (eds) (1998) *Feminist Visions of Development* (New York: Routledge).

Kabeer, N. (1994) *Reversed Realities. Gender Hierarchies in Development Thought* (London: Verso).

Kofes, S. (1993) 'Categorias analítica e empírica: gênero e mulher; disjunções, conjunções e mediações', *Caderno Pagu*, Vol. 1, no. 1.

Lamas, M. (1996) 'Usos, Dificultades y Posibilidades de l Categoria "Género" ', in M. Lamas (ed.), *El Gênero: La Construccion Cultural de la Diferencia Sexual* (México: PUEG/UNAM), pp. 327–66.

Nicholson, L. (2000) 'Interpretando o gênero', *Revista Estudos Feministas*, Vol. 8, no. 2: 9–41.

Oakley, A. (1972) *Sex, Gender and Society* (New York: Harper and Row).

Oudshoorn, N. (1994) *Beyond the Natural Body. An Archeology of Sex Hormones* (London and New York: Routledge).

Piscitelli, A. (2002) 'Re-criando a (categoria) mulher?', in L. M. Algranti (ed.), *A Prática Feminista e o Conceito de Gênero. Textos Didáticos*, no. 48, November (Campinas: IFCH/UNICAMP).

Prá, J. R. and M. J. Carvalho (2004) 'Feminismos, políticas de gênero e novas institucionalidades', *Revista Labrys* (Brasília: UNB), available at <www.unb. br/ih/his/gefem>, accessed 20 November 2005.

Radcliffe, S., N. Laurie and R. Andolina (2004) 'The Transnationalization of Gender and Remaining Andean Indigenous Development', *Signs*, Vol. 29, no. 2: 387–420.

Razavi, S. and C. Miller (1995) *From WID to GAD: Conceptual Shifts in the Women and Development Discourse* (Geneva: UNRISD).

Saffioti, H. (1992) 'Rearticulando Gênero e Classe', in A. O. Costa and C. Bruschini (eds), *Uma Questão de Gênero* (Rio de Janeiro and São Paulo: Rosa dos Tempos and Fund. Carlos Chagas), pp. 183–215.

Sardenberg, C. M. B. (2004) 'Estudos Feministas: Um Esboço Crítico', in C. Gurgel (ed.), *Teoria e Práxis dos Enfoques de Gênero* (Salvador: REDOR-NEGIF), pp. 17–40.

— (2002a) 'A Mulher e a Cultura da Eterna Juventude: Reflexões Teóricas e Pessoais de uma Feminista Cinquentona', in E. Rosendo and S. L. Ferreira (eds), *Imagens da Mulher na Cultura Contemporânea* (Salvador: NEIM-UFBA).

— (2002b) 'Da Crítica Feminista à Ciência a uma Ciência Feminista?' in A. A. Costa and C. M. B. Sardenberg, *Feminismo, Ciência e Tecnologia* (Salvador: NEIM/UFBA: REDOR).

— (2000) 'Introducing Gender Sensitizing to Elementary School Teachers in Rural Bahia, Brazil', in P. Theherani-Kröner, M. Schmitt and U. Hoffmann-Altmann (eds), *Knowledge, Education and Extension for Women in Rural Areas* (Berlin: Humboldt-Universität zu Berlin), pp. 46–54.

Sardenberg, C. M. B. and A. A. A. Costa (1994) 'Feminismos, Feministas e Movimentos Sociais', in M. Brandão and M. Clara Binghemer (eds), *Mulher e Relações de Gênero* (São Paulo: Ed. Loyola), pp. 81–114.

Sardenberg, C., A. A. Costa and E. Passos (1999), 'Rural Development in Brazil: Are We Practising Feminism or Gender?', *Gender and Development*, Vol. 7, no. 3: 28–38.

— (1998) 'Análise Crítica do Pró-Gavião na Perspectiva de Gênero', CAR/SEPLANTEC, internal document.

Scott, J. (2001) 'Millenium Fantasies: The Future of "Gender" in the 21st Century', in C. Honegger and C. Ani (eds), *Gender – die Tuchken einer Kategorie* (Zurich: Chronos), pp. 19–37.

— (1988) *Gender and the Politics of History* (New York: Columbia University Press).

Simião, D. S. (2002) 'As coisas for a do lugar. Gênero e o potencial de programas de geração de emprego e renda', in C. Buarque (ed.), *Perspectivas de Gênero: Debates e Questões para as ONGS* (Recife: GT Gênero – Plataforma de Contrapartes NOVIB/SOS Corpo, Gênero e Cidadania), pp. 80–93.

Back to women?

Souza-Lobo, E. (1991) *A Classe Operária tem dois sexos* (São Paulo, Brasiliense: SMC), pp. 47–62.

Stoller, R. (1968) *Sex and Gender* (New York: Science House).

Thayer, M. (2001) 'Transnational Feminism: Reading Joan Scott in the Brazilian sertão', *Ethnography*, Vol. 2, no. 2 (June): 243–72.

Valente, V. V. (2003), 'Presupuestos sensibles al género: las expericencias en América Latina', ponencia presentada en el panel internacional titulados 'Presupuestos nacionales para la equidad', Quito, available at <www.unifemandina.org/docu.html>, accessed 10 May 2003.

# 5 | Battles over booklets: gender myths in the British aid programme

ROSALIND EYBEN

Between 1986 and 1999, the British government's development cooperation ministry[1] published a series of information booklets to publicize its policy in relation to women and development (ODA 1986, 1989, 1992, 1995; DFID 1999).[2] These were colloquially known in house as 'WID glossies'. They aimed to state the government's policy position at the moment of publication. Three years or so later, that position had shifted and a new booklet was required.

The cover of the 1986 publication has a photograph of a group of sullen, immobile sari-clad women, one very obviously pregnant and in a rural setting. The cover on the next booklet, in 1989, shows a more modern image of female technicians in white coats, in a laboratory and on a research station. In 1991, it is a lively young woman teacher in a *shalwar kameez*, sharing a joke with a group of laughing girl pupils. The fourth booklet, published for the Beijing conference in 1995, reverts to tradition: a sari-clad woman frowns in concentration as she makes a basket. Finally, in 1999 the title *Breaking the Barriers* returns to the educational image. A group of school girls *and boys*, is depicted, representing the shift in British aid policy from Women in Development (WID) to Gender and Development (GAD).

The choice of these covers was a small but significant element in contests within the ministry about the pictorial and textual content of each booklet. These contests were an important arena for the making, confirming and disputing of the government's evolving policy on women: a battle between those who wanted each booklet to stop further change by drawing a line in the sand and those seeing it as a pointer towards a more progressive policy.

I write this chapter as an erstwhile protagonist in these contests, as a social development adviser and gender specialist in what was then a hierarchical and highly patriarchal organization.[3] Fellow protagonists and I saw ourselves more as guerrillas than missionaries (Miller and Razavi 1998). Thus, I describe dreary, bureaucratic arguments over the choice of words and pictures as 'battles' because that is how I experienced them – as battles to illuminate, challenge and change the norms and meaning embedded in government policy (Fraser 1989). Although I cannot represent the UK gender and development lobby, it seemed to me that many women in that group also saw engagement as a battle, in which the construction of the policy document was a key field.

I begin by describing each booklet's policy context. I then provide a historical account of the specific policy processes that shaped each booklet and follow this by analysing the stories, that is the myths and fables, that the booklets contain. I conclude by briefly touching on the advantages and perils in deploying such stories as an instrument for policy change.

## The policy context

Policy tends to be a response to interest. If no one outside government is interested, an issue will probably fade away and disappear. That interest can come from another part of the government machinery, from Parliament, the business sector or from civil society. Foreign or international interest may also require a policy response. Communicating that response is a process whereby what is said, how it is said and to whom it is said shapes the nature of the policy. The frequency of the WID booklets can be explained by the attitudes of policy-makers inside the ministry and by the sources of the external pressure.

Officials can manage the effects of external pressure. They can be very influential in encouraging or discouraging ministerial interest in an issue. In my time, all three ministers were favourable to the theme of gender, but either did not see it as fundamentally important or thought it politic not to express too much enthusiasm. Most senior civil servants never saw gender as genuinely significant, or as warranting a change in the content of policy dialogue with aid recipient governments or a shift in expenditure patterns. Some officials described gender as a tedious matter of 'political correctness'.

Apart from the influence of officials, ministerial interest on a topic tends to be related to the frequency of Parliamentary questions, comments in the media, the number of letters from the general public and the energy of the relevant lobby group. Ministers must respond by answering the questions and letters and by making speeches to the lobby. Officials may also propose that a concern for the matter be demonstrated through appropriate publications. In the case of gender, ministers made few speeches, compared for example with those on the environment. Ministers tend to speak to lobbies representing formal organizations, such as trades unions, the churches or business associations. However, the gender lobby was a loose network of (usually marginalized) representatives from non-governmental development organizations and universities, not sufficiently numerous to make up an audience for a speech. Speeches take time. Even when an official writes the speech, the minister must be physically present to make it. A booklet, on the other hand, requires no more ministerial time than a rapid read and signing a personalized foreword. Furthermore, the ministry received a steady trickle of letters and inquiries from the general public concerning its policy on women. Each time such a letter was received, an answer had to be sent. An up-to-date booklet performed a labour-saving function. WID booklets were thus a satisfactory means of responding to not very politically significant domestic pressure.

While for most senior managers the booklets could placate a lobby without influencing their own practice, for social development advisers (the gender specialists in the ministry), the booklets' stories were statements of aspiration, potential instruments for changed behaviour and attitudes. If the stories were sufficiently convincing, giving the impression of gender-sensitive practices *already* occurring in the ministry's projects and programmes, middle management readers might come to believe they were laggards and be stimulated to catch up with the (mythical) mainstream portrayed in the booklet.

Apthorpe (1997) comments that policy documents serve more to please and persuade than to inform and describe. The text of the WID booklets reflected internal tensions between senior managers' wish to please (but not change) and social development advisers' wish to persuade (and change). In the case of the WID booklets, there was one audience to please and another to persuade. Senior management was trying to please the external lobby and the gender specialists were trying to persuade the ministry staff. While allowing management to keep the whole issue of women in an apparently safe symbolic domain, the myths provided scope for subaltern subversion. Our political intent was Sorelian – that the booklet should make real what was still largely imagined.[4]

### The history of the booklets

I joined the Overseas Development Administration (ODA) in late 1986, shortly after the appointment of a new minister, Conservative MP Chris Patten. This was his first ministerial post and he was keen to show himself open to new ideas and approaches, including the role of women in development. He had inherited a ministry which included many older staff who had started their career in the colonial service. Natural conservatism had been reinforced by severe cuts in the early 1980s. Many in senior positions were, by conviction, neo-liberal economists. It was also an organization where the wives of many senior managers stayed at home and did voluntary work. Women in the office knew their place as filing clerks and secretaries.

The few in senior positions dressed in grey and brown, working quietly in efficient obscurity.

The international women's movement and the Women's Decade had, however, already made some impact on the ODA. It had recruited a 'social development adviser' to represent the country at the 1975 United Nations Conference on Women in Mexico. Ten years later, there were two such advisers working at the head office on societal aspects of development, including 'women's issues' (Eyben 2003). The ministry was responding to the pressure of an external lobby largely consisting, since the 1970s, of a loose network of women academics working in the field of gender and development studies, joined by some women in development non-governmental organizations (NGOs) and the British Council. By 1980, the lobby had formed itself into the 'Decade Network' with a keen interest in the performance of the British aid programme. At the 1985 United Nations Conference on Women in Nairobi, the network actively lobbied UK government representatives. ODA responded with its first WID booklet in early 1986, prior to Patten becoming minister. The booklet was also responding to parliamentary interest from the All Party Group on Population.

Another source of external pressure was the Women in Development group of the Development Assistance Committee (DAC) of the OECD.[5] Established in 1983, it had become a strong network, providing mutual support to often-beleaguered women responsible for their agencies' WID policies. This support included friendly rivalry over WID glossies, as symbolic expressions of evolving policy among the membership. Following Nairobi, the DAC group had agreed Guiding Principles for Women in Development and a system for monitoring these. They judged the British performance in implementing these principles as one of the worst among its members. Officials hoped that the booklet would mollify that source of criticism.

The first booklet describes 'how the ODA looks after women's interests' (ODA 1986: 6) and contains three key messages:

- The ODA never attempts to influence the social policies of recipient governments nor to undermine national culture and traditions.[6]
- Improvements for women can only be achieved if there is greater prosperity for all.
- In certain circumstances, it is essential to consider women's role.

The conservative tone reflects both the absence of an internal feminist lobby inside the ODA and of a minister with any interest in the topic, and the booklet was badly received by the network. Yet it was an important step. While it appeared to be merely stating what had been until then unexamined policy, the statements themselves illuminated the possibility of alternative policy.[7] That there was now available a written policy to attack galvanized the lobby to propose changes. Patten's arrival, combined with the fortuitous appointment of a feminist social development adviser, provided the opportunity.

Patten instructed his officials to start a dialogue with the gender lobby.[8] In the first few meetings of the Patten era, the contrast between the 'dark grey suited male' officials and the women lobbyists appeared to me very striking. The men were clearly very uncomfortable with these women, who were so very different in behaviour from their own wives and secretaries. They wore long earrings and flowing, brightly-coloured garments. They cut their hair very short like men, or, flagrantly feminine, wore it loose down to the waist. Their bangles jangled discordantly when they thumped the table to make a vociferous point. Certainly, the default, normative discourse of aid with its emphasis on efficiency and modernism appeared to be harder to maintain when challenged by these disorderly women.

The dialogue required a new booklet that could attempt to refute the principal tenets of the first. By late 1988, there were three social development advisers working out of London on projects across the globe (Eyben 2003). Our energy and enthusiasm had led to the integration of WID issues in an increasing number of existing projects as well as to our taking the lead in designing some new ones. We had also established cordial informal links with the lobby, playing a brokerage role between the ministry's male managers and the disorderly women. The hostile encounters of the past were becoming a distant memory. This was the context of the second booklet (1989). It was written to publicize the ministry's decision to adopt a WID strategy, as required by the DAC Guiding Principles. The booklet's introduction stressed that 'we are listening to those who can advise us on what more should be done' (ODA 1989: 7). Social development advisers wrote the first draft, exercising considerable self-censorship, but also seeking through an apt choice of words and stories to communicate a radical shift in policy. The economist in charge of social development advisers modified the text and shared this second draft with the gender lobby who (with behind-the-scenes encouragement from the social development advisers) proposed amendments and changes that would have led to a much more radical text than the initial first draft. The negotiations over these eventually resulted in a final version that looked very much like the first draft.

Our biggest challenge was to convince senior managers that women's unequal status was a socio-cultural rather than a biological construct. By early 1989, management was persuaded that the new booklet could contain language that appeared to reverse the policy position taken in 1986.

Whereas *then* the ODA would never interfere in other people's cultures, the ministry was *now* prepared to admit that culture might be a problem – 'and not only in developing countries' (ODA 1989: 5). Nevertheless to reach agreement on the text was a long and difficult process and the cracks show. Thus, while: 'The cultural and legal status of women is often circumscribed, resulting in narrower occupational opportunities, limited property rights and restricted social outlets.' We also read: 'The governments of most developing countries accept that women are disadvantaged ... They recognise that development is hampered while half the population is unable to participate fully in economic and social activities, but usually wish to improve the position of women within their countries' cultural tradition' (ODA 1989: 5).

By 1992, the UK had repaired its damaged reputation in the DAC WID group and relations with the lobby had become very fruitful. With younger staff coming into the ministry, and most by now having participated in gender training courses, the issue of women had become routinized and less threatening. One senior manager wrote to another: 'It is about time we give women a fair crack at the whip.' It was the intensive programme of gender training that served as the primary impetus for the third booklet. The readership was the staff attending the training courses that had been designed and initially run by Caroline Moser and myself using her gender planning methodology (Moser 1993). The foreword by the new minister, Lynda Chalker, confirmed the Patten approach to dialogue with the lobby.

The UN World Conference on Women in Beijing set the scene for the fourth booklet. While the booklet was still interested in influencing ODA staff, the writers by this time had little difficulty in identifying projects and programmes to include as examples of progress on gender and development. A large number of ODA country programmes were themselves supporting government and civil society preparations for the conference. Aid recipient countries were a key audience for the fourth booklet. The booklet covered a wider range of themes than in previous versions, reflecting the UK response to the strategic areas of concern in the draft Beijing Platform for Action. It was also a more expensive and larger product, demonstrating the enhanced access to budgetary resources of the social development advisers now running our own policy department. It was the booklet with the fewest myths and stories. The apparent success of mainstreaming obviated the need for stories to either please or persuade.

Two years after Beijing, in 1997, the ODA was transformed under the new Labour Government into the Department for International Development (DFID). Clare Short, as Secretary of State, replaced Lynda Chalker. Social development advisers were keen to produce a new glossy to confirm the new government's commitment to the Beijing Platform for Action. The two-year delay in publication was due to the social development group's putting their energy into mainstreaming gender in the new White Paper, the major policy document of the new government on development aid (DFID 1997). As ever, despite a supportive minister, the civil servants drafting the White Paper did not attribute much significance to gender. The purpose of the fifth booklet was primarily to remind DFID staff that gender still mattered. At the same time, it had to reflect not only DFID commitment to Beijing, but also the new emphasis on tackling gender inequality as an aspect of eliminating global poverty.

## Themes, myths and fables

Although much of the content of the booklets changed radically over time, some policy issues, and associated myths and fables, continued to appear from one publication to the next. By policy issue, I mean a topic such as family planning or structural adjustment. I take 'myth' to mean something poetic or metaphysical that is used to provide a normative explanation for the state of the world and the social order (Weiner 1996). Fables are less normative and grand than myths. Like myths, the *Oxford English Dictionary* notes that they may not necessarily be founded on fact, but the dominant meaning is a story (true or not) that is told to convey a lesson. What were the sources for our stories? Primarily they came from our two external interest groups, the gender and development network in Britain and the DAC WID group. The latter may have played a very influential role in the international circulation of gender myths. Sharing and comparing our glossies facilitated the spread of the stories of official development assistance across the world.

Although I saw the booklets as aspirational statements, some elements of reality were also required. Typically, each booklet provided some current gender myths illustrated with examples of projects and programmes funded by British aid. These examples were fables that had a basis in truth. Because we could not too often use the same fable, we needed real world changes to be able to write the next booklet.[9] The impetus of the need to produce a new booklet (to demonstrate change) contributed to our efforts to reshape or introduce new projects in the country programme expenditure. Thus, for example, in the second booklet (1989) it was with great satisfaction that I was able to include at the last very minute the first ODA-funded rain-fed farming project that had just been approved by senior management.[10]

The battle about the booklets concerned the disputed interplay of themes, myths and fables. The result was that each booklet contained a dominant descriptor of women with minor and sometimes contradictory descriptions entering into the text and or the illustrations. A dominant descriptor in one booklet emerges as a minor theme in a subsequent one, and vice versa. The myths and fables in each booklet serve to support and justify the descriptors. In 1986, the dominant descriptor was that 'women have babies'. In 1989 women are 'agents of development'. In 1992 they have a triple role and in 1995 they have rights. In 1999, women are 'poor'. In what follows, I briefly look at each of these.

*Women have babies* That women have babies gave rise to fables that other women – voluntary health workers – are needed to stop them having too many babies and to teach them to feed the babies properly when they do have them. The *voluntary woman worker* appears in various guises in the 1986 and 1989 booklets. In 1990, Caroline Moser and I visited a British-funded health programme in India. We observed the performance of power when the male doctors harangued serried ranks of women voluntary workers. I was determined that fable should disappear from future editions of the booklet, if not from the real world. In the 1995 booklet, a gender analysis is introduced into the theme and the low demand for family planning is attributed to men not allowing women to go to clinics. Men are also part of the problem in the 1999 booklet, which makes the point that women are especially vulnerable to HIV/AIDS.

Women in their reproductive role continue to appear in other guises. Domestic water supply projects are a response to women's needs and therefore unsustainable without women's involvement (ODA 1986, 1989, 1995). In 1986, just as women need water so they need firewood and, by collecting it, they damage the environment. In subsequent editions, we were able to promote women to the status of environmental managers, hinting at the earth mother figure that conserves and protects nature.

*Women as agents of development* By the late 1980s, the DAC WID group had decided to use the efficiency argument as a way of 'talking to the boys' (Elson 1998) who ran the official aid business. In any case, this suited our own self-image of women in development better than the previous representation in which WID issues were confined to 'safe motherhood'. The message of the 1989 booklet, typified by the cover illustration, was that to include women in projects led to greater efficiency and effectiveness: 'If they themselves are healthy and knowledgeable, if they have greater access to knowledge, skills and credit, they will be more economically productive' (ODA 1989: 6). It was thus 'essential to recognize the role of women – as both agents and beneficiaries of development' (ibid.: 22). A new descriptor appeared as part of this argument, namely that women are the dominant influence on the next generation. This reappears in 1995, when investing in women's human development contributes to social and economic progress.

Despite the new and strong efficiency theme in the 1989 text and cover, old fables lingered on in some of the illustrations. Community workers were still teaching women nutrition and health (ibid.: 6, 37) and visiting them in slums (ibid.: 16). They were still having babies (ibid.: 25, 26) and benefiting from clean water (ibid.: 23). The photographs had been selected by staff in the ministry's information service. When challenged, they stated with some truth that it was difficult to find in the photographic archive illustrations of women matching the way the text of the booklet was seeking to portray them.

*Women's triple role* Women's triple role appeared in the 1992 booklet as a direct outcome of Moser's influence on the ministry's emerging gender and development policy. In her training work, Moser had also stressed Molyneux's strategic and practical gender needs framework, but this was a concept that senior management refused to incorporate into the booklet. In the ministerial foreword, reference is simply made to 'women's needs' as being possibly different from men's needs. Nevertheless, in the same foreword strategic change is introduced as a minor theme through the assertion that 'women are prime movers in the process of change', thus justifying the consequential statement, 'and yet women's needs and opinions are ignored in deciding how to plan change'.

We introduced strategic gender needs implicitly in the four key issues that the booklet states as the challenge to women in development: legal rights, access to education, access to planning public services and social status. Once again, the illustrations lagged behind the text. They reflected the message of the previous booklet. Like generals, our photographs were always fighting the previous war. They showed women as productive agents of development, not struggling for their legal rights or seeking to change their social status. The only representation depicting women being educated was the photograph on the front cover that I had taken on a visit to Pakistan.

*Women have rights* By 1995, the two main protagonists in the battle of the booklets had both been promoted, respectively as Principal Social Development Adviser and Chief Economist. More was at stake. Top management, previously unconcerned by what had always seemed a marginal issue, was applying pressure to prevent too radical a shift. Thus, we took this new battle to a more intensive pitch in the effort to represent ODA policy to the wider world that would meet in Beijing. The key issue was the language of rights. The title, *Making Aid Work for Women*, was an explicit challenge to the efficiency argument which makes women work for aid.

In 1994, following the 1993 United Nations Conference on Human Rights in Vienna, the Minister, Lynda Chalker, accepted an invitation to speak at the University of Oxford's Queen Elizabeth House on the subject of women and development. Her speech emphasized that women as well as men have rights. Top civil servants strongly disliked this rights language and instructed the Chief Economist to control its use. The minister was discouraged from putting Beijing into her diary.[11]

The text and illustrations in the fourth booklet reflect this conflict. Chalker's foreword starts with the old, comfortable myth of village water systems needing women to maintain them. Later, the language changes to incorporate for the first time a Gender and Development approach. Echoing the language in the draft Beijing Platform for Action, it speaks of transforming the partnership between men and women, while 'because most women in many countries have fewer choices open to them than most men, we need to make a special effort to support their empowerment' (ODA 1995: 3). Overall, despite the breadth of the subject matter, the use of myths and fables was in decline, although some old ones were reprocessed and new ones introduced, including women as peacemakers, reflecting the increase in conflict taking place around the world following the collapse of communism. Again, the booklet's text was partly subverted by the illustrations. The cover page shows a woman making a basket and this picture is reproduced again on page 6 under the rubric 'Creating Opportunities'. Elsewhere, however, the new message of equal gender relations is illustrated by pictures of boys and girls at school and of men listening to family planning advice.

*Women are poor* The dominant descriptor in the 1989 booklet of women as agents of development was supported by a minor descriptor of women as poor. This reflected part of the wider shift that was beginning to take place in development thinking at that time. The gender lobby had raised the issue of the negative impact of structural adjustment programmes on women. The language of the booklet had to be very carefully chosen to reflect the government's neo-liberal position, while recognizing a need to refocus the attention of international aid on to poverty. Thus, in this booklet the myth that 'women make up the greatest part of the poorest of the poor' appears for the first time.

That women are poor became the dominant descriptor in the 1999 booklet. Others have noted the constraints the poverty framework imposed on addressing gender equality as a human rights issue (Jackson 1998). While the emphasis on gender inequality as barrier to poverty reduction may have contributed to the reappearance of efficiency arguments, the greater use and abuse of gender myths can be attributed to the personal interest taken by the minister in the production of the booklet.[12] Because of their potential to communicate messages to a wide audience, she liked fables to support policy statements. In the field of gender and development, she found a rich seam to mine and a large number of myths reappeared from earlier booklets.

Mythical numbers appear in support of the efficiency argument. It is *70 per cent* of women who are poor (p. 1) and women in Africa typically spend more than *five hours a day* travelling mostly on foot to meet the basic needs of their families (p. 15). Investment in education for girls is the single most effective way to reduce poverty (p. 9). Women also protect the environment, maintain peace and keep societies together, make up most of the labour force and pass on knowledge to the next generation (all on p. 1). They also have a better track record than men in paying back loans (p. 4).

The myths sometimes sit uncomfortably with the detailed social analysis and textual descriptions of the various projects and programmes that the booklet describes DFID as supporting, in relation to the Beijing objectives. There is a discursive disjuncture between the politician and the gender analyst. The former prefers the resonance and emotional potency of myth and fable, with less interest in the actual 'facts of the case' and the latter attempts to provide a grounded description of gender relations in a specific context. Nevertheless, common ground between the two is apparent in a section of the booklet that robustly breaks old barriers with the triumphant political slogan 'More power for women', illustrated by a full-page photograph of two smiling women raising clenched fists. This has come a long way from the static group of sullen and silent pregnant women portrayed on the cover of the first booklet.

## Conclusion

Various contributors to this book have discussed myth-making as a struggle for interpretative power. Because myths are resonant, enduring and good for galvanizing action, they are particularly attractive to activists and politicians such as Clare Short. They are also ambiguous and perilous. They can be reduced to slogans, captured by non-feminist and conservative forces that may then use them for their own ends, as with the message of the efficiency myths that women must work for aid, rather than aid work for women.

The strength of myths is that they can be simultaneously believed and not believed. Reflecting on the battles of the booklets, I realize that, while I rationally exploited some of the available myths as a means to getting gender on the agenda, at the same time their power encouraged action and energy that could not be sustained by dry and rigorous analysis alone. The sense of relative powerlessness in an indifferent, not infrequently hostile bureaucracy, made symbols and images important spiritual resources to the small group of people working to mainstream gender within the ministry. The drafting of a WID glossy was the occasion for a discursive battle with a symbolic outcome. Pfeiffer (1981) notes that such a symbolic outcome may be achieved even when the underlying facts and decisions remain unaltered and that for various reasons such symbolic outcomes may be all that was desired by those making demands of or within the organization. I am still reflecting to what extent that was true in this instance.

## Notes

I am grateful to Elizabeth Harrison and Jane Esuantasiwa Goldsmith for commenting on earlier drafts of this chapter, and especially to Jane for background information concerning the gender and development lobby.

1 This was the Overseas Development Administration (ODA) until 1997, when it became the Department for International Development (DFID).

2 A sixth booklet, *Poverty Elimination and the Empowerment of Women*, was published by the DFID in 2000 in the international development targets strategy series and is not included in this present analysis.

3 I worked as a social development adviser in ODA/DFID's head office from late 1986 to 1999.

4 Sorel on myths: 'We should be especially careful not to make any comparison between accomplished fact and the picture people had formed for themselves before action' (Sorel 1961: 42).

5 The DAC is the coordinating mechanism for official bilateral aid. Within the DAC separate working groups pursue particular themes of common interest to all bilateral donors in an effort to improve collective performance. The DAC WID Group was one such.

6 As Goetz pointed out (cited in Razavi and Miller 1995), the reservations about interfering in other people's cultures with respect to the role of women did not apparently dampen aid bureaucracies' enthusiasm for interfering in other ways, such as population control.

7 See Nancy Fraser's (1989) discussion on how the very act of articulating normative constructs exposes the hegemony and thus weakens it.

8 The network, to increase its numbers and legitimacy, invited to this first meeting with Patten women from a wider part of the UK voluntary sector, whose organizations, such as the Girl Guides movement, were members

of the international section of the Women's Organizations Interest Group (WOIG) within the National Council for Voluntary Organizations (NCVO). The international section of WOIG subsequently became the development section of the National Association of Women's Organizations and was the means by which the gender and development lobby continued to meet ministry officials during the whole period under discussion.

9  I use 'real world change' in the sense implied by Pfeiffer (1981) when he refers to changes in allocation of resources.

10  This was one of the first ODA projects to seek to mainstream participatory approaches and in which the project documentation sought a role for women that went beyond supporting them in the production of handicrafts. What subsequently took place, and the broadening of the agenda by the women community workers, is discussed in Jackson (1998).

11  She did go – and personally distributed copies of the booklet at a meeting of all the Commonwealth heads of delegation.

12  Until 1997, the battle about the booklets had been between civil servants with the minister signing off on the agreed text. Under Short, the principal contest on this (and many other matters) was between the minister and her civil servants. Unlike her predecessors, she took an intense and micro-level interest in the production of all policy statements. Gender policy was no exception. She read and annotated every draft of the booklet.

## References

Apthorpe, R. (1997) 'Writing Development Policy and Policy Analysis: On Language, Genre and Power', in C. Shore and S. Wright (eds), *Anthropology of Policy* (London: Routledge), pp. 43–58.

DFID (Department for International Development) (1999) *Breaking the Barriers: Women and the Elimination of World Poverty* (London: DFID).

— (1997) *Eliminating World Poverty: White Paper on International Development* (London: Stationery Office).

Elson, D. (1998) 'Talking to the Boys: Gender and Economic Growth Models', in C. Jackson and R. Pearson (eds), *Feminist Visions of Development* (London: Routledge), pp. 155–70.

Eyben, R. (2003) 'Mainstreaming Social Development into the Overseas Development Administration, a Partial History', *Journal of International Development*, Vol. 15, no. 7: 879–92.

Fraser, N. (1989) *Unruly Practices: Power, Discourse and Gender* (Cambridge: Polity Press).

Jackson, C. (1998) 'Rescuing Gender from the Poverty Trap', in C. Jackson and R. Pearson (eds), *Feminist Visions of Development* (London: Routledge), pp. 39–64.

Miller, C. and S. Razavi (1998) 'Introduction', in C. Miller and S. Razavi (eds), *Missionaries and Mandarins: Feminist Engagement with Development Institutions* (London: Intermediate Technology Publications in association with UNRISD).

Moser, C. (1993) *Gender Planning and Development, Theory, Practice and Training* (London: Routledge).

ODA (Overseas Development Administration) (1995) *Making Aid Work for Women* (London: ODA).

— (1992) *Women in Development* (London: ODA).

— (1989) *Women, Development and the British Aid Programme. A Progress Report* (London: ODA).

— (1986) *Women in Development and the British Aid Programme* (London: ODA).

Pfeiffer, J. (1981) *Power in Organizations* (Massachusetts: Pitman Publishing).

Razavi, S. and C. Miller (1995) 'From WID to GAD: Conceptual Shifts in the Women and Development Discourse', *UNRISD Occasional Paper* no. 1 (Geneva: UNRISD).

Sorel, G. (1961) *Reflections on Violence* (New York: Collier Books).

United Nations (1995) Fourth World Conference on Women: Platform for Action (New York: United Nations).

Weiner, J. (1996) 'Myth and Mythology', in A. Barnard and J. Spencer (eds), *Encyclopaedia of Social and Cultural Anthropology* (London: Routledge).

# 6 | Not very poor, powerless or pregnant: the African woman forgotten by development

EVERJOICE J. WIN

## The appeal of the myth of the poor and powerless African woman

For decades now, the development industry has thrived on the stereotypical image of an African woman who is its 'target' or 'beneficiary'. Always poor, powerless and invariably pregnant, burdened with lots of children, or carrying one load or another on her back or her head, this is a favourite image, one which we have come to associate with development. From the United Nations, to large international agencies, to multilateral/bilateral donors, to small non-governmental organizations (NGOs), most of us have used and abused this image time and time again. Like the fly-infested and emaciated black child that is so often used by international news agencies, the bare-footed African woman *sells*. Without her uttering a word, this poor woman pulls in financial resources. Any researchers worth their salt have to go to the 'most remote' village to find her for their statistics on issues like access to water to be valid. Similarly, the gender programme officer in any institution always has to demonstrate that her work is about the very poor and marginalized woman for her to be regarded as legitimate.

But is this image an accurate one? Does it tell the full story of black African women's complex realities? And does this image encompass all levels of 'marginalization' and 'disempowerment' that development work must deal with? In this new era of rights-based approaches, is this the only woman that development organizations should be concerned about? Is resource poverty the only lens through which we should look at women's rights denial and violations? As one of those women often forced to negate my own needs and experiences in the work that I do, I seek to challenge this image and consequent focus.

## HIV/AIDS: the new lens

If there is one good thing to say about HIV/AIDS, it is the fact that it has finally enabled feminists like me to articulate more clearly all the issues that I have often raised which did not seem to make sense to others. And it is by focusing on an issue that I have personally experienced as a middle-class woman that I am able to demonstrate adequately my frustration with the way the development industry constantly delegitimizes my voice and

### *Notice:* **For the Development Bulletin Board**

*Attention: Researchers, donors, policy-makers, Northern feminists, Southern practitioners and other such-like*

*Sighted*: 'New' African woman – not very poor, powerless or pregnant

A new African woman has recently appeared on the margins of the development stage. From reports received, this woman does not fit the usual stereotype that many of us have become used to in our work. Please find below a rough description of this new woman. You are all advised urgently to start looking out for her and to find ways of engaging and working with her. Please be warned that this woman is rather more complex than the old one we have come to know, whom we see as much more simple and straightforward. You are therefore advised to exercise the greatest of caution when you approach her and spend a bit more time understanding her.

*Geographic location*

This woman can be found in many countries of Africa, particularly the sub-Saharan region. At the local level, she can be found in rural villages or in the urban areas. She moves between the two locations with ease. It is difficult to say specifically if she is fully a

denies me a space. I will therefore use this example in exploding the myth of the poor, powerless and pregnant African woman.

It is now a well-established fact that gender inequalities are driving the HIV/AIDS pandemic. Women's inability to protect themselves and exercise choices, sexual violence and the lower status accorded to women and girls are some of the many aspects of women's greater vulnerability to HIV. Research has clearly shown that it is also women who bear the disproportionate burden of care for the sick, and yet suffer a lack of access to treatment for themselves. All of these facts apply not just to resource-poor women in remote rural areas, they apply to all women regardless of all the variables that we know: class, location, age, and so on. The defining factor is unequal power relations between women and men. While resource poverty is an important factor, mediating the differences among classes of women, it is still a fact that generally most women experience unequal power relations regardless of class.

resident of one of the two. Her work spans the two as well. Some of her work is directly in her own village, while some is in the urban area where she also lives. Lately she has been elected as a representative in her local government.

It is at national level, though, that she is most active and she also appears at the regional and international level. You are likely to see her presenting a keynote speech at a regional donor conference, or running round the lobbies of powerful international institutions lobbying policy-makers on the issues she is passionate about. The following week you will meet her again in the villages of her country, facilitating workshops, or organizing economic activities with resource-poor women.

### Class and other social characteristics

The new woman is mostly middle to upper middle class – such as there is in sub-Saharan Africa. She is not very poor, nor can she be called very rich. Although she is relatively comfortable, in comparison to the majority of women in her communities, the new woman's comforts tend to be wiped out by the reality of her existence. For example, she is the one most likely shouldering the burden of HIV/AIDS; paying fees for orphans; buying anti-retrovirals for the infected and generally stepping in when governments and others fail.

As a middle-class woman, I am intimately affected by HIV/AIDS. I find it as hard to negotiate safe sex as any other woman. I have the same fears about the consequences of my actions as any other woman. I am afraid of what society thinks of me, I am afraid of what my family will say, I do not want to be constantly seen as a bad woman. Sexual violence stalks me wherever I go. Even when I travel to what some would see as exciting places – out of my country, to conferences – I worry about my safety and security in hotel rooms. I personally do not sleep in any hotel room without pushing a chair against the door, just in case!

My class has not been spared from the reality of HIV/AIDS. We are both infected and affected. Of course there are no class-disaggregated statistics. Stigma still knows no boundaries. I constantly get pointed out as 'the one whose mother has lost three children to AIDS!' The burden of care and support for the affected and infected falls on the shoulders of the middle-class woman. She is the one with access to money, so she pays fees for the orphan here, takes the dying relative to hospital the next day, and generally the whole clan looks to her to pay for everything that is needed. She even sponsors the funerals. If she is married she has to do this for her own family and for *his* family.

The bottom line, when it comes to a problem like HIV/AIDS, or violence against women is *I am the woman*. The issues I talk about are issues that I live with and experience. I am the one who mops up after everyone and on behalf of the state. I am the marginalized and oppressed. I am not working 'for' *the woman out there*, who is nameless or faceless. This is about me. I do not have to ratchet up 'grassroots women' to speak on behalf of, because I am that woman and I speak on my own behalf.

The big difference between development's favourite woman and me lies merely in the degree to which we each experience these problems. As they say, money does not buy happiness – but it helps; equally, education, geographic location and access to resources do not buy gender equality – but they help. It is important to note, though, that I am constantly hovering on the brink of becoming the poor woman in the posters because of something like HIV/AIDS or violence. Many of us have been reduced to a hand-to-mouth existence by the demands placed on us by those around us. Because we are still subjected to practices like property grabbing, there is the ever-present possibility of finding oneself as destitute as the mythical development target.

## Silencing of the middle-class woman

Despite all of this, the middle-class woman is completely silenced and erased from the images of development and rights work. She is constantly reminded that development is about eradicating poverty and so it focuses on those defined as 'the poor' (read as resource-poor). Therefore her story and her experiences are not part of the narrative. In essence, this means women's lives are put in a kind of league table and it is those that qualify which get addressed.

If the non-poor woman dares give herself as an example, she is reminded that she is too distant from the lives of the *women out there* to matter. If she works in development, she constantly has to demonstrate how she is connected to the women at grassroots level. It is not acceptable to claim any knowledge of the issue/s at hand. Many a women's organization and its leadership have had to provide physical evidence of links with the grassroots poor. This can even go to ridiculous lengths; for example, women's rights NGOs have been forced to take 'their grassroots poor' to a UN meeting or international conference, just to prove their legitimacy.

The most disturbing aspect of all this is that none of these requirements is put on Northern feminists or other rights organizations. It is quite acceptable for a Northern academic feminist to present her paper in Beijing, or for her activist colleague to lobby the UN on HIV/AIDS. The world does not yet know how to deal with the articulate non-poor African feminist. Is it because she talks back? Is it because she does not fit the image of the charity case? As African feminists, we have learnt to laugh at the comment made by our Northern colleagues: 'Oh, you are *sooo* articulate, Everjoice!' We ask ourselves, what we were supposed to be? Incoherent?

## The dual identity

Because for many years the work of the African middle-class activist has had to focus on and be based in rural poor areas, she has one foot at the micro-level and the other in macro-spaces. This dual identity can only result in schizophrenia! It becomes extremely difficult to hone one's skills and expertise.

'Villagization' of non-poor activists has resulted in the often-heard refrain, 'Africa has no policy analysis capacity'. The results are all too visible; it is still largely Northern academics or feminists who write and get published; it is their work which is used by policy-makers and is quoted in international media. The 'village-based' micro-analyst, or anecdote-telling African activist is not that well respected. Her work often gets relegated to the human-interest stories section. At international conferences, it is the conceptual papers that get discussed, rather than the practical experiences or suggestions. Any academic journal will show the power imbalances between Northern and African feminists. Rarely does one find an article written by anyone on the front line.

The most recent fashion is for co-authored articles by Northern and African 'writers', but one can still pick out who contributed what to the piece. Donors are equally reluctant to support work by African women that is not practical and grassroots-oriented. Donors hardly ever support feminist academics on the continent – in strategic thinking processes or macro-policy work (including advocacy); but they have no problem giving resources to an institute of development studies, or a women's studies centre at a Northern university. Clearly, the Northern colleagues are not asked in what way their work is going to impact directly on the lives of poor African women. Nor are they asked to involve the grassroots.

How are African feminists and activists expected to strengthen or develop our intellectual capacities when we are too busy running small projects, while others have all the space, the resources and the support they need?

Not very poor

## The personal is no longer political

A more worrying offshoot of all this is that many African feminist activists find it difficult to live out the principle that the personal is political. By articulating issues that affect the other, the non-poor woman distances herself from even those struggles that should be hers. In the process she loses the ability to position herself within the solutions that she ultimately 'prescribes' for others. So, for example, on HIV/AIDS she will spread prevention messages that she herself has not even tried or, worse, knows do not work.

In the end she cannot really win, can she? On the one hand, she is seen as illegitimate if she does not dredge up the grassroots, and on the other she cannot get close enough to the same grassroots, because she does not identify with their reality. It would enrich development work were non-poor women accorded the right and the space to tell their own story and work on issues that concern them. There would even be resonance and solidarity with Northern women who also have made telling the stories of others into an art-form. Just like us, they suffer from violence, have the same concerns about HIV/AIDS and reproductive rights etc. – even if there is a difference in degree and other nuances. But the principal villain we are dealing with is the same: patriarchy and power relations. It would also enrich all women's lives were they to share stories, strategies and create solidarity platforms. But this can only happen if both sides come to this common space with honesty and without 'othering' the other.

## Conclusion: creating new images and using new approaches

The development community's new fad is the rights-based approach. Perhaps this might offer a way for us to begin to move away finally from some of these stereotypes and myths about the African woman. The rights-based approach creates new opportunities for reconceptualizing our understandings of poverty, for example. As various authors have shown, poverty is not simply resource poverty but includes violence, denial of personhood, silencing, marginalization, denial of choice and other freedoms. All of these are experienced by the so-called 'poor and other women'.

Therefore, in rights-based approaches, resource poverty ceases to be 'the' central distinguishing factor. Rather, what matters is the denial and/or violation/s of rights, which is based on nothing other than sex and gender. This, however, is not to suggest that all women are the same and that all women regardless of class, race and other factors should be treated the same. Development agencies can still choose among the various categories of women whom they want to focus on and work with.

What I am suggesting is that there is a need for conceptual clarity and a strategic shift from conceptualizing poverty in very simplistic terms, and consequently choosing partners also based on such simplistic understandings of the complexity of African women's lives. This shift would also enable development practitioners and donors in particular to move away from the simplistic 'magic bullet' solutions that they often propose for African women, examples of which include income-generating activities and awareness-raising campaigns. Just looking at non-resource-poor women, who do not need income-generating activities, and yet suffer from domestic violence or are infected with HIV/AIDS, would answer the question: So, what else needs to change?

This strategic shift would see us moving beyond our favourite African woman, to strategic engagements with those other women who not only need support, but who can be strategic allies and leaders in development. But of course this means the power relations between Northerners and African women must also shift dramatically: from seeing us as objects of charity – which those of us who are not poor or powerless and not likely to get pregnant are not – to seeing us as agents of our own change; from seeing us as junior partners with the anecdotes, to seeing us as analysts and macro-level actors in our own right. And when we talk back and challenge, we would perhaps no longer be labelled 'so difficult to work with' or 'too sensitive'.

Rights-based approaches give those of us who are not resource-poor a space within development discourse and practice to participate fully in change processes. This would help to re-energize us, as we become more emotionally and spiritually invested and uplifted by the work we do. Because as long as we feel that 'development' is about 'others' far removed from our own realities, we will not see what we do as more than a job that we get paid for. Personal investment gives us the tools to live out the personal as political.

Most importantly, the strategic shift to rights-based approaches would mean that we develop the courage to tell the good African stories, and show the positive images of African women. This might even begin to suggest redundancy for the missionaries among us. And then, hopefully, we can support the poor, powerless and pregnant one to deliver her babies and take a well-deserved rest.

# 7 | 'Streetwalkers show the way': reframing the debate on trafficking from sex workers' perspective

NANDINEE BANDYOPADHYAY WITH SWAPNA GAYEN,
RAMA DEBNATH, KAJOL BOSE, SIKHA DAS, GEETA DAS,
M. DAS, MANJU BISWAS, PUSHPA SARKAR, PUTUL SINGH,
RASHOBA BIBI, REKHA MITRA AND SUDIPTA BISWAS

Trafficking of women and children across and within nations is said to have escalated dramatically in the last decade. At the same time, we are told how much political commitment to, and funding for, anti-trafficking interventions, preventive and punitive legislation have grown. For both propositions to be true there must be something wrong, either in the definition of trafficking or in the ways it is being tackled. Despite the media headlines on desperate Third World men dying in their hundreds in closed containers that haul them across international borders, there remains a steadfast conviction that those who are trafficked are predominantly women and children. After all, the most persistent of all trafficking myths asserts that the destination of all trafficking is prostitution, all prostitutes are women and as no woman can deliberately choose to be a prostitute, all of them are trafficked. The principal causes of trafficking are commonly believed to be the so-called 'push factors' of poverty and gender inequality. Moreover, it is supposed that organized gangs of traffickers carefully orchestrate all trafficking, both internationally and within national borders. Then it is assumed that those who are trafficked remain in a situation of everlasting powerlessness, unless rescued by external agents, preferably anti-trafficking non-governmental organizations (NGOs) ... and the list goes on.

The problem with such positions and conceptions is not just that they are misleading. More importantly, they fail to examine the experiences of those who are trafficked into a range of labour markets every year and deny them any possibility of autonomy or agency, for ever banishing them to a silent world of eternal and relentless victimhood. To understand the realities of trafficking from the point of view of those who are trafficked, this chapter will recount the stories of some women who now work in the sex industry. It will also briefly examine the ways in which Durbar,[1] an organized forum of sex workers based in West Bengal, has intervened in the debate on trafficking and has offered alternative ways of thinking about and acting on the issue.

**First the stories ...**

*Shohagi's story* Shohagi[2] was born to a poor family in Murshidabad. Her parents could barely make ends meet, working as they did as agricultural labourers, but Shohagi did not mind, as she was much loved by her mother and grandmother. As a child she had loved going to school and had taken much pleasure in learning to embroider from her grandmother. When she was fourteen her father married her off to a much older and much married man, whose only qualification was that he did not demand any dowry. Although Shohagi was heartbroken to leave her home and school friends, and disappointed in her father's choice, she resolved to be a good wife. To her horror, soon after her wedding she found her new husband was extremely violent. He regularly thrashed her black and blue and seemed to derive enormous pleasure in threatening to kill her if she dared protest. Unable to stand it any longer, six months into the marriage, Shohagi returned to her parents. Her father and elder brothers were livid at her effrontery in rejecting a husband they had chosen and threatened to kill her when she refused to return to him, as her 'waywardness' would bring ignominy to her family. Her mother and grandmother tried to intervene on her behalf, but were ignored.

So Shohagi ran away from home. Taking shelter in a bus station, she came across an older woman who listened to her tale of woe with sympathy. She offered to take Shohagi to Calcutta and find her a job as a domestic help. After a long and confusing journey, it was evening when Shohagi's new-found benefactor brought her to a crowded neighbourhood in Calcutta, with well-lit narrow roads, old, dilapidated mansions and numerous men milling around. Shohagi's companion took her to a formidable-looking woman, who after a brief discussion handed some money to the older woman and shoved Shohagi into a small room. Tired after her ordeal, Shohagi fell asleep.

Next morning Shohagi woke up to find two or three young women crowding around her. Responding to her nervous queries, these women said she was in a brothel and patiently explained to Shohagi what she was expected to do. Shohagi was shattered. She pleaded with the *malkin* (brothel manager or madam) that she be spared and allowed to go. The *malkin* argued that she had invested money in Shohagi, and could not let her leave till the amount had been repaid. However, she conceded that Shohagi could do household chores in the brothel until she became accustomed to the idea of working as a sex worker.

During the first month or so that Shohagi spent in the brothel working as a housemaid, the prospect of sex work lost its initial horror. Young though she was, she had already been initiated into sex by her husband,

and often had to have sex with him against her will. In the brothel she found that the sex workers had more of a say with their clients, and could even refuse them. Also, they got paid for the act. The clients paid the *malkin*, which supposedly went towards paying off her investment in the sex workers and their upkeep. But if the clients were happy with the sex worker they would pay her some extra which she could keep. As Shohagi swept the brothel, she considered her options. Given her situation, working in the brothel seemed less hazardous than going home to inevitable violence. Soon after, Shohagi, nearly fifteen now, started working as a *chhukri*.[3] She worked hard and saved harder, determined to get out of bondage and become independent.

One year later, Shohagi ran away from the brothel. She took shelter with another sex worker whom she met at a protest rally organized by Durbar. Her *malkin* found out and came to her new home demanding that she pay her debt. The sex workers of the area rallied together and persuaded the *malkin* to leave Shohagi alone, saying she had already made enough money from Shohagi and threatening dire consequences if she ever harassed her again. Shohagi rented a room in the red-light area and started operating as an independent sex worker. Every once in a while she thought of her mother and her grandmother, and even sent them money and gifts, but never considered going back for good. She still has the room and still works as a sex worker – it has been ten years now since she last ran away.

*Jharna's story* Living in a village in Bangladesh, Jharna[4] was happy enough with her uncle and aunt who had raised her after her parents died, as long as she could roam around with her friends, climbing trees and swimming in the river. However, when her guardians said that they had fixed her marriage, she rebelled. The man they had chosen was much older and Jharna loved a boy from the village who had left to seek his fortune in India. An older woman from the neighbourhood suggested that she run away from home and assured Jharna that she would help her find her lover. Jharna, determined to find her love, left home with this woman, crossed the river Padma and walked across the border to reach India. After staying with the woman for a few days, Jharna started pressing her to take her to her boyfriend. The woman took her on another journey, this time to a red-light area in Calcutta. She took her to Meera, a local *malkin*, who paid off the woman and contracted Jharna as a *chhukri*. So began Jharna's working life as a sex worker.

A few months later, Meera took Jharna to Bombay and put her in another brothel there. As it happened the brothel was raided by the police that very night. Policemen broke open the door of the brothel and kicked her out.

With many other sex workers she was pushed into a police van and taken to a remand home. At the remand home she and the others were persistently abused. The social workers warned her that she would be allowed to leave only if she promised to give up sex work and accepted a rehabilitation package offered by the government. Jharna was quite ready to accept the proposition and get out; but the authorities had another stipulation – that unless her guardians came to take her into custody, Jharna would not be allowed to go under her own volition. Jharna was in a fix. She had not let on that she was a Bangladeshi because that would have landed her in another protracted bureaucratic wrangle. So where would she produce her guardians from? This is when Meera – her first *malkin* – came to her rescue. Meera paid a hefty bribe to the home authorities and took Jharna back to Calcutta, this time to work for another *malkin*, Parul.

For a year Jharna worked hard to pay off her debt to Meera; all she earned went to Meera and Parul. To escape the debt trap and once again to find love, one day Jharna ran away from the brothel with a client she fancied. She lived with him for a while but, not being able to tolerate his father's persistent sexual advances, she left him and came back to the sex industry to work as an *adhiya*.[5] With the money she saved and the help of a friend she finally managed to rent a room independently in a cheaper red-light area. She says although she never found the elusive love that she had sought, she derives great satisfaction from the fact that she is now her own *malkin*.

*Madhabi's story* As a teenager, Madhabi[6] had fallen in love with a distant relative, Mukul. However, her parents did not approve of Madhabi's love affair. When her parents insisted she end her relationship, Madhabi ran away from home with him. They rented a room in the suburbs of Calcutta and started living together. Mukul had no income nor did he have any skills to find a job in the city. They managed to survive the first couple of months by selling Madhabi's jewellery.

One morning, Mukul left home in search of a job and did not return. Two days later Mukul's friends turned up saying they had come to take Madhabi to a hospital where Mukul had been admitted following a serious accident. Travelling for more than an hour by bus and tram Madhabi found herself in a strange street. 'How could it be a hospital?' she mumbled. She had never seen so many women standing in the street, dressed so brightly or talking so loudly. As she hesitated, Mukul's friends dragged her to the staircase of the nearby building. Suddenly they heard a stern voice from behind asking them to stop. Unknown to Mukul's friends, Durbar activists had been following them since their arrival in the red-light area, finding their movements to be suspicious.

Madhabi was brought to the Durbar office for counselling and support. The other volunteers found Mukul lurking in the brothel Madhabi was being taken to and took him and his friends to the local police station. After a brief dialogue, the officer in charge asked Durbar members to hand over Madhabi to the police so that he could register a case of trafficking against Mukul, saying that without taking custody of Madhabi no case could be booked. The activists returned to the Durbar office. A debate soon ensued.

What was being debated was Madhabi's fate. Should she be handed over to the police so that Mukul could be punished? Or should she be allowed to follow a course of action of her own choice? Durbar members knew that putting Madhabi in police custody meant indirectly 'forcing' her into the sex industry. When a trafficked woman is rescued from the sex industry and put in police custody, the police put her up in the government remand home, which is notorious for corruption and unofficial linkages with brothel managers. Durbar's experience is that *malkins* have a system worked out to get the woman back by paying a bribe to the remand home authorities. They then extract an inflated repayment from the trafficked woman by making her work without wages. Moreover, Durbar members felt that the process from police custody to judicial custody to remand homes, is not only a lengthy one, but also extremely hazardous. The police, as well as the caretakers of the remand home, were likely to treat Madhabi with disrespect and violence. At the end of such a process her already restricted options would be reduced to none.

## Challenging the associations between poverty and trafficking and other myths

While Durbar members debate over what is to be done with Madhabi, let us now look at what these stories tell. These stories and numerous others, recorded during the course of recent research,[7] indicate that, contrary to popular belief, poverty in itself does not inevitably lead to trafficking. Poverty and lack of viable livelihood opportunities can and do prompt people to migrate. Of the sixty sex workers interviewed, most came from very poor households, where they had little or no access to education or training in marketable skills. However, in the majority of cases they left home by their own choice, in search of better livelihoods, to escape parental or marital violence or drudgery, or to seek love. After deciding to leave home, many of the respondents sought information about possible employment from neighbours or relatives who seemed to them to be more knowledgeable about the ways of the world. It was these people who brought them to their future recruiters – be they brothel managers or owners of small factories or labour contractors in the building industry – and made a profit out of it. At every level, a string of individuals carried out different functions, such as helping undocumented migrants to cross international borders illegally, or introducing them to potential employers, rather than the process being masterminded and controlled by an organized mafia of traffickers.

Some respondents chose to become sex workers when they left home, finding out about the industry from neighbours who had been sex workers and had used the services of the same kind of agents to find their way to the cities. Others were tricked into being employed by a *malkin*, while they thought they were to get some other job. Only one respondent said she was actually forcibly abducted as a child from her school in Uttar Pradesh by a group of four men who tried to bring her to Calcutta. Ironically, one of the policemen who then rescued her from her abductors was the one who actually brought her to Calcutta and sold her to a brothel.

Not all the respondents were recruited into sex work directly after leaving home or being trafficked. Some of the respondents were recruited as domestic help and a few in small, informal manufacturing units, where they got very low or no wages, were abused verbally and physically, sometimes sexually harassed and often summarily dismissed when they dared to protest. Some of them were, of course, directly brought to red-light areas and sold to brothel managers, as some of the others were subsequently.

A significant number of respondents left home for love and the dream of romantic adventure and marital bliss. It was the boyfriends they absconded with who introduced them to the sex industry – sometimes after a brief and half-hearted attempt at conjugality. Many of the respondents never saw the man they left home with again, once they had been paid off by the brothel manager, while a few of the men stayed on for a while, living off the women's income.

Most women who came into the sex industry stayed on, even when they notionally could have returned to their earlier lives. Looking at why, it was found that, contrary to popular belief, coercion by brothel managers or other gatekeepers of the sex industry was not a serious deterrent. Rather, it was the stigma attached to being a sex worker and apprehension of social rejection that closed that option for them. Having become a sex worker, they feared that their parents, family or neighbours would not accept them back, or even if their parents did, their neighbours would shun them. Brought up as dutiful daughters, they were more concerned about protecting their parents' or families' interests than doing what they wished. The other important reason was that sex work provided them with a viable income with which to sustain themselves, their children and their families. Many did not want to return home, fearing violence from their husbands.

The study further helped to dispel another popular misconception regarding trafficking. Dominant discourses describe a trafficked person as eternally doomed, for ever trapped in the condition of victimhood, without rights and without ever regaining control over her life. The respondents' experiences showed that being trafficked is a temporally, time-bound and reversible phase in any person's life. At the time of the study, none of the respondents trafficked into the sex industry had remained with the original brothel manager to whom she was sold.

## The question of agency

What enabled these sex workers to get out of the trafficked situation? Support from fellow sex workers, especially those who were more experienced and street smart, was the most important and frequently cited factor that spurred the respondents to seek a practical way out of the trafficked situation. These colleagues provided advice, courage, loans and contacts with more friendly *malkins*. In some cases, members of Durbar acted as counsellors and guides. For some respondents, regular clients or *babus* came to the rescue, offering moral and financial support to set up independent establishments. In some cases, the *malkin* herself helped the respondents to change their situation, such as by encouraging them to save money. In one case, the *malkin* encouraged the respondent to get rid of the boyfriend she had run away with, who had sold her to the *malkin*. In another, the *malkin* loaned money to rent a room in the red-light area from which to operate independently. Of course, not all *malkins* were as sympathetic or fair-minded. Many respondents recounted escaping when everyone else was asleep. In these cases, too, other sex workers provided information about and contacts in other red-light areas. In none of these cases did the *malkins* or other gatekeepers seem zealous about finding and reclaiming the runaway sex workers.

While outsiders, whether colleagues, friends, *babus* or *malkins*, provided support and practical help, it was the respondents who had to take the initiative and find the conviction to make the move. In no case did they meekly submit themselves to their situation or passively wait to be rescued. Their own sense of agency and determination to act, as well as their resourcefulness, was critical in regaining control over their lives.

When asked what needed to change for sex workers to work with autonomy and security, sex workers named local thugs,[8] the police, political party workers at the local level, and *malkins* as those who persistently exploited and oppressed them. They said that if sex workers were to work with dignity and security there should be mechanisms to stop these people harassing and exploiting them. Some mentioned the role of sex workers' organizations like Durbar, while some others looked to the state to intervene on sex workers' behalf. Almost all respondents were of the opinion that it was social stigma that makes sex workers' lives vulnerable and their security precarious. They felt that the way to destigmatize the profession was to give it the same social and legal recognition as any other work, and to recognize their rights as workers. Although most were not aware of exactly what individual rights they would gain as workers, they were clear in their demands for an ideological recognition of sex work as a legitimate and valid occupation.[9]

### Durbar's position on trafficking and its interventions against it

Durbar sees trafficking as an *outcome* of a process whereby people are recruited and moved within or across national borders without informed consent, coerced into a job against their will and as a result lose control over their lives. As sex workers' rights activists, they are against trafficking for a number of reasons. The first set of reasons has to do with Durbar's aim of safeguarding the interests and rights of workers engaged in the sex industry. Durbar sees sex work as a contractual service, negotiated between consenting adults. In such a service contract, no coercion or deception ought to be involved. Trafficking into sex work by definition involves women and children being employed against their will, either through direct force or through deception, violating their fundamental rights to self-determination and autonomy over their bodies. Durbar has also been persistent in protecting and promoting the rights of sex workers in other contexts, such as police harassment, forcible eviction of sex workers by landlords or builders' mafia and unethical use of sex workers in medical research without their informed consent, so intervening to stop people from being trafficked into the sex industry was an obvious arena of intervention.

Durbar holds that for sex work to be established as a legitimate profession, those practising it have to comply with certain non-negotiable norms. Two fundamental principles have been identified on which these norms are based: first, anyone becoming a sex worker has to be of age, that is eighteen years or older; and second, she has to exercise informed consent. As trafficking violates both these norms, Durbar is determined to eliminate this as a way of recruitment into sex work. Moreover, Durbar aims to dissociate sex work from all criminal links so as to clean up its image as a profession and also to eliminate middlemen or agents profiteering from sex work through the exploitation of sex workers. As trafficking involves both, it needs to be eliminated.

The second set of arguments that Durbar posits to assert the necessity of sex workers' direct involvement in combating trafficking into sex work has to do with efficiency and effectiveness. Durbar argues that no degree of stringency in patrolling international borders has ever managed to stop illegal crossing of borders. Such severe measures put the lives of those being trafficked more at risk, as they force traffickers to use more hazardous routes. They also hold that no amount of policing by the state or intervention by social workers has managed to control intra-country trafficking. Durbar feels that one effective way of deterring trafficking, at least for the purpose of sex work, would be to ensure that within the sex industry itself, no trafficked person gets recruited as a sex worker. They are in a good position to help develop and enforce these norms, working with sex workers to develop confidential, efficient and independent communication channels for finding out whether any of the new entrants in the sex work sites have been trafficked into it, to which outsiders – be they the police or social workers – would not have access.

The third reason is a more strategic one. Every time sex workers have claimed their rights, those who see prostitution as a moral malaise have used the issue of trafficking to clamour for abolition, silencing sex workers' voices and demands. Contemporary discourses on trafficking are mired with the same anti-sex, and anti-sex-worker, stances. Durbar feels that unless it carves out a space for itself in the public arena to offer alternative perspectives on trafficking, the current focus on trafficking will be overtaken by the abolitionist agenda of the moral right.

### What is to be done?

Ending trafficking in sex work calls for measures to ensure all brothel owners and managers abide by norms barring them from recruiting trafficked sex workers. Durbar rejects the raid-and-rescue operations favoured by the police, social workers and anti-trafficking NGOs. These rescuers never consult sex workers to find out what *they* want, violate their rights by evicting them from their homes and workplaces, often insult and physically abuse them during the raid and then imprison them in remand homes for destitutes and delinquents, in a process not at all dissimilar from trafficking. Rehabilitation can be equally coercive and can create the conditions for further exploitation, with brothel-keepers or petty impostors posing as guardians and later extorting money from the sex worker or making her work like a slave.

To make a real dent into the practice of trafficking, Durbar realized it would have to formalize its efforts. In 1999, they established local self-regulatory boards in three red-light areas in Calcutta, with the aim of ending the exploitation of sex workers within the industry by establishing certain business norms. By 2005, such boards were established in almost all formal sex work sites across West Bengal. These boards have ten members, six sex workers and four non-sex workers who can be members of local clubs, locally practising lawyers and doctors, and local councillors or *panchayat*[10] members. The boards established in Calcutta red-light areas also included representatives from the state Social Welfare Department, the Labour Commission, the State Women's Commission and the Human Rights Commission, and in some cases well-known social workers and feminist activists.

Boards serve to mitigate violence against sex workers by brothel-keepers, room-owners, pimps, local hooligans or the police; to establish channels of information within the red-light area through which the board members can monitor whether any children or adults are trafficked into sex work or whether anyone is being made to work against her will; to identify those who have been trafficked, and encourage them to seek the help of the board to come out of the situation; to provide trauma counselling and health services; in the case of children, to organize repatriation, with representatives of the boards accompanying them to their homes, or if they do not want to go back, to government residential schools, and to maintain contact with them to ensure that they are not stigmatized or re-trafficked.

The principal challenge the boards face is their lack of legal standing. While the law is ambivalent about the legality of selling sex, it does not recognize sex work as a valid occupation. Social discourses frame sex workers as aberrant women, associated with criminality, who cannot be trusted with the welfare of other women and children. In an attempt to overcome this bias, Durbar members involved representatives from mainstream society in the boards, to render their activities transparent and public. Strategically, Durbar involved state representatives in the boards, to gain the tacit approval of the state. However, there continues to exist a degree of discomfort between Durbar and the state, particularly the police. Such tensions become even more obvious and acute when Durbar refuses to submit the rescued individuals into police custody, as is required by the law.

## Restoring control to trafficked women

People have always left home in search of new lives, better livelihoods, or adventure. Traditionally, rigid gender norms and lack of opportunities have prevented women from exploring opportunities. With radical and rapid changes in the politico-economic and social realms across the world, realignment of social and cultural relations and sweeping changes in the labour market, more and more women are now breaking away from homes, looking for more viable livelihood options or a preferred way of life.

For Durbar, this is seen as a positive and even potentially transformative development, opening up a window of opportunity for challenging existing gender and class inequalities. As feminists and rights activists, they are against any measure that restricts women's mobility in the name of stopping trafficking.

Durbar has taken a stand that its chief interest is in restoring a degree of control to the trafficked individual and not in convicting the trafficking agent, the latter being the responsibility and concern of the state. It has decided never to put a trafficked individual in police custody for the sake of filing a case against the traffickers. Moreover, experience has shown that trafficking takes place with the help of numerous agents, often unconnected with each other and many of them known to the trafficked individuals, be they relatives or lovers. Thus, arresting or convicting some of them sporadically is unlikely to have any impact. In many cases, Durbar has managed to establish working relationships with local police, and the higher-ups in the police administration, whereby Durbar continues to recover and repatriate trafficked sex workers with the implicit knowledge of the police. However, the issue becomes more complicated when the trafficked individual comes from another country. This poses a potential threat to Durbar's intervention in this arena, as its extra-constitutional role can be used against it if the state so wishes.

The other challenge is a more practical one. While sex worker members are eager to take action against exploitation, non-sex worker members are more hesitant. Durbar members suggested that boards should be brought up to speed with Durbar's thinking on trafficking, so that they do not lapse into the usual 'raid and rescue' mode of intervention, or just pursue welfare activities. They also suggested visits between board members from different areas, to develop a wider understanding of the issues involved, and in turn, a more institutional character. The boards' effectiveness also depends on the confidence and support of local sex workers. In order to gain their trust, and involve non-sex worker members more actively, the self-regulatory boards have embarked on a series of developmental activities in the red-light areas. These include helping sex workers to acquire ration cards and access government schemes for the poor, repairing roads, arranging regular clearing of garbage, proper water supply and sanitation and so on. These activities bring succour to sex workers, get non-sex worker members involved and give the boards visibility and a certain legitimacy. Through these activities, Durbar reiterates sex workers' claims to amenities and benefits to which they are entitled as citizens.

NGOs' positions and practices also pose a challenge to sex workers' intervention into trafficking. On one hand, the conflict is ideological. Sex workers and trafficked persons taking the initiative to deal with their own problems as actors rather than passive beneficiaries challenge the conventional role of NGOs and the enlightened middle classes of working on behalf of the poor. On the other hand, there is also an immediate conflict of interest. If more and more sex workers' organizations gain the capacity and the confidence to implement anti-trafficking intervention activities themselves, NGOs would become gradually redundant. In fact, sex workers and trafficked persons' demands for the right to self-determination and autonomy represent an ideological challenge not just to NGOs' anti-trafficking practices, but to all discourses that reduce the marginalized, and particularly women, to submissive victims of their circumstance, devoid of human agency, unable to steer their own destiny unless 'rescued' by benevolent others.

## Changing the frame

Overcoming this challenge calls for a discursive shift in the way sex work and sex workers are framed. It was Durbar that introduced the word *jounokarmee* as Bengali nomenclature for sex workers, as a way of claiming an identity as workers. While the debates rage on about whether sex work can be considered a valid occupation and be decriminalized, the word *jounokarmee* has made its way into everyday language. Local newspapers, both in English and Bengali, hardly ever use other, more derogatory terms for sex workers unless the reporter deliberately wants to deprecate the sex workers' rights movement.

For this shift in discourse to have an impact on anti-trafficking practices on the ground, and for sex workers to be accepted as equal players in anti-trafficking forums, where they could effectively challenge the anti-sex worker and anti-human rights slants in the dominant discourses and interventions, establish their own perspectives and protect their interests, much more has to happen. However, the stories related here tell us that sex workers themselves, together with organizations like Durbar, can perhaps show ways in which any marginalized group of poor women can claim citizenship rights through voicing and actualizing their demand for self-determination and participation in the public sphere.

## Notes

'Streetwalkers show the way' is the translation of a popular slogan of the sex workers' movement in West Bengal: '*Rastar meyerai path dekhachhey*'.

Swapna Gayen, Rama Debnath, Kajol Bose, Sikha Das, Geeta Das, M. Das, Manju Biswas, Pushpa Sarkar, Putul Singh, Rashoba Bibi, Rekha Mitra and Sudipta Biswas are sex worker activists who conducted the action research and helped in analysing the data. Swapna and Rama were the elected secretary and president of DMSC – Durbar's agitational front. Kajol was the president of the sex workers' own cooperative society, Usha. Durbar fieldworkers Akshay Mukherjee, Arati Dutta, Bishwajit Modok, Mahashweta Bhattachrya, Shoma Dutta and Shubra Mitra also helped in conducting the interviews.

1 *Durbar* in Bengali means 'indomitable'.

2 Her real name has not been used at her request.

3 *Chhukris* are virtually bonded to their brothel managers, who usually make a down-payment either to agents who traffic sex workers or to the sex worker's relatives or associates who bring her, for contracting the services of the sex worker. A *chhukri* is obliged to work under the *malkin* until she earns enough to pay off the amount advanced. However, in reality, a *chhukri* ends up paying off her debt several times over before she is allowed to move on. The conditions of work are extremely harsh, as the *malkin* tries to extract as much income from the *chhukri* as possible, allowing her neither leisure nor much choice over clients and sexual practices.

4 Her real name has not been used at her request.

5 *Adhiya* is a particular contractual arrangement in sex work. *Adhiyas* are those sex workers who work for a *malkin* and share 50 per cent of their income with her. Some *adhiyas* graduate to this status from originally being *chhukris*, while the majority start their career in sex work as *adhiyas*.

6 Her real name has not been used at her request.

7 Action research for a programme on Gender Citizenship and Good Governance conducted by Durbar in collaboration with Royal Tropical Institute (KIT), the Netherlands, in 2000–02.

8 They mentioned '*parar chheley*' or neighbourhood boys and '*mastans*' or petty criminals who live on extortion and petty crime. In most cases they are synonymous. In red-light areas, and indeed in most poor neighbourhoods, these young men are a common phenomenon, often enjoying the patronage of one or other political party. In red-light areas these men are sex workers' sons, their boyfriends or husbands. Some also come from families that own the brothels.

9 They wanted sex work to enjoy the same status as any other work ('*aar panchta kajer mato kaj*') and claimed workers' rights or '*srameeker adhikar*', so that the *shamaj* (society) would respect them.

10 Elected local government body.

TWO | **Institutionalizing gender in development**

# 8 | Gender, myth and fable: the perils of mainstreaming in sector bureaucracies

HILARY STANDING

This chapter is concerned with the ways in which gender and development discourses and frameworks have been appropriated into a particular area of development policy and practice, namely gender mainstreaming efforts in developing country sector bureaucracies. Its origins lie in practical encounters with these efforts while working over the last few years in health sector development programmes in poor countries that are funded by substantial amounts of external aid. It is an attempt to understand why these efforts cause me considerable unease. The myth, in this context, is not a single overarching one. Rather, it is a set of linked mythical assumptions about the nature of social and political transformation and how it is brought about which led to, and became encapsulated in, the practice of gender mainstreaming in bureaucracies. The chapter also argues that there are fables embedded in some of the common discourses of gender and development. The common thread is an inadequate understanding of the policy domain and how gender and development advocates can engage with it.

Gender mainstreaming in the sector bureaucracies of poor countries has been associated particularly with sector-wide programming in areas such as health and education. Rather than each financing discrete projects, agencies seek to work with governments in a coordinated way to move towards an agreed strategic planning and financial framework with a common funding pool. Progress in embedding gender equity goals in processes such as this depends on building some level of national and local ownership of these objectives (Foster 1999). While, clearly, in many countries there is advocacy for gender issues from civil society and grassroots organizations, this is much more rarely the case in national and local bureaucracies. This has sometimes led to considerable efforts by donors at developing bureaucratic advocacy for gender goals, mainly through gender training and financing and encouraging institutional means of mainstreaming, particularly gender cells, or the designation of focal points in ministries such as health. Yet a common complaint from gender advocates is that of 'policy evaporation' – the tendency for policy commitments to gender equity to be lost, reinterpreted or heavily watered down as they move through (or become mired in) the bureaucracy.

To borrow from anthropology, myths can be good to 'think with'. For projects of transformation, they offer powerful ways of capturing and framing complex messages in pursuit of desirable outcomes. They can equally be problematic in reducing the complex to the banal and seeming to promise the riches of political change without the long work of politics. As one of the major policy tools with a direct lineage in feminist-inspired gender and development, gender mainstreaming in bureaucracies can be an uncomfortable bearer of some of its more mythical thought and practice. The first task is to assemble the mythical elements through an actual event.

## The scene

A workshop is taking place in the Ministry of Health (MoH). We are here to discuss the draft gender equity strategy which three external consultants have been putting together. The MoH has been under pressure for some time from the donor consortium that funds the health sector programme to incorporate a gender strategy. Consultants have come and gone. There has been commitment and useful input from some of the women's groups and non-governmental organizations (NGOs), but no movement within the MoH itself. Finally, one of the donors brought in the three new gender consultants in a final attempt to move the process forwards. I was one of them.

The workshop brought together three sets of actors: staff at various levels in the MoH, donor and international agency representatives and a sprinkling of women's group and other 'civil society' representatives.

The external consultants, who are facilitating, start, as requested, with an overview of gender analytical frameworks. They have decided to take a low-key, eclectic approach to this task. The staff are from different levels in the hierarchy and have varying competence in English. Most of them are unfamiliar with 'gender' language and there is not a readily accessible set of terms in the national language for translating gender concepts. The consultants stress that there is diversity in views and understandings of gender, women, power and powerlessness. They are anxious to avoid prescribing 'right' and 'wrong' ways of engaging with gender and to encourage the staff in particular to make links with their understanding of the broader programme goals.

The discussion which follows is largely appropriated by donor representatives, who are concerned to lay down a correct line on what is gender and how the term should be used. They scold some of the bureaucrats for their 'misunderstanding' of gender, particularly in talking about women's health, rather than gender relations. The effect is to confuse and silence the very people who are expected to operationalize the strategy.

## What is going on?

At one level, there is an easy reading of this. The gender and development industry, as epitomized in bureaucratic gender mainstreaming, is a
soft target. Here, we have all its less attractive elements. First, there is an
agenda driven by outside agencies, often as part of the conditionality for
aid. In this case, gender is to a significant extent an externally imposed
(and in parts of the bureaucracy resented and not understood) requirement for continuing support. Second, there is capture of language and
resources by the particular kinds of elites which the aid industry throws
up. Postgraduate and other training programmes in gender and development have produced a new cadre of frequently young, enthusiastic, but
barely experienced development professionals who nevertheless occupy
influential positions in funding agencies. Third, there is a policing and even
shaming of less powerful groups whose discourses do not fit the gender
and development hegemony that the dominant voices represent.

At the same time, there is a greater complexity to be addressed here, of
which gender mainstreaming in the bureaucracies of subaltern countries
is but one important practical manifestation. I feel the need to start from
the premise (admittedly a self-serving one in this instance) that all the
apparatus which sustains gender mainstreaming – dedicated consultants,
training, masters degrees, institutional mechanisms – is not just a massive
exercise in bad faith or a way of finding jobs for the girls (although it can
certainly turn out that way), but rather, that there has been good faith in
it and a commitment to gender as a transformative project. So what happened between the passion for social justice which fed the debates, and
the reality in many countries of a great deal of official apparatus around
gender but massive 'policy evaporation' in practice?

I will discuss two interwoven aspects of this. The first is how the project
of social transformation became translated into practice in the increasingly
professionalized world of gender and development. The second is the way
in which the links between theory, policy and practice were rendered relatively unproblematic by naïvety about 'policy' and how progressive change
comes about.

## Bureaucracies – drivers or followers of change?

Sector bureaucracies have become a major focus of mainstreaming
efforts in aid-dependent countries. It is not difficult to understand why.
Programmes are largely negotiated, designed, managed and monitored by
international and national bureaucrats, not by and along with politicians
and civil society groups. Of course, the idea is that bureaucracies do this

on behalf of these key constituencies. In practice, there may be initial con-sultation processes (again a condition of aid) which do reach out to other stakeholders, but they rarely go beyond this or develop into sustainable ways in which programme implementers can be brought to account.

The reality in many countries is that there is often a dearth of institu-tional and political mechanisms through which citizens can have voice and influence or can monitor what governments do (or fail to do) in their name. Instead, influence may be exercised through forms of personal and political patronage and be heavily skewed towards elites. The poor, and particularly poor women, have little or no access to alternative forms of influence. Bureaucracies are often heavily politicized with officials balanc-ing conflicting demands as they struggle to protect their interests.

Gender mainstreaming in this environment is therefore a paradoxical affair, subject simultaneously to over-politicization and depoliticization. It becomes over-politicized when linked to resources to be competed for. It becomes depoliticized as the demand for 'industrial' or mass production models of gender mainstreaming in the form of toolkits and checklists grows. This in turn produces a bigger industry of gender professionals, with careers dependent upon a steady demand, from development agencies in particular, for their services.

These processes lend themselves to easy caricature – a political project becomes reduced to a scramble for study tours and a 'tick the box' manage-ment of the gender requirements of the programme. There are easy targets for blame: opportunistic bureaucrats aware of the possible rewards for talking 'gender'; and cooption of a previously politically grounded gender advocacy to often apolitical and prescriptive forms of gender training. I would argue, however, that this kind of depoliticization is largely a con-sequence of a deeper problem with the way the transformatory project in gender and development came to be understood. As advocates became engaged in translating feminist analysis of gender and development into attempts to influence policy agendas, the site of these efforts shifted increasingly to institutions, and particularly to national bureaucracies. What was lacking was bringing together the theoretical insights of gender and development with an equally sophisticated analysis of institutional roles and functions and how they are linked to or disconnected from the possibilities for change.

Gender mainstreaming in sector bureaucracies is one manifestation of this. It entails a mis-specification of the nature, role and functions of bureaucracies. Bureaucracies are not engines of social and political transformation. Indeed, as Orwell, Kafka and others remind us, we need to be ever-vigilant that they are not. In this sense, we have cause to be grateful that gender mainstreaming efforts in bureaucracies tend to become depoliticized. Bureaucracy and ideological fervour can make undesirable bedfellows. The appropriate space and place for driving transformation is in the political arena. Mainstreaming objectives which place the onus on a bureaucracy to drive social transformation, especially where the political legitimacy of the institutions of government is already fragile, will therefore continue to run into the hot sands of evaporation. It may also be noted that in the UK we do not expect our bureaucracies to spearhead gender transformation in this way. We simply expect them to do their job.

The role of a health sector bureaucracy is to improve health systems' functioning. That was at least understood by the bureaucrats at our workshop, even if the reality falls short of the vision. That was why they persisted in talking about how to improve women's health because the sector programme clearly headlines the health of women and girls as the major strategic objective. But instead of being encouraged in this, they stood accused by the donor representatives of what has become the cardinal sin in this version of mainstreaming – namely of 'only' meeting women's practical needs rather than their strategic gender interests. What began as a contextually grounded political analysis of different styles of advocacy and became an off-the-peg gender training tool, ended up used as a stick to belabour the bureaucrats with.

What was needed was not a ticking off for focusing on women's health, but a reinforcement of this understanding in terms of enabling the bureaucrats to understand in their own terms the links between improved health systems functioning and 'gender equity' and to understand the role they could play. For instance, the major complaints of women about health services are the absence of drugs in the facilities, illicit charges and indifferent and disrespectful treatment by health workers. It is within the remit and capacity of the Ministry of Health to do something about these. If it did, poor women would benefit enormously and there would be knock-on improvements in other areas of their lives. Such objectives are consonant with the primary task of the health system as an organization and the links to 'gender' can be brought out and understood in these terms.

I would argue, therefore, that the main myth in gender mainstreaming in sector bureaucracies is not so much a myth of political transformation without politics, but more a mythic relocation of the possibility of political transformation to an inherently non-transformatory context. This mythic relocation requires supporting myths. The first, and most powerful, is that the empowerment language of politics and advocacy can be transferred into bureaucratic mainstreaming without its meaning being changed. Yet institutions always appropriate language and turn it to the service of their own interests. Second, there is the myth of a right and a wrong way to 'do' gender in policy contexts; and third, a myth that gender training can produce a desirable and predictable behavioural outcome.

As with all such myths, the relationship to reality is a complex one. There are undoubtedly better and worse ways of 'doing' gender, but working out which they are requires a high degree of sensitivity to the context, and a large and often indefinable dollop of wisdom derived from experience. These are often at variance with the pressure for mass production of gender tools and the rapid development of a cadre of trainers. The jury is still out on the value of gender training in bureaucracies. There have been few systematic evaluations. One of the few reviewed training in development partner organizations, not in national bureaucracies (Porter and Smyth 1998). It was equivocal about the impact. Given the demand for training, however, more attention needs to be paid to defining exactly what it is trying to achieve, the contexts in which it is effective and the approaches which are of value.

### Naïve notions – policy as a route to transformation

Despite continual challenges from social science, there has been little recognition in gender and development practice of the very problematic link between policy and implementation and the implications of this for social transformation. This is despite the excellent work of individuals writing on constraints to change from an institutional perspective (e.g. Razavi 1997: 1111; Kardam 1995: 11).

This naïvety towards policy takes a number of forms. First, and linked closely to the bureaucratic mainstreaming model of change already discussed, is the issue of bypassing political processes. Second, is the assumption of a prescriptive and predictable relationship between policy *intention* and policy *outcome*. Third, is the tendency to treat discourse and terminology as if they are in themselves independent agents of, or impediments to, change. Let us consider these further.

*Political bypass* I have already argued that it is not the role of bureaucracies to transform gender relations and bureaucracies should not be used as a proxy for this. Transformative actions enshrined in progressive policies on gender require political coalition-building, not just a statement on a statute book and a directive to the bureaucracy to carry them out. It follows from this that the apparatus which has been created from professionalizing gender and development can play only a modest supporting role in the transformative project. It cannot substitute for the work of politics.

*Intentions and outcomes* The complexity and sophistication of gender and development frameworks have not extended to their translation into the policy environment. There has been an almost mechanical belief in the power of intention to determine the outcome of policy implementation. This has generated the myth that policies can be judged on a prior reading of their intent. This is particularly clear in the appropriation of the practical needs/strategic interests distinction to the gender policy toolkit. We have not taken seriously the doctrine of unintended consequences. If we had then we would have understood better the inherently messy and unpredictable nature of this relationship.

In their examination of local economic development projects in a poor urban area of Durban, South Africa, Beall and Todes (2003) give a compelling account of the ways in which carefully crafted 'gender-sensitive' planning led to unexpected outcomes, partly because women did not simply respond as anticipated and partly because some (well-meant) aspects of project implementation inadvertently damaged women by reinforcing elements of existing social relations and inequalities.

They note that ultimately it was those women who were politicized already, through engagement in earlier political struggles or engaged in local politics, who were able to advance a progressive political and social agenda for women. The technical activities of gender planning were a largely irrelevant sideshow to the political arena. They note also that the struggle has been slow, uneven and unpredictable. The experience causes them to question the whole value of externally promoted gender-based planning, particularly in a context where an internally developed politics of transformation already exists.

One important lesson from this is that women are social agents. As agents, they have the capacity to subvert intentions, good or bad. This may be by turning paternalism to their advantage or by 'refusing' to be progressive if they construe their interests in a different way from the planners. At the same time, policies can also 'misbehave': well-intentioned ones can have bad outcomes, and vice versa.

Over-reliance on intention as the arbiter of good and bad policies is linked to an overconfidence that gender and development planning can identify women's interests and devise a pathway for meeting them. This is despite a rich theoretical debate in gender and development on the concept of interests and who is entitled to define them, as well as practical examples that should serve as warnings (Razavi and Miller 1995). For instance, writing on the difficulty of conceptualizing women's interests as separate or separable from those of their households, Whitehead (1990) notes that in the context of policies that may increase their household

labour burdens, women may feel the trade-off between labour intensification and outcomes is worth it if the outcome advances the interests of the
household as a whole. Yet labour intensification occupies a large space in
the canon of gender and development 'ills'.

*Misbehaving discourses* The richness of theoretical work in gender and
development owes much to discourse analysis, which has unpacked the
histories, assumptions and political trajectories of different strands of
development thinking in terms of their gender implications. Again, however, this has been to the neglect of an equally rich exploration in the policy
domain of the relationship between discourses and outcomes.

We have instead substituted fables for evidence-based assessments.[1]
These are often in the form of binary oppositions. Two particularly tenacious ones are the discourses of equity versus efficiency, and instrumentalism versus equity or advocacy. There has been a great preoccupation with
critiquing the development corpus in terms of these discourses, along
with exhortations to institutions and actors in the development field to
choose the 'right' discourse. Much less effort has been expended on understanding how, if at all, these discourses connect to policy implementation
in all its complexity.

Instead, we have attached a moral hierarchy to these gender fables,
ranking them against each other in a way that abstracts them from their
political and social context. Critiques of instrumentalism have been made
most strongly on what might be termed absolutist discursive grounds.
Instrumentalism is therefore ultimately a 'bad' discourse as opposed to
equity, which is a 'good' one, although we might concede that it is occasion-
ally necessary as a tactic if all else fails. But as with bad stepmothers, bad
discourses must be ousted and shamed. Razavi (1997) makes a powerful
case against this tendency in her discussion of policy advocacy strategies.
She points to the weaknesses of discursive absolutism when faced both
with the complex realities of women's and men's lives, and the constraints
of working within institutions to try to bring a gender perspective into
the policy frame.[2]

Her analysis of gender policy discourses notes the difficulties that gender
advocates face when working within institutions on gender issues. There
is not only hostility and indifference to the idea of gender itself, but also
the everyday political battles and sectional interests which are present
in all organizations. Faced with these realities, internal advocates need
to use whatever discursive means make sense to fight their corner. She
argues that charges of 'instrumentalism' from outside are therefore unhelpful. Advocates have both to render their arguments meaningful to an

ungendered audience, and to do it in a way that makes them more likely to be accepted and acted upon. As Razavi points out, this kind of internal advocacy within institutions is again not an inherently transformative project. It only becomes so when those outside the institution – activists and researchers – can connect it to the political world and to pressures for change. We can add to this that the discursive framing will itself then be transformed by this political connectedness.

Razavi also makes an important plea for using or rejecting discourses on the basis of evidence. Here is one of the key lessons from the history of policy engagement. By no means can all battles for gender transformation be won by informed advocacy, but evidence and rational argument remain our most powerful tools in engaging with institutions. This must include interrogating our own discourses and rescuing them where necessary from the realms of the fable.

## Concluding reflections

I have argued that gender mainstreaming in developing country national bureaucracies has been a flawed project based on a myth about how social transformation in gender relations occurs. Associated with this has been an inadequate theorization of the relationship between theory, policy and implementation and particularly the roles and functions of institutions which set 'policy' or mediate its implementation.

Why did some of us, whether as academics, advocates, practitioners or combinations of these, end up understanding mainstreaming and policy in these particular ways? Was it a certain naïvety about how real world institutions work? Or was it an inevitable byproduct of professionalizing gender and development, particularly in contexts where many of the practitioners do not come from a background in political activism?

There is some truth in both of these. The main route to professionalization of gender and development has been through academically-based courses taught mainly by academics, often with a background in feminist advocacy. This has provided an excellent basis for theoretically rigorous analysis. But we have struggled to carry this forwards into the recalcitrant arenas of policy and implementation. We did not make sufficient use of the experience of our students who came from a policy background, nor did we pay enough attention to the skills they would need to go back into those environments and operate more effectively. These skills cannot just be advocacy-based but require a grounding in how institutions work, how to develop contextually-based strategies and create workable alliances in constrained environments.

Instead, the focus of application has been on off-the-peg tools and frameworks, fuelled by the demand for gender mainstreaming. These are not necessarily bad in themselves and I would suggest that the charge of depoliticization is often misplaced. It is perhaps unavoidable that, in needing to provide an orderly route map for busy people, they exclude context and complexity and become banal and mythic. For instance, one of the results has been a too-automatic privileging of gender relations in practical and policy discourses (Razavi and Miller 1995) to the detriment of other contextually important signifiers of difference and inequality.

More troubling is how this industry speaks to power relations through its embeddedness in international aid programmes. The professionalization of gender and development took place in large measure through the demand from and financial support of development agencies. Most funding of work in gender and development derives from international and bilateral agencies. As bureaucracies themselves, they have led the efforts at mainstreaming. Many of us depend for our livelihoods on doing this work on their behalf. We also need to stand back and examine our practice more critically.

In particular, we need to develop a more situated analysis of the shifting and complex relationships of gender, class, culture, North and South encapsulated in events such as the workshop described above. What are the different sorts of power operating here and who is using or abusing them? How do we begin to think about the dynamics of power in encounters between, for instance, young, often female and white, aid bureaucrats and older, often male officials of national bureaucracies?

How far does any of this matter? I think the answer is again a paradoxical one. It matters both a little and a lot. The logic of my argument about bureaucratic mainstreaming is that it matters less than we have tended to think. The apparatus of mainstreaming can at most make a modest contribution to political transformation. It matters a lot in three senses. First, we could do it better by rescuing it from an impossible project to transform gender relations to a more modest adjunct to improving necessary things which can make a difference in women's and men's lives. Second, we could 'do' policy much better by paying the same rigorous attention to it as we do to the political economy of gender relations. Third, we need to acknowledge and explore the less obvious power relations which a professionalized gender and development industry has brought into being.

## Notes

Thanks to Gerry Bloom for insightful comments on an earlier draft.

1 I use fable in the sense of a story told to convey a lesson, not to represent a body of evidence.

2 See Razavi's (1997) discussion of the dilemmas experienced by gender advisers in the World Bank.

## References

Beall, J. and A. Todes (2003) 'Headlines and Head-Space: Challenging Gender Planning Orthodoxy in Area-based Urban Development', paper prepared for the conference, 'Gender Myths and Feminist Fables: Repositioning Gender in Development Policy and Practice', Institute of Development Studies, Brighton, 2–4 July.

Foster, M. (1999) *Lessons of Experience from Health Sector SWAps* (London: Centre for Aid and Public Expenditure/Overseas Development Institute [CAPE/ODI]).

Kardam, N. (1995) 'Conditions of Accountability for Gender Policy: The Organizational, Political and Cognitive Contexts', *IDS Bulletin*, Vol. 26, no. 3: 11–22.

Porter, P. and I. Smyth (1998) 'Gender Training for Development Policy Implementers: Only a Partial Solution', *Oxfam Working Paper* (Oxford: Oxfam).

Razavi, S. (1997) 'Fitting Gender into Development Institutions', *World Development*, Vol. 25, No. 7: 1111–25.

Razavi, S. and C. Miller (1995) 'From WID to GAD: Conceptual Shifts in the Women and Development Discourse', *UNRISD/UNDP Occasional Paper* 1 (Geneva and New York: UNRISD and UNDP).

Whitehead, A. (1990) 'Rural Women and Food Production in Sub-Saharan Africa', in J. Drèze and A. K. Sen (eds), *The Political Economy of Hunger, Vol. 1: Entitlement and Wellbeing* (Oxford: Clarendon Press).

# 9 | Making sense of gender in shifting institutional contexts: some reflections on gender mainstreaming

RAMYA SUBRAHMANIAN

For many speakers at the 'Gender Myths and Feminist Fables' conference, on which this book is based, 'gender mainstreaming' has become a hollow discourse, a generator of myths that simplifies the complexity of gender in ways that are counter-productive, and in many ways a constraint on political action by feminists. These criticisms are not entirely new. As long as gender mainstreaming has been an aspect of the feminist engagement with development, there have been those who have warned of the dangers of political dilution, those who have opposed the takeover of feminist agendas by the state, and the dangers of cooptation. Yet engagement with the state has been critical for furthering inclusive citizenship, and commitments to gender equality and women's empowerment are ubiquitous and often genuine. How do we make sense of these diverse trends? This chapter offers some reflections on gender mainstreaming, arguing for reviewing its achievements both in the wider context of transformative possibilities, and also in more modest perspective, scaling down expectations of what it can achieve.

As feminists have sought to alter the terrain of 'mainstream' development, and as this effort has been increasingly internationalized, gender 'mainstreaming' has been the fundamental Gender and Development (GAD) buzzword. The World Conference on Women held in Beijing in 1995 and the enormous agenda of transformation and change that was identified gave an impetus to a process that had started with the earlier conference in Nairobi. As Staudt (1997: 3) notes, the 'explosion of women's organizational activity and political agenda' unleashed by the UN Decade for Women (1975–85) coincided with developments over time that resulted in states seeking to 'legitimize themselves through public policy and participation-based accountability'. Feminists have, therefore, sought out the state as a key partner for change, and gender mainstreaming has been the label associated with strategies adopted by feminists to make the state an agent of transformative change for women.

Partnership with the state has brought with it clear agendas for feminist action in development, based on reversing the 'lens' through which development is analysed, and making explicit the underlying rules of social relationships that have legitimized inequality in resource allocation and redistribution. The agenda for influencing the 'mainstream' includes altering public policies, improving implementation and delivery of policies through clear programmes for change in administrative systems, and directly benefiting women through targeted actions and programmes. This is an ambitious agenda, at the core of which is the effort to advocate for change, through training, institutional mechanisms for making gender a more explicit criterion for development programming and effectiveness, and developing 'tools' that can help organizations think more deeply about gender relations, away from the earlier 'add women and stir approach'. During this time, feminist analysis has also been enriched, partly as a result of greater feminist engagement with mainstream academic institutions and spaces, and has become increasingly more sophisticated, and more politically acute. This has had the effect both of creating greater expectations of state institutions and the gender feminists who occupy advocacy and implementation positions within them, as well as widening the analytical gap *between* differently located feminist advocates. Standing (this volume) links the ever-widening gulf to the supplementary effect that gender feminism has had – the development of intermediaries in this process, such as consultants, and people skilled through higher education and training programmes on gender and development. 'Gender mainstreaming', as a sub-set of the development institutional landscape, has itself begun to have implications for both feminist movements as well as development spaces.

The decade of mainstreaming experience has uncovered many lessons. Many of these are about the nature of the state and its institutions, and the kinds of spaces that are available for promoting transformative change. A key criticism about gender mainstreaming has been the 'narrowness' of the strategy despite the complexity of gender relations and the contextual variations in the processes and outcomes related to gender inequalities. Most mainstreaming 'machinery' looks the same irrespective of the country; most are located at the national level, rarely reaching sub-state levels where development change may be more manageable, and may more closely reflect the needs and priorities of particular sub-groups. The institutional coverage of mainstreaming actors and efforts has been narrowly within the development 'industry' – largely within agencies of development cooperation and national governments, thus narrowing the field of engagement often to donor-initiated debates and programmatic interventions. 'Gender mainstreaming' has thus *imposed* narrowness on what are actually very diverse processes, conflating policy reform with changes in bureaucratic practice, and confining the analytical gaze to the advancement of women's 'cause' within institutions with often little mandate and power to effect real change.

A second key criticism has been that gender mainstreaming efforts have necessitated simplifying concepts relating to gender inequality and gender relations, which have in turn fuelled unreal expectations of the ways in which social change takes place. The 'implicit' models of social change that continue to hold sway, extend older, and somewhat discredited approaches, which viewed investment of resources in women as the key to their 'liberation' from relations of subordination. Messages that gender inequality can be managed through adjustments in bureaucratic practice and policy have necessarily relied on discursive strategies that are 'instrumental' – i.e. that suggest that investment in women has high pay-offs. By providing a few 'jobs for the girls' in this enterprise, the project of emancipating women was seen to have been set in motion. Quite how this emancipatory project was expected to roll out is not clear. Yet, gender mainstreaming has legitimized this approach in its zeal to portray the achievement of gender equality as a matter of getting development cooperation, development policies and development institutions 'right' for women. Mostly, this has resulted in the 'conflation of a particular institutional strategy with processes of social change' (Woodford-Berger, this volume).

A third criticism has been about the way in which this implicit model of social change put forward has taken the steam out of the inherently political nature of feminist transformative visions, and has thus meant that 'gender' is not seen as explicitly political (unlike, say, race or class), but more as about giving visibility to *women* and their capacities and needs. Complaints about policy evaporation – the process through which gender fades out of the explicit commitments and actions that follow rhetorical claims of the importance of gender and development – and the lack of analytical clarity about what 'gender' means continue to dominate assessments of gender mainstreaming. Recent literature on international instruments of policy and resource coordination emphasizes both analytical weakness and policy evaporation (Whitehead 2003; see Subrahmanian 2004a for a review). The lack of attention to organizational structures is also noted to act as a constraint on following through more impressive policy statements (Kanji and Salway 2000). When the conceptual clarity within organizations attempting to mainstream gender is itself poor, the lack of translation into policy and practice is unsurprising. 'Gender mainstreaming' itself is a hollow term, as its usage commits the user neither to a clear agenda on gender transformative action, nor to a clear institutional transformative agenda. This gives rise to highly varied approaches to mainstreaming, and underdeveloped definitions and understandings of what it is that these processes and strategies are meant to achieve.

## Placing gender mainstreaming in context

This discursive 'hollowness' may be what makes gender mainstreaming attractive to development agencies (or actors within them), who may prefer not to commit to such a demanding transformative agenda, that appears to, regardless of how sophisticated the advocacy discourse is that accompanies it,[1] require some form of disempowerment for men in practice. The notion of the 'complementarity' of the sexes in terms of their roles and inclinations is influential, and hard to disembed. Talk of women's empowerment, while attractive because of its progressive ring, also suggests disturbing a particular equilibrium that is often viewed as part of some natural or created social order.

However, the hollowness may also reflect wider economic and political processes, which constrain spaces for transformation, particularly within development institutions. Fine (2003) argues that although the neo-liberal framework has 'softened' somewhat, based on the criticisms that faced the main Bretton Woods institutions following the perceived failure of their policies to address poverty through structural adjustment policies, not much has changed substantively. Although the post-Washington consensus acknowledges the importance of history, institutions, processes and social dynamics as relevant to the understanding of development and change, he argues that the frameworks and intellectual tools still accord primacy to neo-classical economics and the dominance of the market. In analytical terms, economic analysis is now applied to social dimensions of life, resulting in reductionist analysis, i.e. where economic and social relations are interpreted 'through the narrowest of explanatory prisms' (ibid.: 7). Within such a hegemonic approach, the objective of complexifying institutional understandings of the ways in which gender impacts on development is doomed not to succeed.

Education provides an illustrative case for examining some of these issues, as it appears at a distant glance to represent a success of 'gender mainstreaming'. In education there has been tremendous progress associated with increasing the visibility of gender goals within broader policy efforts. Gender parity, for example, is now widely accepted as a central goal to which governments aspire. International agencies have backed concerted campaigns to promote girls' education. The run-up to the year 2005, and the target of eliminating gender disparity in primary and secondary education in both the Millennium Development Goals (MDGs) (Goal 3, target 4) and the Education for All (EFA) goals, unleashed numerous international reports and conferences. While gender equality in education, a goal for 2015 in the EFA process, is not defined clearly, the impact of gender advocacy on the normative acceptance of gender equality as important to development has been significant. On the redistributive side, too, there have been many gains in terms of efforts to improve female access to education.

However, it is hard to identify the extent to which this change is the result of 'gender mainstreaming' in its narrow sense of coordination mechanisms within bureaucracies. Instrumentalist arguments for girls' education have indeed paid off (the mantra of improved productivity, declining fertility, better child health, better mothering). However, these arguments have perhaps thrived because they have conformed to the wider and hegemonic economic discourse within which policy advocacy is played out. Neo-liberal economic discourse is increasingly shaping the way in which policy approaches in other spheres – social policy, governance systems – are evolving. Education has always been particularly prone to this form of ideological capture, given the private nature of the returns arising from investing in it (Subrahmanian 2004b). Several tensions arise. While the case for public investment in education has been fought for and made central to education policy, particularly in the face of human resource crises in many countries, these developments have taken place in contradictory political and institutional environments. The case for universal education (and the attendant realization that the state is a key agency for this), for example, has been made simultaneous to an assault on the state and its capacities, particularly in the era of structural adjustment. For many, promoting the visibility of women in ways that strengthen policies that continually undermine the conditions under which women are gaining rights is a pyrrhic victory.

This raises the fundamental question of how we should evaluate or assess 'gender mainstreaming'. I suggest that the approach taken should be both broader and more specific. Locating 'gender mainstreaming' (in its composite sense as a set of strategies) within the broader context of development discourses, ideologies and trajectories is important. Equally, insisting on more specific and precise definitions of what these strategies are can only help to clarify the nature of transformation and change that is being pursued. We need to analyse it simultaneously from an overarching perspective of the diversity of development processes and actions focused on transformation, and also from *within* the sub-set of development it represents, that is efforts to influence aspects of state (and development institution) practice.

Criticisms of gender mainstreaming tend to be focused somewhere in between these two levels of analysis, resulting in an overburdening of expectations on institutions that are inadequate to the task. Not only then does this result in conflating particular institutional strategies with a much larger process of social change, as argued earlier, but it also results in conflating what is in effect a fairly specific set of institutional strategies, practices and processes, with a variety of feminist actions and debates, both within and outside of the state, to influence social change. By characterizing gender mainstreaming as a 'monolith', and without disaggregating what it entails, who is involved, and what processes and strategies it comprises, in clearly situated contexts, evaluations of 'its' effects or impacts become impossible. This 'mythical beast' is then invested with the powers to effect social change, and the underlying and implicit assumptions (and models) of institutional and social change associated with it remain uninterrogated. If expectations are scaled down, then the achievements of gender mainstreaming may be more realistically assessed, and may actually be positive in some cases. At the least we may develop a better 'handle' on understanding the processes of change that explain certain outcomes, as well as focusing sharper attention on the politics surrounding these processes of change.

Blackmore's (2004) account of educational change in Australia provides an important historical perspective of the phases undergone by the push for gender equity reform in education. Her analysis locates specific institutional mechanisms within the context of wider political shifts and policy agendas. She notes that several variables determine the extent to which gender equity reform can succeed – the kind of state, the kind of feminism within which 'gender equity' is being advocated, the overarching political ideology of the state, the position adopted about gender inequality, the level of state feminism, the kind of institutional design that is put in place to support reform, among others. Her careful periodization of change in educational policy in Australia shows the fundamental importance of political ideology (a Labour government) and bipartisan feminist advocacy, in creating the fertile ground for state feminism. A key to the promotion of state feminism was the appointment of feminists as bureaucrats. These 'femocrats' 'were expected to be advocates and their divided loyalty to feminism and the bureaucracy was seen to be good for the state' (ibid.: 4). Femocrats were key brokers of multi-sited and potentially oppositional strategies. 'Top-down/bottom-up' parallel processes helped to create pressure from below as well as initiative from the top. For instance, the grass-roots activism of feminist teachers and parents' bodies both complemented and challenged the work of femocrats, provoking greater creativity in the development of strategies and initiatives.

Other institutional mechanisms that supported these parallel movements were the integration of the women's unit into government, rather than its isolation as a separate unit, which allowed femocrats to develop 'cross-portfolio initiatives' (ibid.: 5). Further, the Women's Budget Program made explicit the kind of discrimination experienced by women and re-distributive programmes by uncovering the low financial allocations. This gave femocrats concrete evidence on which to base claims and advocacy. Further, in line with other developments, the gender equity focus in schools also meshed and refined itself through encounters with other social justice advocacies, including indigenous groups and non-English-speaking groups. As Blackmore notes, this meant that the particular discourses of advocacy and equity reform were themselves transformed: 'gender equity reform for girls benefited many students perceived to be "at risk" and indeed came down to being "good pedagogy" for all students by addressing their specific needs' (ibid.: 7).

However, these changes were not all-transforming. With the underlying discourse being assimilationist (i.e. bringing women into leadership posi-tions), and proceduralist (removing obstacles to girls' advancement) and oriented towards recognition of girls, harder issues such as structural and institutional barriers, though recognized, remained off the agenda. Thus, while the infrastructure of change existed at all levels, these were built on the liberal feminist premise which had: 'a focus on improving aspirations, self confidence, skills, and the competence of individual women and girls rather than to challenge cultures of masculinity or change schools. The policy problem with regard to gender equity was defined as the problem lying with women and girls ie [sic] a deficit model' (ibid.: 8).

Blackmore's account offers rich and multilayered insights, of which the above are only a few. Her subsequent analysis of the discursive and ideological shifts that led to the introduction of neo-liberal and socially con-servative policies demonstrates how quickly progressive infrastructure can be made to give way to new pressures. In particular, the impact on the state bureaucracy of performance and outcome-based resourcing policies, and its accompanying discourses of effectiveness and efficiency, have reshaped the concept of 'equity'. In Australia, the call for gender 'mainstreaming' in this context seems to have set off alarm bells: 'the discourse was about mainstreaming of equity that many femocrats opposed as being premature as most managers neither accepted the notion and did not see the lack of women as a problem' (ibid.: 9). With the return of neo-conservative governments both at federal level and in a few states in 1996, equity policies were relegated further to the background, a result of the combination of 'social conservatism (self-help, women return home) and radical economic policies (deregulation of labour market and privatisation)' (ibid.: 10). This has seen the subsequent dismantling of the gender equity structures, a concern with the effect of gender equity reform in education on boys, and the individualization of disadvantage. In state governments which still had a Labour government, there has been an effort to counter these federal moves, but some trends have continued none the less, particularly the rise of 'audit' culture and its impact on the culture of work within the bureaucracy.

The case from Australia, drawing extensively on Blackmore (2004), is used here to highlight the importance of viewing gender mainstreaming strategies in the context of the wider political, ideological and discursive shifts, as well as to demonstrate the multiple ways in which feminist advocacy and actions need to function in order to move forward equity reforms. This case demonstrates the complexity of change processes, and the impossibility of garnering impacts on all dimensions of social and political life through selected state-based strategies.

## Final thoughts ...

As a construct, 'gender mainstreaming' constrains realistic assessment of change processes within bureaucratic institutions, and allows for the blurring of analyses of what are, fundamentally, political reform processes. Liberating gender mainstreaming from these shackles requires three actions: to discard the term altogether, and instead break up its component parts (policy reform, administrative reform, analytical and conceptual strengthening, political advocacy) and name each more accurately; to analyse gains and setbacks in terms of a disaggregated view of gender mainstreaming; and, finally, to recognize the wider political contexts within which these component parts are operating.

Two specific issues are relevant here. First, as Standing argues in this book, expectations of effecting social change through bureaucratic action alone are overwrought. Those who expect bureaucracies to effect miraculous impacts on women's gender identities and their relationships with men are inevitably confronted with the disappointing realization that this is not what bureaucracies can do. Learning how best to leverage bureaucracies for transformative change requires some strategic rethinking. As Standing suggests, this may entail identifying what it is that bureaucracies are placed to deliver, and strengthening them to do so, *within* their operational mandates. Equally, where these operational mandates may not include an explicit commitment to serving citizens, it may mean finding ways to shift and expand them along broader axes of social and economic inequality and marginalization.

Second, and following on from this, women (and men) within gender machineries and those who serve as intermediaries in the transformation project are unfairly sullied as somehow having failed this project. By expecting them to effect transformations and then criticizing them for failing to do so, there is the danger of overlooking and negating the small victories that their presence and activism, however limited, may achieve. In particular, the danger is in overlooking their own battles with bureaucratic resistance, or with other forms of resistance in their personal lives. Models for understanding transformation and social change processes need to be applied not just to *women out there*, but to also the women who work within these institutions, particularly in the uncelebrated gender machineries that have sprung up everywhere. Apart from Goetz's (2001) study of women development workers, which focused on grassroots intermediaries, there has been little effort to focus attention on intermediaries of change, who often suffer from an enormous burden of expectations, and are expected to succeed in environments often resistant or immune to ideas of social change.

The reduction of expectations from gender mainstreaming is a good starting point for a strategic rethink of what drives change on gender equity. 'Gender mainstreaming' as a discourse and strategy has opened up critical spaces for starting to resource women's development, and, in some areas, there have been significant shifts. That these shifts do not go far enough may just be a reflection of the limitations of the spaces within which these strategies are being played out, and also a reflection of the enormous difficulty of advocating social change more generally, particularly within current neo-liberal and neo-conservative policy environments. Thus, while rights may proliferate, the conditions under which women are exercising those rights are not necessarily improving. Further, the central conundrum which has trapped feminist advocacy in general is something that 'gender mainstreaming' alone cannot tackle, or be held responsible for. This, as pithily put in a recent article in the *Guardian* newspaper, is the dilemma about how to 'reward and support [predominantly female] carers without institutionalising gender roles' (Bunting 2004). There is a need, therefore, not to get caught up in debates about whether 'gender mainstreaming' is good or bad, a success or a failure, but instead to focus more on breaking down these processes of change, understanding them and the context in which they are being played out, and finding more appropriate labels to reflect what they really represent in terms of transformation.

### Notes

1 This includes, for example, the recent UNICEF *State of the World's Children* report which focused on girls' education with the argument that

'In practice, almost all of the reforms undertaken to make the educational experience safer, more relevant and more empowering for girls also help boys' (UNICEF 2003: 59) or, in other words, 'educating girls is good for boys'.

## References

Blackmore, J. (2004) 'Gender Equity and Resourcing: Reflections from Australia', paper presented at the Beyond Access Forum, Oxford, 28 April.

Bunting, M. (2004) 'Let's Talk About Sex', *Guardian*, 29 May: 21.

Fine, B. (2003) 'Neither the Washington nor the Post-Washington Consensus: An Introduction', in B. Fine, C. Lapavitsas and J. Pincus (eds), *Development Policy in the Twenty-first Century: Beyond the Post-Washington Consensus* (London: Routledge).

Goetz, A. M. (2001) *Women Development Workers: Implementing Rural Credit Programmes in Bangladesh* (New Delhi: Sage Publications).

Kanji, N. and S. Salway (2000) 'Promoting Equality Between Women and Men', *SD SCOPE Paper* 2, Social Development Systems for Coordinated Poverty Eradication, University of Bath.

Staudt, K. (1997) 'Gender Politics in Bureaucracy: Theoretical Issues in Comparative Perspective', in K. Staudt (ed.), *Women, International Development, and Politics: The Bureaucratic Mire* (Philadelphia: Temple University Press).

Subrahmanian, R. (2004a) 'The Politics of Resourcing Education: A Review of New Aid Modalities from a Gender Perspective', paper presented at the Beyond Access Forum, Oxford, 28 April.

— (2004b) 'Gender Equity in Education: A Perspective from Development', paper presented at the Conference on Gender Equity in Education, Gordon's Bay, Cape Town, 18–20 May.

UNICEF (2003) *The State of the World's Children 2004: Girls, Education and Development* (New York: UNICEF).

Whitehead, A. (2003) 'Failing Women, Sustaining Poverty: Gender in Poverty Reduction Strategy Papers', Report for the UK Gender and Development Network, May.

**Making sense of gender**

# 10 | Gender mainstreaming: what is it (about) and should we continue doing it?

PRUDENCE WOODFORD-BERGER

The transformation of androcentric, unequal, gender-based power structures has been the objective and project of feminism since the emergence of its earliest forms. In many ways, gender mainstreaming as a strategy and interrogative tool brings together the perspectives of different communities of feminists and others: in academia, from activist circles and those 'femocrats' situated in various development bureaucracies. This may be what accounts for the fact that gender mainstreaming has assumed rather mythic or 'magic bullet' proportions in the world of development industry.[1] Intended to counter 'gender-neutral development planning', the myth behind the myth is that 'gender mainstreaming' can involve and equip almost anyone to promote gender equality in development. It is credited with existing more or less independently of the international politics, power hierarchies and persistent ideas about human nature driving the modernization paradigms and modernity theories that define what development is, without becoming, as it were, tainted itself. At the same time, the way 'gender mainstreaming' comes to be talked about within development also contains elements of a fable in the form of a moralizing edict concerning virtuous behaviour in bureaucrats and others in development as they work to promote gender equality and empowerment for women in real worlds.

The powerful appeal of the notion of gender mainstreaming lies, I think, in the spirit, politics and promise of its early intentions: to imbue all systems, structures and institutionalized cultures with awareness of gender-based biases and injustices, and to remove them. The Beijing Platform for Action points to the promotion of women's empowerment and equality between women and men through, among other measures, the establishment of 'national machineries' to ensure the mainstreaming of gender perspectives *in all spheres of society* (UN 2001: 26, emphasis added). However, mainstreaming also involves efforts to make attention to gender and equality issues the concern and responsibility of everyone in development organizations, as opposed to being only that of specialist persons, units, teams or 'machineries'.

For many of us with feminist backgrounds and convictions of one sort or another who have found ourselves in various social policy contexts, the appeal of gender mainstreaming is that it is founded on, and to a significant extent grounded in, feminist theoretical frameworks. Therefore, as a myth, gender mainstreaming can also be used strategically – potentially at least – to promote political ends. As a fable, however, it is coming under a great deal of attack from a number of directions – including some feminist ones – on the grounds that it is nebulous, elusive and has unclear goals; that it is merely an attempt at a technical solution that in reality demands too little in terms of commitment, analytical skill and resources from those who are supposed to carry it out. Even more damning are charges that gender mainstreaming is not performing well in the service of advancing the situation of many if not most women, especially women in subaltern structural positions due to ethnicity, class and/or colonial histories or to sexual orientation and choice of a partner. Those who are sceptical of gender mainstreaming on such grounds see it as proof that modernizing, Eurocentric development paradigms and theories are alive and well and continue to reign to the exclusion of other frameworks.

My own experiences as a female, African American immigrant in Sweden as well as from several periods of ethnographic research on matrilineal kinship, reproduction and perceptions of gender in another cultural setting (Ghana from 1973 to 1993) have influenced my own feminism, as have nearly twenty-five years of work as a development consultant with gender equality issues at the core. I readily admit that these experiences have been a boon as well as a source of discontent. They have been a boon because they have informed my work as principal trainer for Sida's gender training programme since 1990, and my work at the Swedish Ministry for Foreign Affairs as special adviser since 2002. The discontent stems from the fact that I have contributed to and been complicit in the 'objectification' and relay of certain kinds of knowledge in 'diluted' form in order to coax better development results and effects in the form of better conditions and opportunities for women and girls in the countries we work with.

In this chapter, I draw on these experiences to explore the question of whether gender mainstreaming as an idea and as a prescribed course of action can be extracted from the specific contexts and forces from which its dominant forms emerged, and whether it can continue to be sustained, and usefully converted and applied to other contexts. It draws on exciting recent work on the anthropology of policy (Porter 1995; Shore and Wright 1997; Mosse 2002) to analyse a specific case of feminist politics – that of Sweden, where gender mainstreaming has been on the policy agenda since the 1980s – to explore a particular rationale, interpretation and set of tools. It focuses in particular on the gender analytical frameworks, so central to gender mainstreaming, that are employed in the project of transforming power structures and relationships in the work of international development organizations.

## Gender mainstreaming and development policy

Gender mainstreaming can be defined in a number of ways, all of which are contested in one way or another (see e.g. March et al. 1999: 10). The most common usage in Sweden is as a long-term strategy or systematic institutional approach for promoting/producing gender equality as a policy outcome. Although there is a great deal of confusion and contestation surrounding the concept itself (see e.g. Sida 1996: 1), there appears to be a relatively high degree of agreement about its aim. Gender mainstreaming seeks to produce transformatory processes and practices that will concern, engage and benefit women and men equally by systematically integrating explicit attention to issues of sex and gender into all aspects of an organization's work. Gender analytical frameworks are used to impose tangibility and procedurability on what is ultimately a political project based on certain theoretical underpinnings. Such frameworks are usually designed to fit into the planning requirements and routines of development bureaucracies, used in training courses and 'gender sensitization' or 'gender awareness-raising' exercises to marshal support for specific values and interpretations.

Gender mainstreaming emerged in the late 1980s and was slow to take off. Indeed, it continues to compete with earlier praxis and modes of thought that focused generically on women, Women in Development (WID) frameworks and on separate measures for compensating women for disadvantages and discrimination experienced by them in development processes. Since the 1995 World Conference on Women in Beijing, gender mainstreaming has increasingly gained currency at the higher levels of national and international policy-making. At the meetings and negotiations of the 47th Session of the UN subsidiary body, the Commission on the Status of Women (CSW) in March 2003, a resolution was adopted concerning the mainstreaming of a gender perspective into all policies and programmes of the UN system. Likewise, a similar resolution was proposed for adoption by the meetings of the UN Economic and Social Council (ECOSOC) in 2003 and 2004. The 49th session of the UN Commission on the Status of Women in March 2005 marked the tenth anniversary of the Beijing conference. The ministerial, outcome document from 'Beijing+10' reaffirmed the Beijing Declaration and its Platform for Action, as well as gender mainstreaming as the global strategy for promoting gender equality and women's empowerment. This reaffirmation was echoed in the outcome document from the September 2005 World Millennium Summit issued by 180 heads of state and government.

These resolutions, declarations and outcome documents issued from the highest policy levels globally define gender mainstreaming as a critical, globally-accepted strategy for the promotion of gender equality, and provide indications of how it should be implemented. Examples of measures include formulating and implementing gender equality policies and strategies; developing and using data disaggregated by sex; gender-specific studies and information; gender analyses of budgets where relevant; establishing or strengthening institutional mechanisms, such as gender units/focal points, networks and task forces; and strengthening staff skills and capacity to integrate gender perspectives into policies and programmes.

These measures may be seen as comprising specific kinds of concrete practices that lend substance and give meaning to the creation or production of the elusive goal of 'gender equality'. The assumption is that these and other activities and practices are affirming to policy as well as to particular models of social change that are to be encouraged. The hope or conviction is that carrying them out – for example, in development planning and through various models for intervention design – will promote change in such a way that the goal of gender equality will be achieved. Thus, they become elements in institutional and personal practice, and as such are products of policy. At the same time, they also work to produce, protect and legitimize policy (and at the same time themselves). To a significant extent, the emphasis on mainstreaming in planning at the expense of mainstreaming for social transformation (it is necessary to work with both) is due largely perhaps to the complexity of policy-making and the correspondingly perilous translation of policy into manifestations of operational practice.

In recent years, many of us fear that less emphasis is being put on affecting the 'mainstream' of societal structures, processes, organizational cultures and politics through gender mainstreaming as a tool for social transformation, while more is being put on the 'mainstream' of development administration's policies, planning routines and processes, programmes and projects, i.e. through the use of gender mainstreaming as a purely instrumental technique. The increasing demand for useful, usable practical tools or frameworks and for accessible reference materials has led to a considerable number of these. Recent years have also seen a renewed and enhanced emphasis on rights-based frameworks as well as a revival of 'efficiency dimensions' of promoting gender equality.[2] Women's human rights are focused and this focus has been greatly enhanced since the introduction of language concerning sexual and reproductive *rights* in the programmes of action from the 1994 UN International Conference on Population and Development and the 1995 Fourth World Conference on Women.[3]

Policy can, of course, be forcibly imposed, but more commonly is dependent upon some sort of positive rationale and incentive to be credible and at least minimally implementable. The substantiation, reification or 'objectification' of policy in Shore and Wright's terminology (Shore and Wright 1997: 5), involves actions, events, discourse and processes of interpretation and instrumentalization to make policy 'real' through the gradual establishment of practices to implement it. The transformation of policy into practice, and through practice into specified products or other results, occurs in turn by means of institutional mechanisms that are perceived to be legitimate, and that supersede the will and agency of individuals. In the context of gender equality and other cross-cutting development goals, 'objectification' involves not just top-down governance and political decision-making, but also the use of emotive idioms and metaphors to translate political activism and advocacy, academic theory-building and development assistance norms, values and practices into popularized communication and actions.

In the objectification process, the various knowledge, interests and 'interpretive communities' of actors (Porter 1995) in these three fields of engagement – activism, academia, development assistance/cooperation – may become involved in struggles over meanings and pragmatic measures both within and between themselves, in order to determine courses of action and pursue specific gains. In this context, myth-making with regard to gender may be the result of these communities each jockeying to get the most out of an idea, so to speak, by settling for 'thin' or 'thick' (Fraser 1989: 163) descriptive concepts, themes, labels or tropes so as to legitimize claims to a range of phenomena or courses of action, and to mobilize resources. At the same time, there is no denying that such myth-making contributes to the dilution of concepts and the generalization of meta-narratives based on rather narrow universes of experiences and interests, rendering them considerably less useful than they could be.

In any event, in the case of 'gender mainstreaming', gallant efforts have been made to make practical use of theoretical developments and research findings in the fields of feminist and gender studies that emerged during the 1980s, 1990s and the twenty-first century thus far, after the relative dearth of such materials during earlier years. These are used to inform, or are translated into concentrated or distilled forms in, inter alia, gender analytical frameworks. Contrary, then, to accusations of 'theory-lessness' directed at some areas of development cooperation work, we neither lack nor ignore mental models, theories or empirical data that can inform gender equality policies and the gender analytical frameworks currently in use. However, it is clear that these by and large are formulated in terms of the inputs-outcomes planning models common to the 'mainstream' of social and development policy and organizational contexts.

## Swedish approaches to gender equality policy

As Rabo (1997) points out, gender equality policy provides a way for the Swedish state, the social democratic government and its historical legacy of safeguarding a comprehensive welfare system, to organize, direct and control the pursuit of gender equality in Sweden. Sweden has a history of 'social engineering', a form of social planning stemming from the 1930s that combines research, politics and an aesthetics of rationality in order to create 'the good society' (*det goda samhället*) and produce a particular kind of new, aware and socially desirable person or citizen (*den nya människan; den nya medborgaren*). Present-day gender equality policy in Sweden is also the result of allying research with politics and a firm belief in and commitment to the production of gender equality and the achievement of political goals through legislation, top-down directives and the adoption of gender mainstreaming as the government's official strategy. Gender equality as fable in Sweden is illustrative of manifestations of cultural belonging that are closely bound up with Swedish identity and notions of justice and social equality.

In the context of Sweden, gender mainstreaming involves a process of objectification in which virtue/virtuous behaviour is demonstrated through the rather ritualistic use of 'gender analysis' as a tool to bring about gender mainstreaming as practice and as a kind of craftsmanship in pursuit of the goal of gender equality. The most common measures for implementing gender mainstreaming in terms of the dimension mentioned above as 'strengthening staff skills and capacity to integrate gender perspectives into policies and programmes'[4] takes place through so-called gender training courses aimed at awareness-raising and at relaying the basics of gender theory and analysis. During such courses, information is provided on reference materials, manuals and handbooks, checklists and guidelines. Gender mainstreaming is also supported through organizational adjustments such as the creation of special units or 'focal point' positions.

The theoretical underpinnings of Sweden's gender equality policy and of gender mainstreaming as a strategy to address gender inequalities are to be found in the works of, inter alia, Swedish feminist researchers such as Y. Hirdman (1988). Contributing to a major breakthrough in feminist research and analytical thinking about gendered structures in Swedish national historical contexts, Hirdman posited the existence of an intractable, hierarchical sex-based power order (*könsmaktsordning*). This was based on two principles: the principle of absolute separation of the sexes (*isärhållningens princip*), and the primacy of 'man'/'men' as the norm (*den manliga normens primat*), standard and yardstick for valuation and evaluation of human behaviour and entitlement. In this perspective, men are superordinate/superior (*överordnad*) and women are subordinate/inferior (*underordnad*) in terms of power and authority. Based on two opposing and seemingly mutually exclusive categories of adult 'women' and 'men', Hirdman's work has been used to analyse not only employment, working life conditions and labour markets in Sweden, but also education, leadership and family life. Her analytical framework is used as an official foundation for the government's gender equality policy, and for the construction of most of the gender analytical frameworks that are used to mainstream attention to gender in national social policy contexts as well as in the practice of gender mainstreaming in international work.

## Doing 'gender' in Swedish international development work

How do representations of sex, gender, 'women' and 'men' in the gender analytical frameworks currently used in Swedish international development work fit with the realities of particular women and men in non-Swedish cultural settings? And how can we better understand and communicate complex realities and situated knowledges so as to make sense of inequalities and injustices and mobilize support for the purpose of doing away with them? To a considerable extent, both of these points concern bodies of theory and practice that involve so-called identity politics, the politics of difference, and the political pursuit of justice and genuine empowerment by disadvantaged or oppressed groups through 'recognition' and inclusiveness, and/or 'redistribution' of goods, ideas, positions and power (Young 1990, 2000; Fraser 1997; Fraser and Honneth 2003). The evidence is that, in many respects, we are clearly gaining ground as far as our claims for 'recognition' and women's inclusion are concerned, while progress continues to be slow with regard to 'redistribution' and true empowerment.

What assumptions might we be making about the way societies are organized and the way 'gender work' is best done, that are stopping us from making more of a difference? How might Swedish ideas about 'gender equality' and the kinds of notions of 'gender' that are supposed to be 'mainstreamed' be perceived from the standpoint of women and men in a very different cultural setting? For example, that of the Dormaa district of the Brong-Ahafu Region of Ghana, where I conducted ethnographic research into such issues as descent, residence, the 'domestic' domain and reproduction, and notions of personhood, female collective identities and interests, connectedness and solidarity during several fieldwork periods from the late 1970s until 1994[5] (Woodford-Berger 1981, 1997)?

In Dormaa, the creation and mediation of social and gendered identities takes place through the Brong Akan matrilineal kinship system. Domestic arrangements are in effect matrilineage sub-systems characterized by duo-local residence for most married people. Living and nurturing arrangements can be dispersed over a number of different residences, particularly for children and young men. Brong Akan motherhood is a highly idealized condition and culturally elaborated process and a primary status marker for women. Female-ness is strongly associated with hard physical work, with the provision of food and care, as well as with prowess in economic ventures in ways that male-ness is not. Women and children do the bulk of the farming and collecting work that provides the bases for people's livelihoods, and women by and large usually have adequate access to cultivable land through their matrilineage, whether or not they are married.

Despite clear distinctions between conceptions of female-ness (*Twi béré*) and male-ness (*nyin* or *nini*), these are for the most part not firmly attached to physiological sex, or to particular duties, ways of being or behaving. Neither do 'female' and 'male' categories or persons necessarily embody notions of dichotomous relations or dually-constructed social persons considered to be the exact opposites of one another. 'Gender identity' can shift over the life course as well as with respect to specific existential situations, conditions and requirements. In terms of power relations, women should defer to men. However, although authority is associated with male-ness, it is also associated with positionality, e.g. with royals, with ritual specialists and with wealthy people regardless of sex.

Conjugality is an important strategic basis for resource mobilization, as well as affection, for both women and men. Both women and men strive to achieve personal economic wealth and independence, as well as a personal power base and the exercise of authority represented in house headship during their lifetimes. Women consciously form various kinds of alliances with men as brothers, fathers, mothers' brothers, husbands, sons and sisters' sons. The degree of actual or potential 'equality' in these relationships varies a great deal, although women have a stake even in unequal alliances and are well aware of this. At the same time, there are clear differences in opportunities and circumstances between most women and most men due to history and to rigid, underlying structural inequalities and biases. These are reflected in gender-based disparities – sometimes extreme – in indicators such as literacy and education levels, morbidity and health status, livelihood security, human security and vulnerability to various kinds of violence, and poverty (ROG and UNICEF 1990).

The most common models for gender analysis used in Swedish gender mainstreaming would face difficulties in capturing the complexities of gendered life in Dormaa. Conventional definitions of the 'household' that continue to be employed, despite our awareness of their limited usefulness, would have little relevance in this setting. The representation of female-headed households as particularly impoverished (see Chant, this volume; see also Moghadam 1997; World Bank 2001) equally finds little place. The assumed oppositional positions of women and men in the social, economic, political and ritual order, the very basis of gender frameworks and of the kind of gender thinking that is so much part of Swedish gender equality work, simply does not match the Dormaa reality. What they work to obscure is the way in which women mobilize resources, their affective as well as economic bonds with the men in their lives and the cross-sex alliances of various kinds, especially among kin, that can be so critical a part of women's livelihoods.

Critiques of the kind of ideas on which most of Sweden's gender equality policy work has been based have been part of mainstream gender theory for over a decade. Swedish anthropologists, writing in Swedish, have taken Hirdman to task for her ethnocentric and static portrayal of gendered relations, her presentation of 'gender orders' as clear-cut and unambiguous and of 'sex' and 'gender' as being unmediated by other differences such as ethnicity and class, as well as on the basis that she simply ignores patterns of differences among women and girls and among men and boys and similarities between different categories of females and males (see Gemzöe et al. 1989; Thurén 1996; Gemzöe 2003). Researchers in Sweden from various non-Swedish ethnic origins have, equally, drawn attention to some of the shortcomings of Hirdman's assumptions and the essentializing dichotomies on which they are based (see de los Reyes et al. 2002). Yet, Hirdman's work remains the mainstay of Swedish government policy for the promotion of gender equality and for gender mainstreaming.

Why is it, we might ask, that gender analytical frameworks have not developed in tandem with, for example, the recent research on men and masculinities (Connell 1995, 2002; Cornwall 2000), or with post-colonial research that calls attention to differences of being, power and privilege among women and among men (Hill Collins 1990; McClaurin 2001; Mohanty 1991; Imam et al. 1997; Kolawole 1998; Mikell 1997)? Why is it that they pay such scant attention to other socially constructed bases for inequality such as ethnicity, class, age, creed, sexual orientation or historical background and their significance for the construction and dynamics of gender identities and gender ascriptions (Bourdieu 1984; Butler 1990, 1993)? Analytically, the point that Connell makes – that we are dealing with not a single, but multiple, *different*, gender regimes and orders – appears to have been overlooked or perhaps even ignored by those who continued to promote the fixed, essentialized models of gender on which much 'gender mainstreaming' has tended to be based.

## Repositioning 'gender' in development policy and practice: in search of the mainstream(s)

Despite decades of struggle, large parts of 'the mainstream' in all our societies, including their androcentrism and male bias, remain stubbornly intact. In fact, many of us fear that the most misogynist and oppressive structures have indeed been reinforced, gaining strength from an increasingly militarized and polarized world community, and the effects of conservatism and of neo-liberal economic reformism. So how then do we go about (re-)discovering the mainstream of situations we want to change with regard to the promotion of gender equality? An important step, I think, is to revive the focus on defining and addressing the mainstream of the situation that is the focus of change. This may involve the identification of several 'mainstreams', in terms of the 'gender regimes' and 'gender orders' in the societal and political situation under scrutiny (Connell 1987).

Nevertheless, I would claim, along with March et al. (1999: 15), that gender analytical frameworks are not in themselves doomed to remain mere superficial, technical and token devices that are totally without the potential for addressing gender inequalities and injustices in society. Used creatively, they can be political instruments by encouraging attention to and dialogue on inequalities for the promotion of transformative change. Obviously, their use must be accompanied by measures to promote attitudinal change and contextual sensitivity, and for the systematic use of research and other more thoroughgoing sources of data. We already know this. It is also essential that the frameworks themselves be used in such a manner that their own underlying assumptions are also critically examined. This we appear to be reluctant to realize.

The challenge we face is not only to discover ways to capture the imaginations and will of non-feminist, well-meaning but not-at-all-oriented development bureaucrats when it comes to working with gender issues. Nor is it only to introduce accountability for gender mainstreaming into planning and reporting systems. It also lies in maintaining a constructive dialogue with those who should be allies. This is difficult to do where those who promote gender equality insist on adhering to gender analytic frameworks in which 'women' and 'men', 'girls' and 'boys' are represented as mutually exclusive categories, and continue to focus on the differences between 'the sexes'. This makes it difficult for the project of 'gender mainstreaming' to identify and work operationally with cross-sex alliances, across different gender identities, let alone with people whose gender identities may be more ambiguous or ambivalent or non-normative than many of us are used to.

To persevere and continue to be self-critical is difficult. There is a tendency to shy away from troublesome, complicating insights ostensibly for the sake of pursuing the higher cause of equality between women and men. But we must become better at daring to incorporate nuances, and to resist simplifications that generalize, homogenize and sterilize realities. We need to get beyond the 'consensus' processes that dry up dialogue and leave us unable to explore, let alone debate, commonalities in our concerns amid the complexity of difference. Essentializing relationships between women and men, by overemphasizing differences and representing women and men as oppositional categories, makes little sense of the complexity of our own identifications and relationships, let alone those of 'others' (in an anthropological sense) who are not as familiar. Not taking into account different kinds of alliances and cooperational arrangements between and among various categories of women and men comprises nothing less than a denial of the many lessons we have learned over the years. And this is the ultimate disservice not just to ourselves who are in the thick of policy-making settings, but ultimately to all those – including ourselves – whom 'gender mainstreaming' and the transformation of power structures are intended to benefit.

## Notes

1 In *Sida's Action Programme for Promoting Equality Between Women and Men in Partner Countries* (1997), gender mainstreaming is defined as ensuring that attention to the conditions and relative situations of women and men pervades all development policies, strategies and interventions. All personnel are expected to have basic competence in gender mainstreaming in relation to the specific issues they are working on.

2 Promoting gender equality as a means of improving the likelihood of reducing poverty is the theme of the World Bank volume *Engendering Development* (2001).

3 The Convention on the Elimination of All Forms of Discrimination Against Women (CEDAW) from 1979, the major human rights instrument relating to women, does not include sexual rights.

4 United Nations Economic and Social Council, Document E/CN.6/2004/L.6, *Mainstreaming a Gender Perspective into All Policies and Programmes in the United Nations System*.

5 I am grateful for research funding from the National Bank of Sweden's Centenary Research Foundation and from Sida/SAREC.

## References

Bourdieu, P. (1984) *Distinction: A Social Critique of the Judgement of Taste* (London: Routledge and Kegan Paul).

Butler, J. (1993) *Bodies That Matter* (New York and London: Routledge).

— (1990) *Gender Trouble: Feminism and the Subversion of Identity* (New York and London: Routledge).

Connell, R. (2002) *Gender* (Cambridge: Polity Press).

— (1995) *Masculinities* (Cambridge: Polity Press).

— (1987) *Gender and Power: Society, the Person and Sexual Politics* (Cambridge: Polity Press).

Cornwall, A. (2000) 'Missing Men? Reflections on Men, Masculinities and Gender in GAD', *IDS Bulletin*, Vol. 31, no. 2: 18–27.

de los Reyes, P., I. Molina and D. Mulinari (2002) *Maktens (o)lika förklädnader* (Stockholm: Atlas).

Fraser, N. (1997) *Justice Interruptus: Critical Reflections on the 'Postsocialist' Condition* (London and New York: Routledge).

— (1989) *Unruly Practices: Power, Discourse and Gender in Contemporary Social Theory* (Cambridge: Polity Press).

Fraser, N. and A. Honneth (2003) *Redistribution or Recognition? A Political-Philosophical Exchange* (London: Verso).

Gemzöe, L. (2003) *Feminism* (Stockholm: Bilda Förlag).

Gemzöe, L., T. Holmqvist, D. Kulick, B.-M. Thurén and P. Woodford-Berger (1989) 'Sex, genus och makt i antropologiskt perspektiv', *Kvinnovetenskaplig Tidskrift*, Vol. 1: 44–53.

Hill Collins, P. (1990) *Black Feminist Thought: Knowledge, Consciousness and the Politics of Empowerment* (New York: Routledge).

Hirdman, Y. (1988) 'Genussystemet – reflexioner kring kvinnors sociala under-ordning', *Kvinnovetenskaplig tidskrift*, Vol. 3: 49–64.

Imam, A., A. Mama and F. Sow (eds) (1997) *Engendering African Social Sciences* (Dakar: CODESRIA).

Kolawole, M. E. (ed.) (1998) *Gender Perceptions and Development in Africa: A Socio-Cultural Approach* (Lagos: Arrabon Academic Publishers).

McClaurin, I. (ed.) (2001) *Black Feminist Anthropology: Theory, Politics, Praxis and Poetics* (New Brunswick, NJ: Rutgers University Press).

March, C., I. Smythe and M. Mukhopadhyay (1999) *A Guide to Gender Analysis Frameworks* (Oxford: Oxfam GB).

Mikell, G. (ed.) (1997) *African Feminisms: The Politics of Survival in Sub-Saharan Africa* (Philadelphia, PA: University of Pennsylvania Press).

Moghadam, V. (1997) 'The Feminization of Poverty? Notes on a Concept and Trends', *Women's Studies Program, Occasional Papers* 2 (Normal: Illinois State University).

Mohanty, C. (1991) 'Under Western Eyes: Feminist Scholarship and Colonial Discourse', in C. Mohanty, A. Russo and L. Torres (eds), *Third World Women and the Politics of Feminism* (Bloomington: Indiana University Press).

Mosse, D. (2002) 'The Making and Marketing of Participatory Development', conference paper for Collegium for Development Studies, Uppsala University.

Porter, D. J. (1995) 'Scenes from Childhood: The Homesickness of Development Discourse', in J. Crush (ed.), *Power of Development* (London and New York: Routledge).

Rabo, A. (1997) 'Gender Equality Policy in Post-welfare Sweden', in C. Shore and S. Wright (eds), *Anthropology of Policy: Critical Perspectives on Governance and Power* (London: Routledge).

Republic of Ghana (ROG) and UNICEF (1990) *Children and Women of Ghana: A Situation Analysis* (Accra, Ghana: ROG and UNICEF).

Shore, C. and S. Wright (eds) (1997) *Anthropology of Policy: Critical Perspectives on Governance and Power* (London: Routledge).

Sida (Swedish International Development Cooperation Agency) (1997) *Sida's Action Programme for Promoting Equality Between Women and Men in Partner Countries* (Stockholm: Sida).

— (1996) *Mainstreaming: Concept, Strategies and Methodologies – a Think Piece* (Stockholm: Sida).

Thurén, B.-M. (1996) 'Om styrka, räckvidd och hierarki, samt andra genusteoretiska begrepp', *Kvinnovetenskaplig tidskrift*, 3–4.

United Nations (2001) *Beijing Declaration and Platform for Action with the Beijing+5 Political Declaration and Outcome Document* (New York: UN).

Woodford-Berger, P. (1997) 'Associating Women: Female Linkage, Collective Identities and Political Ideology in Ghana', in E. Evers-Rosander (ed.), *Transforming Female Identities: Women's Organizational Forms in West Africa* (Uppsala: Nordic Africa Institute).

— (1981) 'Women in Houses: The Organization of Residence and Work in Rural Ghana', *Antropologiska Studier*, Special Issue, Vol. 30–31 (Stockholm: Stockholm University, Department of Social Anthropology).

World Bank (2001) *Engendering Development – Through Gender Equality in Rights, Resources and Voice* (Washington, DC and Oxford: World Bank and Oxford University Press).

Young, I. M. (2000) *Inclusion and Democracy* (Oxford: Oxford University Press).

— (1990) *Justice and the Politics of Difference* (Princeton, NJ: Princeton University Press).

# 11 | Mainstreaming gender or 'streaming' gender away: feminists marooned in the development business

MAITRAYEE MUKHOPADHYAY

This chapter is about taking stock of experiences of mainstreaming gender. It addresses two related concerns. First, that after three decades of feminist activism in the field of development – both at the level of theory and practice – most development institutions have still to be constantly reminded of the need for gender analysis in their work, policy-makers have to be lobbied to 'include' the 'g' word and even our own colleagues need convincing that integrating a gender analysis makes a qualitative difference. Second, by constantly critiquing their own strategies, feminist advocates have changed their approaches, but institutional change continues to be elusive (except in a few corners).

Gender and development advocates cannot be faulted for their technical proficiency.[1] Making a case for gender and development, developing and implementing training programmes, frameworks, planning tools and even checklists, unpacking organizational development and change from a gender perspective, have all contributed to building technical capacity and pushed forward technical processes for the integration of gender equality concerns in development. The literature also acknowledges that gender equality is as much a political as a technical project and efforts have been directed towards creating 'voice' and influence, lobbying and advocacy.

So who are 'we'? I situate myself among those of us who started out in the development movement of the 1970s in a Third World country. I was shaped by the feminist movement in India, was groomed by the international gender and development movement in the late 1980s and into the 1990s, and am now in a Northern institution that undertakes research, training and technical assistance in development policy and practice. My job involves working with international organizations, national governments and national and international NGOs to integrate a gender perspective in policy and practice. In this chapter, I use my own experiences to interrogate how the concerns of feminists from similar locations with the political project of equality are being normalized in the development business as an ahistorical, apolitical, de-contextualized and technical project that leaves the prevailing and unequal power relations intact. This normalization is happening at both the level of discourse and material practice.

## Gender mainstreaming: the bold new strategy

Mainstreaming was the overall strategy adopted in Beijing to support the goal of gender equality. The political rationale for this strategy follows on from what feminist advocates had been struggling to establish – that rather than tinkering at the margins of development practice, gender should be brought into centre-stage (Razavi 1997).

Gender mainstreaming involves:

- the integration of gender equality concerns into the analyses and formulation of all policies, programmes and projects
- initiatives to enable women as well as men to formulate and express their views and participate in decision-making across all issues

The Organization for Economic Cooperation and Development/Development Assistance Committee (OECD/DAC) guidelines state: 'A mainstreaming strategy does not preclude initiatives specifically directed toward women. Similarly, initiatives targeted directly to men are necessary and complementary as long as they promote gender equality' (OECD/DAC 1998: 15). In practice, there are two interrelated ways in which gender equality concerns can be mainstreamed.

The aim of 'integrationist mainstreaming' is to ensure that gender equality concerns are integrated in the analysis of the problems faced by the particular sector; that these inform the formulation of policy, programmes and projects; that specific targets are set for outcomes and that the monitoring and evaluation of policies and programmes capture the progress made in the achievement of gender equality.

The aim of transformative or agenda-setting mainstreaming is to introduce women's concerns related to their position (strategic interests) into mainstream development agendas, so as to transform the agenda for change. For example, one of the ways of ensuring that gender equality concerns are integrated into agriculture is to make sure that extension services address both women and men and that technological packages are appropriate for both women's and men's roles in agriculture. However, the issue might be that women in their own right, and not as wives or dependants of men, have no rights over land. Advocacy for women's land rights is thus necessary to set the agenda for change of mainstream programmes addressing gender inequality in agriculture.

Integration and transformation require work at two different institutional levels. While integration involves working within development institutions to improve the 'supply' side of the equation, a transformative agenda requires efforts to create constituencies that demand change. The latter requires an understanding of the nature of political society, state–society relationships, and the extent to which in particular contexts the policy-making institutions are dependent on, or autonomous from, the influence of international development and financial institutions. Integration depends for its success on transformation. In order to build the accountability of policy-making institutions to the gender-differentiated public they are supposed to serve, the creation of the demand for democratic, accountable and just governance has to go hand in hand.

Much of the work in integration has been concentrated on institutions and involved improving the technical processes in development. Gender advocates have had to make a case for integration of gender issues by showing how this would benefit the organization and meet official development priorities. To do this, they have developed frameworks, checklists and tools for gender integration in policies and programmes and trained people in gender awareness and planning, monitoring and evaluation. The challenge that feminist advocates in development have faced and continue to face is that their work straddles both worlds – the technical and political – but the development business tolerates only the technical role.

Why is this so? Both integrationist and transformative versions of mainstreaming require explicit acknowledgement of equality goals. These goals entail a redistribution of power, resources and opportunities in favour of the disadvantaged, which in the case of gender mainstreaming happens to be women. Many of the reasons why the development business barely tolerates any role for feminist advocates has to do with the understandings of the development process itself. The most influential and pervasive understanding of development is that it is a planned process of change in which techniques, expertise and resources are brought together to achieve higher rates of economic growth (Kabeer 1994).

## From incorporation to rights

In recent years, concerns about the accountability of decision-making institutions to the public, respect for human rights and the need for enhanced voice and participation have tempered this economically defined development agenda. Even so, transformation – as signifying changes in relations of power and authority and growing equality between social groups – is hardly ever explicitly acknowledged as a goal, except where it is instrumental to the development imperatives of poverty eradication, improvement in children's health, family welfare, intra-household equity and fertility decline.

The international policy agenda throughout the 1960s, 1970s and much of the 1980s was less concerned with women's rights than with how to incorporate women into the development process (Molyneux and Craske 2002). It was not until the 1990s that the focus shifted to rights and led to the questioning of women's position in their own societies. This focus on rights was brought about by the burgeoning international women's movements struggling worldwide for the right to have rights and basic civil liberties. While the international conferences organized by the UN in the 1990s provided the spaces for organizing around rights and the forums in which to articulate demands, it was the growing strength of social movements, especially women's movements, which brought back issues of social justice, equality and rights into the development agenda.

Feminist scholars have argued that advocacy on behalf of women which builds on the common ground between feminist goals and official development priorities has made greater inroads into the mainstream development agenda than advocacy which argues for these goals on the grounds of their intrinsic value. The reason, they say, is because in a situation of limited resources, where policy-makers have to adjudicate between competing claims, advocacy for feminist goals in intrinsic terms takes policy-makers out of their familiar conceptual territory of welfare, poverty and efficiency, into the nebulous territory of power and social injustice (Razavi 1997; Kabeer 1999). Even though it has not automatically secured accountability to women's concerns, explaining the world to policy-makers has nevertheless driven the work of feminist advocates in development. It has led to the undermining of radical analytical and methodological tools, as when Molyneux's distinction between strategic and practical gender *interests* (1985) became translated in development planning language as *needs* rather than rights (Moser 1989).

However, there are other reasons why the development business can barely tolerate the technical role of gender and development advocates, while rejecting outright the political project of gender equality. These have to do with deep-seated resentment of and consequent resistance to the project of equality between men and women and the language of politics that assertions of equality bring forward.[2] The language of women's rights is deeply disturbing because it involves separating out the identity of women as citizen-subjects from their identities as daughters, wives and mothers, the subject of social relations. It is threatening not only for development institutions, but also for communities and families who stand to lose when male prerogatives to rights and resources are in jeopardy. Feminist scholarship has devoted much attention to unpacking the inherent male bias in development processes (Elson 1991) and more recently male bias in the construction of rights and law and interpretation and implementation of law (Mukhopadhyay 1998; Goetz 2003). The cumulative impact of these resentments and resistance has been the silencing of the project of equality and its rendering into an ahistorical, apolitical, de-contextualized and technical project both at the level of discourse and material practice.

## Gender mainstreaming means getting rid of the focus on women

While a mainstreaming strategy does not preclude initiatives specifically directed towards women, in the development business it has come to mean exactly the opposite. Initiatives specifically directed towards women are seen as a failure of mainstreaming. Experiences in a project in Yemen, financed by the Royal Netherlands Embassy (RNE) in Sanaa, provide a good illustration of this. The objective of the project was to support the rural women's directorate in the Ministry of Agriculture to reach out to women farmers. Earlier the RNE, under the leadership of the sector specialist for women and development, supported the Ministry of Agriculture in Yemen in developing a gender policy that would pave the way for a better deal for the majority of invisible tillers of the land and tenders of household cattle – that is, the women and girl children of Yemen. The Ministry of Agriculture in Yemen has a section called the Rural Women's General Directorate (RWGD). In each of Yemen's provinces, teams are attached to the provincial agriculture extension offices, which generally consider only men to be farmers, to serve the interests of this silent majority. Our responsibility was to build the capacity of these units and to make sure that they served the interests of women farmers, who are responsible for a large part of the work that contributes directly to household food security. This project received strong support from the Minster of Agriculture, who strengthened the rural women's sections in the provinces, often upgrading them to directorates, so that they had more power within the bureaucracy.

Responsibility for this project at the RNE was shifted from the sector specialist for women and development to the officer in charge of agriculture and rural development, on the grounds that 'gender had to be mainstreamed'. The sector specialist for women and development was keen for this project not to be seen as a 'women's project', but as one that made a difference to the policies and practices of the agricultural sector and to the donor strategy. But she did not succeed in establishing this analysis. Negotiations between the Ministry of Agriculture and the RNE regarding future support for the sector continued to treat the rural women's general directorates as marginal. Finally, faced with budget cuts, the RNE axed the project on the grounds that 'gender had been mainstreamed' and thus there was no need to resource the special emphasis on women. This in a country where extreme gender segregation means that women farmers cannot be approached by male extensionists, even if they wanted to, and where women workers of the ministry are seen as illegitimate occupants of public office because they are women and not men.

## Whose responsibility?

At an international conference held in 2002 entitled 'Governing for Equity' and organized by my department in the Royal Tropical Institute, a panel of gender advocates from international organizations and donor bodies discussed the strategies and problems of their organizations in gender mainstreaming (Mukhopadhyay 2003a). The presentations highlighted the common experiences of international institutions in integrating a gender perspective. While there is recognition and acceptance within institutions of the importance of gender equality in development, the *practice* of incorporating a gender perspective in all programmes and policies is beset with difficulties that are not being overcome by present strategies. The main strategy has been to incorporate gender equality concerns in external policies, to demonstrate the importance of gender analysis as a tool for operationalizing the mandate of the institution, and in some instances the setting up of a gender infrastructure, such as gender focal points or departments. For the most part, however, the integration of gender equality in the work done by these institutions relies on committed gender expertise and the 'good will' of colleagues. Accountability to gender equality concerns throughout policy-making and programme implementation on a sustained basis is hard to pin down.

Gender mainstreaming has been adopted as a tool for gender integration in the UN system and by other multilateral institutions. This strategy raises two kinds of questions regarding accountability. First, gender mainstreaming as a tool does not actually convey to those using it what exactly it is that they are responsible for ensuring. According to the United Nations Children's Fund (UNICEF) representative at the conference, it would be preferable to focus on women's rights, children's rights and men's rights because the rights focus actually tells one what has to be achieved. Second, gender mainstreaming as a tool is supposed to ensure that everybody is answerable for gender equity commitments. This has generally meant that nobody is ultimately responsible for getting it done. The limited success of gender mainstreaming in international institutions is due both to the absence of professional and political accountability and the lack of institutional spaces for enforcing accountability. Who is going to hold UNICEF or the World Bank or for that matter DGIS (the Development Cooperation directorate of the Royal Netherlands government) responsible for not promoting gender equality? And how?

## Gender mainstreaming = more women in organizations

While gender mainstreaming implies the integration of gender equality concerns into the analyses and formulation of all policies, programmes and projects, in organizational practice this has increasingly come to signify that gender equality goals can be achieved solely by increasing the number of women within organizations and in decision-making positions. This line is generally pushed by well-meaning donors.[3] Most gender mainstreaming checklists mention this as an item that has to be ticked off in order to determine whether or not a client government department or a non-governmental organization (NGO) has made progress on gender equality. For them, this is easier to measure than to what extent gender analysis has entered into the formulation of policies, programmes and projects. While it is important to push for equality of opportunity for both women and men within development organizations, this cannot be the be-all and end-all. If such measures are introduced in an ahistorical and de-contextualized manner, they can have serious consequences for gender politics within organizations.

This was evident in a workshop I conducted in Cambodia in April 2003, the theme of which was gender mainstreaming in human rights organizations (Mukhopadhyay 2003b and 2003c). During the workshop, the director of the largest human rights NGO in Cambodia explained that increasing the number of women in his organization was what he interpreted as constituting gender mainstreaming. He had adopted a policy whereby 30 per cent of the staff would, over a period of time, be female. He has faced and is facing stiff resistance from his board and especially from the one female member. She opposes the policy on the grounds that hiring women means lowering the standard of the workforce because women are generally less qualified. Asked what he had done faced with this resistance he replied that he was determined to make the policy work and had continued to hire and promote women. Representatives of the donors for this organization, who were also present at the workshop, saw his stand as vindication of their efforts to push gender equality in human rights NGOs. The director, a man, emerged as the champion of gender equality and the woman member of the board, not present, as the villain. Male leadership is legitimized by the underlying message: attempts at introducing equality policies are opposed by women themselves (read backward) and men are far more open to liberal ideas (read modern). Even more sinister, however, was the account of how this very same NGO had performed 'rather badly' a couple of years ago and that this coincided with the time that the gender policy was introduced. Members of the organization present at the workshop equated poor performance with the *introduction of the gender policy and less qualified women in the workforce*. Asked to give concrete instances of how having more women in the organization had led to poor performance, they were unable to do so. Nevertheless, it had become 'common sense' understanding that the presence of more women leads to lowered standards of performance. The head of the Women's Department kept quiet in this discussion. The adoption of gender quotas and the attempts at promoting women had started a gender war in the organization. This then helped reinforce the dominant culture of misogyny.

## Gender equality in the absence of an institutional mandate for promoting equality

To what extent is it possible to enforce gender equity commitments in institutions and within policy agendas whose main objective is not necessarily the promotion of equal rights and human rights? The main question is not how does one do it – feminists have been doing it all the time, creating a fit between gender issues and the organizational mandate/culture within which they operate (Razavi 1997). Rather we should ask whether it is possible in the long run to use instrumentalist arguments to persuade those not convinced of the intrinsic value of gender equality.[4] What really is the efficacy of internal advocacy without supportive politics?

In 2002, I was requested to undertake a situational analysis of gender mainstreaming efforts in selected ministries in Ethiopia. The report concluded that the Ministry of Education was doing far better than the Ministry of Agriculture, Rural Development and Health (Mukhopadhyay 2002). Each of these ministries has a Women's Affairs Department (WAD). The commitment of the Ethiopian government to address gender equality and equity concerns in development is formalized in the national policy on Ethiopian women issued by the Prime Minister's office in 1993. The policy draws attention to the main areas of concern, enlists strategies for implementation of the policy and sets up gender machinery within government. The national policy on women mandated the setting up of the WAD in the Prime Minister's office; women's affairs bureaux in the regions and the WADs in the ministries and commissions.[5]

Why was the Ministry of Education succeeding, while the Ministry of Agriculture was not? The difference in performance on the gender front seemed to be the main policy line promoted by the leadership and the *political support* that the WADs received from the leadership. The policy line developed by the Ministry of Education was based on a sustained analysis of the education sector in Ethiopia, which showed how achieving gender goals in education was essential to achieving overall goals. The WAD has been closely involved in the development of the new education and training policy which states clear support for girls' education, and a strategy paper for improving girls' education was adopted by the ministry in early 1997 (Ministry of Education 1997). In July of the same year, the country embarked on an ambitious education sector development programme (ESDP) which sought to increase the gross enrolment rates and to reduce the gender gap in education, and which incorporated the strategies that had been developed for improving girls' education.

In contrast, the main policy direction in the Ministry of Agriculture seems to be to work towards rural economic transformation that will entail agricultural commercialization and the development of marketable agriculture. A three-point agenda has been devised: creating an enabling environment for capacity building of farmers; formulation of technological packages for commercial agriculture and increased productivity; and revising the rules and regulations to be able to intervene in the world market. Where do poor women farmers, or for that matter poor men farmers, fit in here? The WAD is left scratching at the margins of this policy because equity considerations are ruled out by these policy objectives. The main policy line does not address how the effects of increased commercialization on the gender division of labour and women's work burdens and welfare will be minimized and how the marginalization of women farmers will be avoided, or how household food security will be maintained.[6]

The main lesson that can be learnt from this contrast is as follows. While the overall policy direction of the Ministry of Education was to promote equality in access to education, there was political backing from the leadership to pay special attention to girls' education. Gender equality was an explicit goal of the leadership (interview, HE Genet Zewdie, Minister of Education, 2002).[7] The WAD within the ministry thus had considerable space for manoeuvre and enjoyed support from the political leadership for its advocacy and for suggestions as to how gender goals could be achieved. The political aim of the Ministry of Agriculture, on the other hand, was to build an agricultural sector that would be internationally competitive and profitable. The political space for the WAD to intervene in the policy objectives was thus limited, since there was no support from the top for the relevance of any gender equity objectives.[8] The gender guidelines produced by the WAD, based on data that showed the importance of women's roles in agriculture and food security and the gender gaps in extension and support services, remained a cosmetic document with little or no power of enforceability.

### Conclusion: fighting back

These different examples illustrate how feminist concerns with the political project of equality are being normalized in the development business as an ahistorical, apolitical, de-contextualized and technical project that leaves the prevailing and unequal power relations intact. Gender mainstreaming is being interpreted as getting rid of the focus on women, regardless of context. In Yemen, that context is of extreme gender segregation, which means that women farmers cannot be reached by male agriculture extension workers, while the interpretation of mainstreaming evades this and other questions of gender power relations. In other contexts, well-meaning donors and compliant organizations have reduced mainstreaming to a one-point programme of increasing the number of women within organizations, while the political project of equality between women and men is being undermined by gender conflict within organizations and by deeply demeaning images of women workers.

While most international organizations claim that there is recognition and acceptance within institutions of the importance of gender equality in development and there is a plethora of frameworks, tools and check-lists available to aid these bureaucracies to integrate gender, there are no institutional mechanisms to check on failures. Gender mainstreaming in the absence of accountability becomes merely a technical exercise without political outcomes. As the Ethiopian example shows, integrating gender equality concerns within policy agendas whose main objective is not necessarily the promotion of equal rights is a near impossible task and one that reinforces the powerlessness of gender advocates and the gender equality agenda.

In repositioning gender in development policy and practice, we need to consider how to get back to the political project while not abandoning the present mode of engagement with development institutions. This was the goal of a three-year programme of work at the Gender Unit of the Royal Tropical Institute in Amsterdam entitled Gender, Citizenship and Governance. It aimed to develop a range of good practices to bring about institutional change – changes in institutional rules and practices that would promote gender equality and enhance citizen participation, changes that build the accountability of public administration institutions to the gender-differentiated public they are supposed to serve. In order to build good practice on institutional change from a gender perspective, the approach adopted was to resource civil society institutions. Partnerships were developed with sixteen organizations in two regions: Southern Africa and South Asia. Each participating organization undertook action research projects on a theme of particular national and regional importance for gender equality. While these were on a range of issues, the initiatives undertaken can be categorized as follows: (1) enhancing and sustaining women's representation and political participation; (2) engendering governance institutions; (3) claiming citizenship and staking a claim to equal rights.

The activities, successes and failures of these action research projects suggest the following lessons (Mukhopadhyay and Meer 2004):

- The importance of establishing citizenship as an intrinsic component of development, where citizenship is understood as feminists have been defining and redefining it: to mean having entitlements, rights, responsibilities and agency. This includes the right to have a right, to politicize needs, and to have influence in producing wider equality in decision-making in development. A good example here is the release of women's agency in the efforts by Durbar (see Bandyopadhyay et al., this volume) to articulate the voice of sex workers by changing perceptions and by foregrounding their real experiences of exclusion from entitlements and rights that they face as women.
- The importance of carving out spaces for articulation and citizen participation. Just as rights have to be articulated, the space for articulation and citizen participation has to be constructed. In Pakistan, the government has set up the National Commission on Women without consultation with civil society groups. Women's groups feared that without a truly independent status, enforcing authority or clear mandate, the commission would be unable to make any significant contribution towards changing the situation of women. Two civil society women's organizations (Aurat Foundation and Shirkat Gah), made the strategic decision to initiate a post-facto consultative process involving all stakeholders, government, commission members, civil society and experts. This reinforced the idea that critical decisions of this nature should involve all stakeholders and that citizens have a right to participate. The consultations with civil society and women's rights organizations at the provincial level served to introduce the members to their constituency and to listen to their expectations. The national consultation brought together all parties – civil society organizations and commission members – in formulating the key recommendations for changes to the power, mandate and composition of the NCSW. Government measures to enlarge the future role and mandate of the NCSW are under way.[9]
- The importance of creating constituencies and 'communities of struggle'. Changes in institutional rules and practices to promote gender equality and enhance citizen participation require that women emerge as a constituency, are aware of their entitlements and are able to articulate these. Sakhi, a women's rights organization in Kerala, found that despite the existence of regulations favouring women's participation in

the decentralized planning process and appropriate budgetary allocations, women could not take advantage of these to further their strategic
interests. They did not have the organization nor the articulation of
interests needed to intervene. Sakhi set about remedying this situation
by helping women to organize. It provided information and training so
that women could undertake a needs analysis and training and support
for the elected women representatives, building a constituency that
could demand gender-fair practices.[10]

- The importance of establishing substantive equality as opposed to formal equality. The lived experience of specific categories of women (the
most marginalized or those who are most affected by the specific lack
of rights) must be honestly represented in constructing substantive
citizenship as against citizenship as formal rights. The end of apartheid
in South Africa in 1994 opened up new political spaces for legal reform.
One concern of the Rural Women's Movement (RWM) there has been
that of customary marriage, which limited women's rights. They linked
up with the Gender Research Project (GRP) at the Centre for Applied
Legal Studies (CALS) a university-based research unit, to research and
advocate on this issue. When it became clear to CALS researchers that
many rural women living in polygynous unions were concerned that
outlawing polygyny would invalidate their unions and threaten their
livelihoods, ways were found to intervene in the law reform process
to address the key concerns of women living in polygynous marriages
– their rights to property and custody of children.[11] By listening carefully
to the worries and difficulties of particular rural women CALS brought
the reform of customary law closer to their lived realities.

These emerging lessons suggest ways of getting back to feminist concerns with the political project of equality. The participating organizations
have worked both within institutions to change norms and practices and
outside institutions to build pressure on institutions to change, be more
responsive and accountable to women's interests. They reconfirm that the
political project of equality requires engagement in politics – the messy
business of creating voice, articulating demand, carving out rights, insisting on participation and mobilizing women's constituencies to demand
accountability.

**Notes**

1 The distinction between the technical, professional and scientific on
the one hand, and the political on the other, is often made in development
institutions. The technical often refers to the processes of planning, implementation, monitoring and evaluation of policies, programmes and projects.

It further refers to how to get things done in a specific timeframe and with set objectives. It relies on models, frameworks and tools for getting things done.

2 This resentment and resistance takes many forms, e.g. in 2003 there was a reorganization in the Royal Tropical Institute where I work. Our existence as a gender unit was called into question on the grounds that 'gender' was too narrow a field and we should be working on wider development issues. As a result we renamed our unit as Social Development and Gender Equity and have constantly to prove our 'social development' credentials.

3 Donor pressure on NGOs and governments to abide by certain conditions such as civil society participation and/or gender integration has led institutions to apply 'checklists' in a mechanistic way. Whitehead shows in her review of Poverty Reduction Strategy Papers in four countries that, in many cases, governments have conducted national dialogue on poverty policy not out of a genuine commitment to participation in policy-making, but simply to fulfil this condition of the Heavily Indebted Poor Country (HIPC) initiative and to access debt relief funds (Whitehead 2003).

4 Meer shows in her review of European Union (EU) and Department for International Development (DFID) gender policy in South Africa that while both have strong gender policies that link gender equality to poverty eradication, these policies are located within an overarching framework of market liberalization which promotes polices that increase the burden on poor women (Meer 2003).

5 See reports cited in this section: Ministry of Education (1999, 2001); the Women's Affairs Department of Ministry of Agriculture (1996, 2000); and the Women's Affairs Department of Ministry of Education (1995, 1999, 2000).

6 According to a study undertaken by the Department of Planning and Programming of the Ministry of Agriculture (MOA) and mentioned in the gender guidelines, 48.3 per cent of labour contributed in agriculture is female.

7 The Minister of Education, Genet Zewdie, also pointed out to me that while a lot had to be done (and is being done) to improve the supply side of education, maintaining the momentum required the empowerment of women to challenge the education system to provide better and relevant services.

8 Whitehead (2003) makes a related point in her review of Poverty Reduction Strategy Papers (PRSPs). She shows that poverty analysis in the PRSPs is limited. The description of impoverished groups does not extend to analysis of why they are poor, so gender relations cannot be advanced as an explanation of women's poverty.

9 Based on a case study prepared by the Aurat Foundation and Shirkat Gah Pakistan for the Royal Tropical Institute (KIT) Gender Citizenship and Governance Programme and summarized in Mukhopadhyay (2003a).

10 Based on a case study prepared by Sakhi, India, for the KIT Gender Citizenship and Governance Programme and summarized in Mukhopadhyay (2003a).

11 Based on a case study prepared by Centre for Applied Legal Studies (CALS) for the KIT Gender Citizenship and Governance Programme and summarized in Mukhopadhyay (2003a).

## References

Elson, D. (1991) 'Male Bias in the Development Process: An Overview', in D. Elson (ed.), *Male Bias in the Development Process* (Manchester: Manchester University Press), pp. 1–28.

Goetz, A. M. (2003) 'Conceptual Paper on Applied Research for Gender Justice' (draft), prepared for Gender Unit of the International Development Research Centre, Ottawa.

Kabeer, N. (1999) 'Resources, Agency, Achievements: Reflections on the Measurement of Women's Empowerment', United Nations Research Institute for Social Development (UNRISD) Discussion Paper DP108 (Geneva: UNRISD).

— (1994) *Reversed Realities: Hierarchies in Development Thought* (London and New York: Verso).

Meer, S. (2003) 'Closing the Gap: Putting EU and UK Gender Policy into Practice in South Africa', mimeo report, One World Action.

Ministry of Education (Ethiopia) (2001) *Education Statistics Annual Abstract 1993*, E.C./2000–01 (Addis Ababa: Ministry of Education).

— (1999) *Indicators of the Ethiopian Education System* (quick reference), (Addis Ababa: Education Management Information Systems).

— (1997) *Major Strategies to Strengthen Women's Participation in Education* (Amharic version) (Addis Ababa: Ministry of Education).

Molyneux, M. (1985) 'Mobilisation without Emancipation: Women's Interests and Revolution in Nicaragua', *Feminist Studies*, Vol. 11, no. 2: 227–54.

Molyneux, M. and N. Craske (2002) 'The Local, the Regional and the Global: Transforming the Politics of Rights', in N. Craske and M. Molyneux (eds), *Gender and the Politics of Rights and Democracy in Latin America* (Basingstoke: Palgrave).

Moser, C. (1989) 'Gender Planning in the Third World: Meeting Practical and Strategic Gender Needs', *World Development*, Vol. 17, no. 11: 1799–825.

Mukhopadhyay, M. (2003a) *Governing for Equity: Gender Citizenship and Governance* (Amsterdam: Royal Tropical Institute).

— (2003b) 'Evaluation Report of GAD Cambodia', commissioned by the Royal Netherlands Embassy in Bangkok (Bangkok: KIT Gender).

— (2003c) 'Workshop on Gender Mainstreaming in Human Rights NGOs in Cambodia' (Amsterdam: Royal Tropical Institute).

— (2002) *Situational Analysis of the State of Gender Mainstreaming in Selected Ministries in Ethiopia*, commissioned by the Royal Netherlands Embassy in Ethiopia (Ethiopia: KIT Gender).

— (1998) *Legally Dispossessed: Gender Identity and the Process of Law* (Calcutta: Stree).

Mukhopadhyay, M. and S. Meer (2004) *Creating Voice and Carving Space: Redefining Governance from a Gender Perspective* (Amsterdam: KIT Publishers).

OECD/DAC (1998) *DAC Guidelines for Gender Equality and Women's Empowerment in Development Cooperation* (Paris: OECD/DAC).

Razavi, S. (1997) 'Fitting Gender into Development Institutions', *World Development*, Vol. 25, no. 7: 1111–25.

Whitehead, A. (2003) 'Failing Women, Sustaining Poverty', *Gender in Poverty Reduction Strategy Papers*, report for the UK Gender and Development Network (London: Christian Aid).

Women's Affairs Department of Ministry of Agriculture (Ethiopia) (2000) *Women and Development Guideline: Promoting Women's Participation and Benefit in Agriculture Development* (Addis Ababa: Ministry of Agriculture).

— (1996) *Population and Development in Ethiopia: Prepared for Rural Development Staff* (Amharic version) (Addis Ababa: Ministry of Agriculture).

Women's Affairs Department of Ministry of Education (Ethiopia) 2000 *Note on Gender Sensitive Counseling: Excerpts from Summer Training Course Conducted for High School Guidance and Counsellors*, in collaboration with Department of Educational Psychology, Addis Ababa University.

— (1999) *Improving Retention with a Special Focus on Girls*, in collaboration with the USAID/BESO Project, Addis Ababa.

— (1995) *Some Considerations on Girls' Education*, Addis Ababa.

# 12 | Critical connections: feminist studies in African contexts

AMINA MAMA

Feminism – an international political and intellectual movement to challenge the subordination of women – has many roots and trajectories. The theoretical and practical aspects of this movement draw connections between the local and the global manifestations of women's ongoing subordination, between the various movements that seek to advance liberation and development, and span the various academic disciplines that have to date structured much of what we define as social theory.

The impact of feminism on the global development industry has led to many things, only some of which are as radical and progressive as their instigators dreamed. The interaction between feminism and development has generated a series of approaches to development and a need for gender expertise, which has become something of a travelling circus of experts – gender technocrats touting a new kind of export product, whose brand-name has shifted with the decades, from WID to WAD to GAD to gender mainstreaming. These new women (and some gender-expert men) service the industry, but their value to the alleged beneficiaries of development remains debatable, as conditions of ordinary women and men in the former colonies of the West continue to worsen.

Developmental feminism can be understood as a product of the liaison between feminism and the development industry. It can be traced back to the initiation of the global development interest in women, and was early manifest in the UN Decade of the 1970s and 1980s.[1] If one were to take a long view, one might be tempted to draw an analysis that examines developmental feminism, tracing it back to precursors in feminist internationalism and the idea of global sisterhood. These were roundly challenged for their ethnocentrism when women from Africa, Asia, Latin America and the Caribbean joined North American and European women on the international stages of the UN Decade for Women (1975–85). Nationally-based expressions of feminism took various forms, some radical, some liberal. Both state feminism and development feminism are organized round a liberal politics of entryism. Both display pragmatic tendencies that have taken on new importance in the era of neo-liberalism.

Whatever trajectory one traces, it is clear that developmental feminism has been the result of at times quite complex negotiations that reflect the rapid growth and proliferation of feminist thought and strategy on the one hand, and the long arm of much more powerful players in the development industry on the other. This unequal power and authority has ensured a dynamic of appropriation and incorporation that constantly subverts and depletes transformative feminist agendas. The only evidence I have for this assertion is the fact that, in real terms, women at the post-colonial periphery have seen their prospects deteriorate further with each new development era. A few years ago I noted that:

> The United Nations response to international feminism might have been a case of radical politics being incorporated and neutralised, but it nonetheless signalled the growing currency of feminist concerns within the global arena. ... [T]his created ... institutional needs for WID expertise, which in turn generated a bureaucratic discourse on women in development. The fact that this bureaucratic discourse developed largely within the practical exigencies of conducting rapid appraisals and developing politics and project proposals meant that it was often far removed from the liberatory concerns of the international women's movement. (Mama 1997: 417)

African feminist scholars have articulated stringent critiques of the manner in which anti-democratic African governments jumped on to the WID bandwagon in ways that in the end failed to advance more radical and liberatory feminist agendas. For example, it has been noted that although a number of governments across the region established national machineries for women, these were never properly resourced and thus remained largely ineffective. Others, like those in Ghana and Nigeria, set about pursuing grandiose projects run by the wives of dictatorial heads of state, and so served as mere foils, set up to confer legitimacy on otherwise discredited dictatorial regimes (TWN 2000; Mama 1995; 1998; Ibrahim 2005).

Today, now that the state has been rolled back, and in some instances collapsed entirely, one might want to speak less of bureaucratization and more of marketization. The poorly defined and even more poorly understood logic of 'market forces' has largely supplanted the hegemony, and some might say the protection, of the state. That this shift has been accompanied by financial stringencies that thwart and subvert social justice agendas whenever these do not 'add value' in the immediate term only makes it harder to live with. It produces a levelling down instead of a levelling up of the various public and educational services that a tax-paying public might reasonably expect not to have to pay for.

Within the world of global development, feminism has made com-

**Critical connections**

plicated inroads that are sometimes hard to decipher. This is because they are the product of complex negotiations within and across the hierarchies of power that imbue the complex of organizations currently dominating the development industry. Each apparent advance has generated its own challenges and risks; each manoeuvre has been greeted with new manoeuvres. As we enter the 'knowledge society', a key concern must be the global inequalities played out in the arena of knowledge production, in which I include feminist knowledge production. Feminist intellectual work has been dispersed, but much of it can still be found under the institutionally negotiated rubrics of gender and/or women's studies.

## Women's studies, gender studies, feminist studies

Apart from the various structures, policies and projects that have resulted from WID, WAD and GAD approaches to development, feminism has also generated a large and diverse body of theoretical and conceptual tools, a corpus of methodologies and approaches to knowledge-building, an impressive array of pedagogical innovations and adaptations that are deployed by teachers, a substantial body of new knowledge, and an internationalization of women's studies.

Chandra Mohanty (2003: 518–23) describes three types of Western feminist interest in the non-Western world: the feminist-as-tourist/international consumer, the feminist-as-explorer who is more open-minded but no less voracious a consumer, and finally the feminist solidarity/comparative feminist studies type. All three are US-based, and, while we might recognize the 'types' and even encounter them all quite frequently, I am more concerned to address the epistemological and practical challenges that face feminist scholars living and working in the rest of the world. To do this, I will draw on the African contexts with which I am most familiar.

It is worth recalling that one of the major contributions of feminist epistemology, enriched as it has been by the interventions of Southern-based feminists, is an insistence on being constantly alert to the politics of location and diversities of class, race, culture, sexuality and so on. Feminist epistemology also seeks to build understanding of the connections between the local and global, between the micro-politics of subjectivity and everyday life, and the macro-politics of global political economy. This reflects a commitment to a certain holism, to challenging and subverting the disciplinary and locational fragmentations which have tended to demarcate and circumscribe the theorizing of gender and gender relations. Feminist intellectuals, therefore, straddle many intellectual and institutional arenas, in which they face the challenge of keeping global and local levels of analysis in their sights. They thus need to cultivate the navigational skills required to move between the different and at times competing levels of analysis, and to network effectively.

In the academic arena, whether one refers to women's studies, gender studies or the more assertive idea of feminist studies, it is clear that feminist intellectual work has generated a great deal of ferment across all the conventional disciplinary landscapes. Whether one is considering psychology or political economy, biology or fine art, the influence and effects of feminist ideas have been a key feature of twentieth-century thought, one which is continuing to exercise the intellectual and political life of the twenty-first century. Feminist studies have often been deeply subversive, overturning pre-existing assumptions, pre-existing histories of knowledge, and transforming pre-existing accounts of human history with rich and interesting herstories that function to complete and to subvert the masculine-dominated canons that went before.

However, the myth that feminism has generated only good and radical things needs to be constantly debunked. There are nowadays many less-than-radical gender interventions, in which gender is applied as a depoliticized, technical device, generating log frames and statistics, but doing little to challenge unjust gender relations. This is gender analysis denuded so that it ceases to challenge the patriarchal power of the development industry, and instead 'adds value' to existing meta-narratives. It is my intention to explore some of the ways in which the changes in development brought about by local and global feminist interventions have played out in African contexts, with particular reference to the potential of gender and women's studies units as sites for feminist activism. I will discuss some of the strategic implications that arise from this exploration, and end by outlining some of the ways in which African scholars working in gender and women's studies are responding to present challenges.[2]

*African contexts* We are all aware that Africa has for centuries been afforded a special place in Western mythology, a dark and antithetical land of fables and fantasies, imbued with sexuality, violence and taboo. The advent of modern science did little to interrupt this fabulous status, but rather continued to construct the mother continent as a series of myths that grew more gothic with every generation, and which gained currency as underdevelopment gained ground. However, the emergence of modern feminism in African contexts can be traced back to the liberal philosophers of the eighteenth and nineteenth centuries, perhaps earlier, as early manuscripts from Egypt and Southern Africa demonstrate. As independence struggles gained ground, feminist activists emerged in a number of countries; those in Egypt and Nigeria being among the best known. They combined political actions with intellectual work and their writings formed an important aspect of their activism. So it was that the Egyptian Feminist Union established by Huda Sharawi in the 1920s produced a journal, and acknowledged the influence of earlier poets and writers such as Doria Shafik. So it was too that Mrs Ransome-Kuti and Mrs Ekpo, both well-known Nigerian activists, were educators and writers, as well as militant political actors.

Throughout the late twentieth century and into the twenty-first, the connections between feminist activism and feminist scholarship in African contexts have only been partly compromised by the development of Western-style educational institutions that have tended to aspire towards the Western-style separation between thought and action. They have also been complicated by the dominance of developmentalism, something that does not feature so much in Western histories of feminism. In practical terms, however, the uptake of feminism within development has provided women's movements with resources for women's projects, and, although limited in the grand scheme of things, they have supported a plethora of organizations, networks and movements, most of which are yet to be documented with any seriousness.

What can continental feminist scholarship in the field of gender and women's studies contribute to the development and transformation of African societies? To what extent does the work of feminists counter the generalizations of the global development industry and its appropriation of gender? To what extent are feminist perspectives heard in the development industry, in the global academic arenas, or even within Africa's policy-making and intellectual communities? In what follows I review the field, critically examining what it has to offer in the context of, or despite, the sustained external domination of continental intellectual life. I argue that feminist studies represents a critical and independent field of work, one that maintains connections between theory and practice, and across institutions and fields, and which offers valuable critical perspectives furnished by the particular vantage points afforded to the women of Africa.

*Mapping the terrain*[3] Gender and women's studies (GWS) has been a growth area within the African higher education sector over the last two decades. From just a handful of sites in the early 1990s, the field has grown to include thirty or more sites, scattered across Africa's 600-plus higher education institutions. The oldest of these are those at the Women's Documentation Centre in the Institute of African Studies at the University of Ibadan and the Women's Documentation Centre at the University of Dar Es Salaam, while the largest is the Department of Women and Gender

Studies at Makerere University. The greatest concentrations are found in the countries with the most universities, notably Nigeria, with half a dozen centres in forty universities, and South Africa.[4]

The number of faculty and students has increased substantially, too, and there are signs that gender studies is indeed gaining institutional ground, as the number of sites recognized as full academic departments has also risen during the last few years. Of the thirty who responded to the AGI's survey, seventeen have dedicated units with specialized staff, while thirteen more run courses and modules that form part of mainstream degrees. However, of the dedicated units, only four have full departmental status: the University of Makerere's Department of Women and Gender Studies, the University of Buea's Department of Women's Studies, the University of Cape Town's African Gender Institute (AGI) and the University of Zambia's Gender Studies Department (2001 figures).

The intellectual content of the teaching varies, but even a cursory survey indicates that the vast majority of these teach in the area of development. Very few teach, or admit to teaching, in more controversial fields, such as sexuality, and those that do place it under the respectable rubric of health or population studies, rather than treating it as a key aspect of gender, or even gender and development. This suggests a degree of pragmatism, and a willingness to comply with administrative rationales that bind gender studies to developmentalism, and to accommodate feminist initiatives in so far as they present a funding opportunity.

Those engaged in teaching point to a number of substantial constraints. Beyond the salient problems of overload and poor remuneration, a major challenge to the development of locally relevant teaching, which can support and or develop activist agendas with local women's movements, is posed by the limited availability of locally generated research and publications, and the constrained access to those studies that do exist.[5]

Most of the teaching appears to be taking place at graduate level, with only a few sites offering undergraduate degrees, and only two (the AGI and Makerere Department of Women and Gender Studies) offering support all the way through to doctoral level. The limitations on graduate offerings are most evident at doctoral level, something which reflects the dearth of senior level capacity, as there are hardly any full professors with specialized skills in gender studies. This in turn reflects the overall deficit in senior women academics, such that only 3 per cent of Africa's professors are women, and we make up as few as 12 per cent of faculty (Ajayi et al 1996; Mama 2004). Women have a tough time within mainstream departments, but the existing GWS programmes and departments also present their own challenges, especially for women pursuing academic and research careers and hoping for an upward trajectory within the academic establishment.

The wider reform effort at the largest department, at Makerere University, has created a situation in which there are now over 1,000 students enrolled at the Department of Women's Studies. The expanded teaching load has been accompanied by competing demands coming from stakeholders within and outside the university. From within the university have come demands related to gender mainstreaming policy, as women's studies are expected to include responsibility for ensuring that various institutional players and academics are kept aware of the cross-cutting importance of gender. From outside the university come additional demands from government and from international donors seeking quick-fix consultants, or requesting staff training. The department has tried to respond to these needs by negotiating partnership arrangements with Northern institutions. These enabled the department to establish an outreach programme in gender training, which set out to achieve the commendable goal of creating 'a critical mass of development workers who would work directly with communities to enhance their capacities to meet women's practical needs and to advocate for change where required'.

However, despite its popularity with the constituencies for whom it was designed, the gender training programme could not be sustained once donor funding was discontinued.[6]

The situation at the AGI – established in 1996, five years after Makerere's Women and Gender Studies Department – bears some similarities, in terms of being subject to competing demands from multiple stakeholders. While the AGI has been formally recognized as an academic department since 1998, it has not been staffed or supported by the University of Cape Town, so its teaching programme has remained much smaller, and only partially able to respond to student demand for places, especially at graduate level. It has also not been able to sustain externally funded research and writing workshops for the various governmental and non-governmental constituencies seeking them. The AGI has had to develop linkages with donors, and it has used these to carry out intellectual development work, the best known aspects of which are the continental feminist studies network, the curriculum development initiative, and a number of research and publishing activities. It has utilized donor resources to develop a broad continental initiative, rather than to sustain the core academic programmes that it provides to the university.

Establishing a new and cross-disciplinary gender studies programme has been an uphill struggle in the context of the complexities of the higher education reform process, and the contradictions between political rhetoric and institutional realities. While the mission of University of Cape Town depicts the university as an African institution, there is little consensus over what this means, and hardly any engagement with what this might require. In terms of institutional policy, concerns over gender are played off against concerns over racial equity, the latter being given more airtime than the former, presumably because 'race' is perceived to offer better political capital than gender in the post-apartheid context.

The AGI has foregrounded its own dual agenda of delivering intellectually rigorous teaching and research in gender studies grounded in the particular challenges posed by various African contexts. To sustain its own work both intellectually and financially, the AGI has been compelled to rely substantively on external funding, in so far as this confers a greater degree of academic freedom than the strictures of a cash-strapped faculty based on conservative discipline-based academic departments. In this way the institute maintains a small, but continentally networked, critical space from within which it can better service and support the long-term agenda of producing socially conscious intellectuals skilled in feminist analysis, theory-building, research and pedagogical skills. Such people, however they are named, are envisaged as having a critical role to play in the social and political transformation of Africa. What this has meant in practice is a focus on teaching and research as political praxis, and a commitment to working within African institutions of higher education. This has been pursued by sustaining a taught academic programme while simultaneously developing a continental intellectual development programme aptly referred to as the Strengthening Gender Studies for Africa's Transformation project.

## Conclusions

The transdiscplinary field of gender studies has emerged through the nexus between feminism and development, and this has been responsible for as many constraints as opportunities, as can be seen from the myths and fables currently circulating under the variously named rubrics of women in development, women and development, gender in development, gender and development, and gender mainstreaming. While many of these terms suggest broadly emancipatory agendas, using the term feminist to denote the more radical conceptualizations would confer greater clarity on this increasingly complex and contested field. Feminist approaches to development are, after all, modes of feminist activism and intervention. These seek to resist the mystifications and appropriations that have complicated the terrain.

Feminist approaches to development rely on and include an intellectual aspect. This has been discussed here under the broader rubric of GWS.

Critical connections

Here, too, the more radical and transformative teaching and research are informed by feminist pedagogies, epistemologies, theories, and as such could simply be referred to as feminist studies.

Feminist theories and intellectual capacities provide the critical analysis that is required to think and act beyond the myths and fables currently obscuring and curtailing the transformative potential of potentially radical gender work being orchestrated by feminist movements and carried into the international development arena. Such a conceptual clarification will enable us to move towards liberatory rather than liberal feminist development praxis. GWS in Africa straddles and links different institutional arenas and academic disciplines, representing a key site for locally grounded knowledge production. The knowledge generated by feminist analysis in African contexts is distinctive and original, being rooted in the locally diverse lived realities and experiences of the effects of global development policies. This is significant because hegemonic political and economic dogmas still emanate largely from international financial institutions and development agencies that are very far removed from the lives and struggles of women in Africa, even though they continuously invoke them (poor, rural, African women) to justify their operations. Feminist research carried out by gender-conscious and intellectually capacitated women in Africa, or indeed in any other location peripheral to the still-patriarchal centres of global power today, has the potential to generate new possibilities and insights regarding the connections between the local and the global dynamics of development/underdevelopment. These connections have become all the more salient as globalization has advanced, and an understanding of how they function is a necessary resource for those seeking to intervene and resist the growing inequalities and disparities in evidence in the current emphasis on economic reforms that jeopardize the hard-won gains women made at the end of the twentieth century (UNRISD 2005).

As a mode of activism, feminist scholarship also offers to restore the political, to counteract the depoliticizing influence of narrower approaches to development, dominated as these are by economic reductionism and technicism. Indeed, thinking beyond the myths and fables requires this clarity of perspective. It means that those engaged in teaching and research need also to be cautious with regard to their sources of support. GWS units are often called upon to provide 'gender experts' to perform consultancy and advisory services and to carry out the institutional work of implementing reforms – sometimes under the rubric of gender mainstreaming – both within and beyond universities. There is always the danger that providing such services, while it confers legitimacy on the field and may raise income, may undermine the intellectual autonomy and blunt the critical edge of feminist scholarship. Alternatively, because these instrumental demands draw on the same pool of scholars as harder-to-come-by opportunities for independent research, they may serve to drain the capacity for feminist intellectualism.

The better known GWS centres these days find themselves inundated with invitations to participate in collaborative relationships with Western gender studies departments seeking to establish links as a means of ensuring their own survival by demonstrating that they have become global, in the context of their own cash-crunch. Such assistance, while it may be presented as a gesture of solidarity, is often a condition of funding/ collaboration, whether or not the expertise is actually needed by the African partners. The terms of such collaborations need to be carefully considered and negotiated in full awareness of the history of unequal relations, and the aforementioned persistence of global imbalances in publication and research outputs within GWS.

It is to be hoped that feminism's history of generating new theoretical and practical tools, research methodologies and pedagogies, will enable feminist studies to survive beyond the instrumentalizing effects of these many demands, to continue to produce the critical capacity and the personnel that will ensure the creativity and commitment of feminist scholarship and development activism. Keeping open this critical space is necessary if we are indeed to continue to engage with, and where necessary resist, globally hegemonic development doctrines, and to continue to challenge the international development industry's inherent tendency to conserve and reinscribe patriarchal power.

## Notes

An earlier draft of this paper was presented under a different title at 'Gender Myths and Feminist Fables' conference, University of Sussex, 2–4 July 2003.

1 For an elaboration of UN feminism see Mama (1997: 416–17).

2 This section draws on the African Gender Institute's current programme to strengthen gender and women's studies in African contexts.

3 This section draws on the work of the GWS Africa project team based at the African Gender Institute.

4 Details with map available at <www.gwsafrica.org>.

5 See AGI (2002) 'Strengthening Gender and Women's Studies in African Contexts', workshop report available at <www.gwsafrica.org>.

6 This experience with donor funding has been repeated at many other sites, including a number of continentally based NGOs purposely dedicated to providing gender training.

# References

AGI (African Gender Institute) (2002) 'Strengthening Gender Studies in African Contexts', workshop report, Cape Town, South Africa, January; available at <www.gwsafrica.org/workshops/main2.html>, accessed July 2004.

Ajayi Ajayi, J., L. Goma and G. Ampah Johnson (eds) (1996) *The African Experience with Higher Education* (Oxford and Accra: James Currey/Association of African Universities).

Ibrahim, J. (2005) *Feminist Africa 3, National Politricks* (Cape Town: African Gender Institute).

Jackson, C. and R. Pearson (1998) *Feminist Visions of Development* (London: Routledge).

Mama, A. (2003) 'Restore, Reform but Do Not Transform: The Gender Politics of Higher Education in Africa', *Journal of Higher Education in Africa*, Vol. 1, no. 1: 101–25.

— (1998) 'Khaki in the Family: Gender Discourses and Militarism in Nigeria', *African Studies Review*, Vol. 41, no. 2: 1–18.

— (1997) 'Afterword', in A. Imam, A. Mama and F. Sow, *Engendering African Social Sciences* (Dakar: CODESRIA).

— (1995) 'Feminism or Femocracy? State Feminism and Democratisation in Nigeria', *Africa Development*, Vol. 20, no. 1 (Dakar: CODESRIA).

Mohanty, C. (2003) '"Under Western Eyes" Revisited: Feminist Solidarity Through Anticapitalist Struggles', *Signs: Journal of Women in Culture and Society*, Vol. 28, no. 1.

Sall, E. (ed.) (2000) *Women and Academic Freedom in Africa* (Dakar: CODESRIA).

Tripp, A. M. and J. Kwesiga (2002) *The Women's Movement in Uganda: History, Challenges and Prospects* (Kampala: Fountain Publishers).

TWN (Third World Network – Africa) (2000) *National Machinery Series* (Accra: Third World Network).

UNRISD (United Nations Research Institute for Social Development) (2005) *Gender Equality: Striving for Justice in an Unequal World* (Geneva: UNRISD).

## Websites

<www://gwsafrica.org>.
<www://feministafrica.org>.

# 13 | SWApping gender: from cross-cutting obscurity to sectoral security?

ANNE-MARIE GOETZ AND JOANNE SANDLER

Stephen Lewis, the United Nations special envoy to Africa on AIDS and an increasingly vocal and frankly agonized campaigner for women's rights, recently made his strongest condemnation yet of the way in which gender has been 'mainstreamed' in the UN system. In a speech to a conference on UN reform and human rights at Harvard Law School on Saturday 26 February 2006, he detailed the many ways in which the UN had failed women, and argued that women 'need a new and powerful voice. They need an advocate that never allows the world to forget the sorrow it perpetuates. They need a women's agency.' He dismissed gender mainstreaming as a 'pathetic illusion of transformation', leading to nothing but a 'cul de sac for women'. In an earlier statement he described the situation at the UN, in spite of the existence of several agencies whose work affects women, as resulting in a fragmentation and dispersal of efforts by a handful of under-funded and maligned agencies: 'Nobody is responsible,' he said. 'There is no money, there is no urgency, there is no energy.'[1]

Lewis's insistence that there should be a large and powerful women's UN agency, with, as he says, a budget of at least a billion dollars a year in order to compete with the wealth and clout of other UN agencies, begs the question of why there is not one already. And not just within the United Nations. There are large human rights organizations, such as Amnesty and Human Rights Watch, but why is there no equivalent specifically focused on women? There are large international non-governmental development agencies, like Oxfam International or CARE, but why are there no equivalents specifically focused on women? In countries worldwide, there are ministries that are supposed to include women as key constituencies – like Ministries of Health – that have budgets of hundreds of millions or billions of dollars, but why are there no ministries of women's affairs with such generous budgets? There are certainly UN organizations, international non-governmental and human rights organizations, and ministries that speak out on behalf of women; but mainstreaming has meant that integration has been sought, rather than the establishment of entities that advocate specifically for women with the resources and position to have maximum influence, outreach and representation in countries worldwide. What price have we paid for this?

We are at a critical moment on the winding path to gender equality. We see that moment as being between a rock and a soft space. The rock is the 'miasma of sexism' that Lewis cites and that continues to pervade the spaces in which women organize. The soft space includes the strategies and practices that women's rights advocates have promoted, which have resulted in some positive and incremental changes in the enabling environment for gender equality but, increasingly, are recognized as having limited impact on the majority of women's options and opportunities. That soft space includes promoting a 'two-track' approach to achieving gender equality and women's rights (women-specific programming and gender mainstreaming), a tactic that has resulted in massive conceptual confusion and the deployment of tens of millions of dollars into 'gender training' for development assistance agency staff.

Our contribution to this volume is to use our positions as gender equality advocates working in one of the UN's smallest funds – the United Nations Development Fund for Women (UNIFEM) – to bridge the scholar–practitioner debates on strategies for achieving gender equality with a hard-headed assessment of how bureaucracies respond to change mandates. We write from the perspective of 'insiders' in a bureaucracy but having spent as much or more time outside than inside. Joanne, currently the deputy director of UNIFEM, worked with non-governmental women's rights organizations focusing on domestic US and international development issues for twenty years before coming to the UN, while Anne-Marie, currently UNIFEM's thematic adviser on governance, peace and security, has a twenty-year background in gender and development studies in the UK. Inevitably we draw on our own experiences doing UNIFEM's work advocating a gender-equality perspective in the UN's development and security work as well as on our backgrounds as feminist activists and academics. We use the challenges and positioning of UNIFEM within the UN system as a metaphor for the treatment of gender equality issues in the mainstream in general. This is particularly timely in the context of contemporary UN reform, where the gender architecture within the UN is being scrutinized, where an opportunity exists to bank on women's power, to jump out of the 'mainstream' on to the solid ground of decision-making; to build a power-house for women's rights rather than contenting ourselves with hitching a ride on the tailgates of the development bus.

The 'soft space' in which we operate is characterized by two deficits, one of which is within our remit to address, while the other requires systemic and cultural change that, while not inconceivable, is profoundly daunting. These deficits afflicting the gender mainstreaming project are found not just within the project of promoting gender equality in the UN, but everywhere. The first is fragmentation, and a lack of emphasis on building on the strengths of women's organizing and women's entities. Within the UN and among women's organizations in too many countries, we become parts of a structure that limits our ability to forge alliances for change. Within the UN, the existence of separate entities for gender equality on the normative and operational side (for instance, UNIFEM as an operational fund and the Division for the Advancement of Women as a normative agency) should benefit from a strong alliance between the two entities. But the opposite is the case, and neither gender equality structure derives full benefit from the other. Too often this fragmentation is replicated in countries where civil society women's rights leaders advocate women being elected into parliaments, only to feel abandoned once their representatives enter the political mainstream with lost opportunities for alliance building. In some countries, decision-makers establish a ministry for women's affairs and then a competing entity with a similar mandate, thereby ensuring confusion and competition for scarce resources. Not surprisingly, there are too few examples of our gender equality entities being able to forge productive alliances across these structures. But it remains within our own capacity to do this.

The second deficit of the gender mainstreaming strategy to date is far more complex and devastating. The abuse of women's rights simply fails to produce a sense of a life-threatening, economy-paralysing crisis, in the same way that humanitarian emergencies, environmental disasters or un-controlled capital flows do. The fervour and despair evident in Stephen Lewis's statements about the urgency of addressing women's needs are uncharacteristic of the way women's suffering is addressed by the major-ity of development decision-makers. Lewis's crusade for a UN agency for women is driven by a sense that there is a profound crisis in women's lives – for him, this takes the form of the young female face of AIDS in Africa where a vast hole is being brutally punched out of the population of women in their earlier reproductive years. As he puts it, this is nothing other than 'Armageddon'.

For the most part, however, callous indifference meets the suffering of women the world over. The fact that up to 6 million women die of gender-related violence every three years (Vlachova and Biason 2005) does not plague the conscience of the world in the way that holocausts and genocide do. Women's suffering is too routine, too normalized to generate shame and outrage. Directly representative of this is the fact that the UN Trust Fund to End Violence Against Women limps along at about $1.5 million annually, in contrast to the Global Fund for AIDS, Malaria and TB that has attracted approximately $4.7 billion since 2001. The fact that the first of the Millennium Development Goal targets to be missed in 2005 – parity in girls' enrolment in primary schools – excited no obvious sense of panic, alarm or need to rethink strategies is likewise indicative of relative indifference, or resignation, to women's secondary status.

From the perspective of our work in UNIFEM – where we are linked to a global network of colleagues and partners that generate almost daily stories of inspiring change – our starting point is not quite as apocalyptic as is that of Lewis, although we agree there is a desperate crisis in women's lives in many parts of the world. But we daily have the opportunity to hear about, reflect on and support enhancements in women's agency in many places. We are privileged to be part of some of the notable shifts in opportunities for women that have occurred recently. These include the ground-breaking family laws passed in Morocco during the past two years, the extraordinarily high percentage of women in parliament in Rwanda, the declaration of the Indian Finance Minister that eighteen ministries submit gender budgets, the election of the first African woman president in Liberia, the agreement by UN member states to Security Council Resolution 1325 demanding a response to women's experience of war, and many other enhancements to the enabling environment for gender equality. These are changes that have the potential to make a real contribution to gender equality, even though they still are far from sustainable transformation. These gains were achieved because of the work of many actors at strategic times and serendipitous places, often helped by enlightened leadership, organizing by women's groups and networks, and much constituency building. Gender mainstreaming played a role, but on its own, it did not and does not take us far enough. We illustrate below why it has produced a logic of marginality, and go on to argue that a hard-headed assessment of how large bureaucracies function militates against continuing with gender mainstreaming as the principal or only strategy for transformation.

## The logic of marginality

One of the ills that afflicts UNIFEM and other gender equality entities – whether women's ministries or women's networks operating in the larger mainstream environment – is that we are often excluded from the decision-making venues that we were set up to influence. UNIFEM, for instance, cannot participate as an equal among UN organizations in the major cross-sectoral and inter-agency committees at the UN which, among other things, set out the priorities for humanitarian assistance, for development or environmental policy, for peace and security. The basis upon which UNIFEM is excluded is 'status'; that is, the position of the head of UNIFEM is not sufficiently high for her to sit at the same table as other heads of UN agencies. This happens to Ministers of Women's Affairs on a regular basis as well; their ministerial rank is not sufficiently high for them to join cabinet meetings. It happens to gender 'units'; because they are a 'unit' rather than a department or a thematic area, they do not sit on management committees.

The pervasive positioning of gender equality in the lower ranks of hierarchies and bureaucracies sends a clear message to colleagues: it is *not* important. This leads to sometimes humorous, but revealing, interactions. For instance, UNIFEM was recently (and uncharacteristically) invited to be one of the seven UN agencies on an advisory board for a new UN fund. One of the first decisions of the committee of seven was that each agency would take a turn at chairing the group, with the chair rotating every year. In the ensuing debate over which agency should have the first crack at chair, two large UN agencies declared their candidacies. A deadlock ensued, with each contender producing increasingly detailed arguments as to their own appropriateness for the first-round chair, as well as pointing out the (diplomatically phrased) deficiencies of the other. Early in this discussion, the UNIFEM representative raised her hand and noted that she would also like to be considered for the first-round chair.

This intervention was clearly viewed as so bizarre that it was barely acknowledged by the group, which carried on with the stand-off between the two large agencies. Each time the discussion reached a point where the chair asked if the group was ready to make a decision, he referred to the *two* contenders, and the UNIFEM representative had to reiterate that there were *three* agencies. After prolonged discussion, when the group finally determined that it was at a stand-off, and the chair said that the contenders needed to join him in his office to decide among themselves, he invited the *two* contenders in. UNIFEM again had to remind him that there were *three* agencies.

The upshot of the story will surprise no reader of this book: UNIFEM did not get the chair. A discussion (in which the UNIFEM representative inserted herself) behind closed doors resulted in the triumph of the most tenacious agency representative. But triumph for the UNIFEM representative was never on the cards, no matter how tenacious she had been, because it was *inconceivable* to the gathering that UNIFEM could chair. Why? Because UNIFEM is not an equal among these other agencies. Because there are countless indications in bureaucratic systems that work on gender equality has little worth for the system, which places defenders of women's rights in positions to become the recipients of, as Lewis notes, 'shameless patriarchal assault'.

## Bureaucratic logic

No, this is not an oxymoron. We have created and pay the price for promoting a 'two-track' approach to achieving gender equality and women's empowerment. We pay the price for having articulated a theory of gender mainstreaming, which positions gender equality as a cross-cutting issue. While in theory gender is indeed a factor shaping interactions across all manner of development sectors, the application of the gender mainstreaming idea across sectors in practice reflects a fundamental misjudgement about bureaucratic logic and bureaucratic reactions to new challenges. Bureaucracies operate a little like armies – they are complex chains of command in which rank is a key determinant of what gets prioritized and becomes actionable. When challenging problems are posed, when an internal or external constituency arises to demand responses to an issue not formerly defined as a concern, when the bureaucracy's failings are exposed, the bureaucracy's response will depend on the level of threat or opportunity. The level of threat will be determined by the extent to which the challenging issue can undermine the funding base or public image of the bureaucracy. The opportunities are measured likewise in terms of the resources in physical or human capital or public relations gains that response to the new issue brings.

When it comes to gender equality and women's rights, both the threat and the opportunities are low. Unlike the environmental interest, women's groups have not been able to threaten the funding base of development agencies, as environmental groups did during the 1990s (Wade 1997) when they threatened congressional appropriations for the World Bank and thereby triggered impressive environmental 'mainstreaming' in that institution. As noted above, women's suffering does not excite the passions or the pity of the international community in the same way that an environmental disaster does, or in the way the suffering of children does. On the contrary, it is only when women's reproductive behaviour threatens economies because they are producing too many or too few children that there is a response from national and international communities. Even then the response often takes the form of new controls on this behaviour that limit, rather than expand, women's reproductive choices. The lack of public sympathy for women constrains efforts to raise funds to support their freedoms. This limits the positive incentive that gender equality advocates can offer to international development bureaucracies in the form of new funds for new operational work. There is some gain to be had from rhetorical commitments to women's rights, and in consequence rather more energy has gone into the elaboration of normative frameworks and treaty-signing ceremonies than translating these high-minded commitments into action.

To a large extent, fear and powerful lobbies are what too often motivate a bureaucratic response to a high-threat or high-opportunity issue. The environment is the only special cross-cutting interest to have been awarded attention in the new rules for aid management outlined in the 2005 Paris Declaration, where amplified aid flows will be contingent on national performance in 'strategic environmental assessments'. Failure of a country to meet standards of environmental protection may at a certain point jeopardize the flow of aid into direct budget support.[2] Similarly, the environment emerges as one of only three areas into which UN operational activities are to be merged into 'more tightly-managed entities' in one of the leading proposals in the current UN reform process; the other two being development and humanitarian assistance (UN 2005). This means that a global institutional power-house will soon emerge to protect the environment: big threat, big money, big institution.

A low-threat and low-opportunity issue such as women's rights gets a different response: gender mainstreaming. We have convinced ourselves that this is desirable for ideological reasons: better that we seek to make everyone a gender equality advocate than to acknowledge that it actually requires specialized and fairly massive expertise, commitment and resources – perhaps, in the UN context, a specialized agency – to deliver for women on an equal basis with men. But this taste for mass conversion has let us down. We have underestimated the technical expertise required to build gender equality; it is not acquired at the stroke of the pen that transforms an already over-worked bureaucrat into a gender focal point. We have underestimated the indifference and sheer hostility that has resulted in resistance at all levels. But most of all, we have underestimated or misunderstood bureaucratic logics that work to absorb and disarm mild threats. By contenting ourselves with the possibility of playing a catalytic role, pioneering pilot projects that would move others into replication and scaling up, we have been duped; this is not how bureaucracies change. We have been assimilated when we were aiming for infiltration and influence. Bureaucracies do not easily tolerate fifth columns or change agents – which is what infiltrators are. Bureaucracies also do not easily tolerate cross-cutting issues – these pose a dilemma: who is in charge? Where are their budgets to be housed and how can they be assigned a budget line? Where do they fit in the command hierarchy?

## Re-positioning gender equality

Uncomfortable as it is to contemplate, we are at a point where we need to be re-examining how we position gender equality. What if we insisted that gender equality be treated as a sector? There has been an objection to this, of course. We cannot equate gender equality with 'health' or 'education'. And yet, because these are sectors, health and education benefit from investments in Sector Wide Approaches (SWAps) at the country level, receiving large amounts of coordinated financial and technical support, and the ensuing delivery systems and services. If gender equality (or gender inequality) were benefiting from a SWAp, we might be able to invest in building for women, on the ground, institutional survival alternatives to dependence on patriarchal systems. Without the ability to deliver the money in the form of real services and resources, women continue, from a disadvantaged position, to advocate for an equal piece of the pie in the name of gender mainstreaming. Instead of systemic change, we have therefore had to rely on palliatives: normative frameworks and rights agreements rather than a massive increase in prosecutions for perpetrators of gender-based violence; micro-finance instead of employment and property rights; quotas for women candidates for public office rather than campaign finance reform and democratized political parties.

We are not dismissing the importance of normative frameworks, micro-finance or quotas. All have underpinned important areas of change. But these changes have failed to permeate the deep structures of patriarchy and inequality (Rao et al. 1999). So, too often, we have the sense that we are going up a down escalator. Yes, we can count the massive number of countries (now over 180)[3] that are a party to CEDAW. Yes, we can tout the high percentage of micro-credit recipients that are women and their high repayment rates. But while these positive changes represent upward momentum, the larger environment is pointing in the other direction. The violence that women suffer continues unabated, and the international community has, for the most part, stood by and watched – in Darfur, in DRC, Northern Uganda and in so many other places. The numbers and ratios of women and girls infected by HIV/AIDS grows steadily and, despite pronouncements to the contrary, HIV/AIDS programming continues to ignore the warning that while the disease is a health issue, the pandemic is a gender issue. If we fail to address the very dynamic that fuels the pandemic – gender inequality – most solutions will fail to stem the tide.

Whether gender equality becomes a sector, a pillar or a theme, for it to receive the attention, status and resources it needs to generate action in bureaucracies, we need to engage head-on with bureaucratic logic. With the current focus on 'gender mainstreaming' as a lead strategy for achieving gender equality, real action will remain elusive.

An analogy might help here: we propose that gender mainstreaming is to the work of achieving gender equality and women's empowerment what trickle-down economics is to the work of achieving poverty alleviation. It concentrates on top-loading and investments in those that are already privileged, in the belief that they will share this privilege and that benefits will flow to change the options and opportunities of those most in need. So we invest tens of millions of dollars in gender training for bureaucrats. We invest in building an evidence base, checking again and again to document the insidious effects of gender inequality to be able to convince our colleagues that this is a real problem. We invest time and money in formulating gender action plans and policies, gender equality checklists and, more recently, gender equality scorecards. In the current bureaucratic logic this makes sense. But just as those who are already wealthy can either use their increased income from tax breaks to create job opportunities for those living in poverty or can simply put it in a savings account, so too can those who receive gender training place it in their own private knowledge bank and fail to turn it into programming that supports greater equality. In the face of the violence that women confront daily in conflict zones, the burdens that grandmothers caring for HIV orphans carry, and the nearly total absence of women from negotiating peace agreements, the logic crumbles and we become co-conspirators in an ineffable abuse of women's human rights.

Gender mainstreaming is not a failed strategy; but it has been coopted, just like rights-based approaches and participatory development have been in some instances. It is insidious when it creates a window dressing to make it look as if there is real engagement with gender equality – we have national or institutional policies, plans, strategies, experts and units and the illusion of change. But there is very little sustainability, very little power sharing, and almost no transformation or connection to the very constituencies on behalf of whom our institutions are engaging in these processes.

## Building power-houses for women's rights

This is not a rant; it is a plea. Instead of bemoaning our failures, or dwelling on the extent of the real and ferocious resistance that we face, we need to start working from our strengths. The world has changed radically since 1995 and the Fourth World Conference on Women. We are facing different challenges for gender mainstreaming now than we were in 1995 when it became the strategy of choice. Results-based management, performance-based budgeting, UN reform, PRSPs, SWAps and the aid effectiveness agenda indicate a new level of cooperation among donors, sophistication on the part of aid recipients, and, for gender equality advocates, they offer new opportunities for participation in decision-making, as well as threats of being squeezed out by the dominant post-Washington consensus. Unilateralism, neo-liberalism, neo-conservatism, extremisms and patriarchal backlash are other emergent features of global politics that seem to limit the space for the social and economic policies favoured by feminists. The looming presence of India and China on the development scene as power-houses of investment for growth raises new questions about the prospects for gender equality when it does not serve the purpose of keeping labour cheap for manufacturing megaliths.

At the same time, blogs and electronic working groups, the major uptake of gender-responsive budgeting in local and national governments around the world, Security Council Resolution 1325, and even the MDGs create new platforms and opportunities that have also emerged post-1995. So, if our work on gender equality, women's empowerment, gender justice and women's human rights – goals that are not interchangeable but mutually reinforcing – needs to be context-specific, our work needs to change too because the contexts have changed.

The strengths and areas to build on are considerable.

*Numbers*  There are some numbers to feel optimistic about. A slowly grow-ing number of countries (seventeen in 2005) have filled their national assemblies with 30 per cent or more women – the 'critical mass' threshold considered necessary for women to work from strength of numbers to effect the changes they want to see. These countries put others to shame for their lack of commitment to effecting the simple affirmative action or electoral systems change that can make it possible for more women to win positions in representative politics. More women are taking up non-traditional decision-making positions once in public office. For instance, there are currently at least twenty women Ministers of Finance, and twenty-one others who are Ministers or deputies of the Budget, Revenue, the Economy, or Development. Around the world, there is a growing number of 'femocrats' in the public administration and in development work. In the UN system there are at least 1,300 gender focal points in the multilateral system's headquarters and field-based offices around the world; and while the majority of these 1,300 are in relatively low-ranking positions and have limited access to influence or decision-making (and too often inadequate training), they represent an internal resource that can be mobilized. In rural development work in poor countries, thousands, even hundreds of thousands of women are gaining employment distributing micro-credit, family planning techniques and other development inputs. There are more women in business than ever before. Women migrants are sustaining whole sub-regional economies with their remittances.

*Beyond numbers* There is a widespread understanding that deep institutional change is needed if the growing presence of women in public
decision-making is to result in changes in the substance of these decisions.
The challenges of making public institutions more responsive to gender
equality concerns are not underestimated, but we know more than before
about the key institutions that need to change: political parties, the judiciary, financial sector institutions, security forces.

*New openings* The new aid agenda and the new generation of governance reforms offer new spaces in which to expose the gender-blindness
of mainstream development policy, and to tackle the necessary deep
institutional change. New aid relationships, through which aid flows are
expected to increase substantially, function on the principle that nation-
states must control and own their own development plans.[4] For the aid
flows to increase, countries will have to meet certain standards of 'good
governance': they will need to have reasonably efficient bureaucracies,
levels of corruption will have to go down, and governments will have to
demonstrate that their proposals for public spending have been produced
in democratic and participatory processes, and will be subject to effective
public oversight. This is where the good governance agenda comes in.
Governance reforms must be challenged to promote gender equality in
public participation, in the responsiveness of the public administration
to the needs of women citizens, and in the accountability systems that
oversee state actions and correct for failures.

At the moment, however, governance reforms are in the main geared
towards building secure environments for private investment, with less
concern for building the capacity of the state to serve as an agent of redistribution and equity. This is the right time for women's rights advocates to engage with governance debates from a perspective that supports
strengthening the capacity of the state to defend equality projects. The
state, as an institution for directing social change and protecting rights,
has been under assault from all sides for the last twenty-five years. It is
discredited as a wanton spendthrift by the Washington establishment,
and vilified as an agent of oppression and social control by progressive
groups, including some feminists. Of course, many of the states deserved
the assault – many have been unaccountable and kleptocratic, many have
so dampened economic activity as to exacerbate poverty, some have taken
their remit to construct a national identity into the realm of genocide or
ethnic persecution.

Yet, as some of the other chapters in this book note, the state is the
main credible site from which to launch a long-term project of social

justice. States still retain the capacities to devise and implement progressive laws – globalization, informalization and privatization notwithstanding. States are the main institutional arenas in which meaningful debates about legitimate social arrangements can be pursued and enforced. And the good governance agenda offers an opening through which we can make states answerable *to* women, and answerable *for* promoting their rights.

*Solidarity* There is no substitute for collective action to back up the change projects of women in positions of power, or of the femocrats making their daily contribution in a range of organizations. Autonomous feminist association is what gives us the moral energy (and sense of humour) to carry on, it is the crucible in which ideas about alternative futures are generated, it must become an institutional basis upon which to ground some of these alternatives, and it also provides the political leverage needed to pursue these alternatives in the 'mainstream'. Collective action also invigorates and inspires, and ways of sharing this sense of inspiration must be shared by others; colleagues, men, other social justice groups. In other words, gender equality has to make sense to others beyond members of feminist groups. This is a matter of cultural transformation, something that has always been high on the feminist 'to do' list, but that ought to be pursued through the same means used by other social groups; media and advocacy campaigns and other initiatives that capture people's (especially young people's) imaginations and energy. This is particularly essential today, when the resentments of so many people about a range of economic, political and cultural injustices have made secular emancipation projects less appealing than a return to the certainties of tradition.

The time is certainly right for the development of better linkages and collective action across the wide-ranging individuals and networks advocating women's rights and social justice in different institutional settings, regions and countries, across the private and public sectors, between civil servants and civil society activists, among women and men. And perhaps the effort will be stronger, and the issues clearer, if we build on the achievements of gender mainstreaming but move on, and say what we mean: this is a struggle for women's rights, and it is a struggle that must be conducted from power-houses that represent the collectivity of women's movements. It will need infiltration of mainstream institutions, not assimilation. Assimilation is what happens when we have no home to return to, no community from which to draw affirmation and support. Infiltration is possible when we can keep one foot outside of the institutions we are trying to change. And building power-houses to defend women's human rights is one essential way of keeping the foot outside the 'mainstream', of keeping us grounded and, at the same time, committed to a vision of equality and lives free from poverty and violence that can inspire future generations.

## Notes

1 <www.nytimes.com/2005/12/30/international/africa/30africa. html?pagewanted=2>.

2 For more information on the principles of the new aid relationships, see the Paris Declaration on Aid Effectiveness; <www.aidharmonization.org/ah-overview/secondary-pages/editable?key=205>.

3 There are 98 signatures and 182 accessions, successions and ratifications.

4 For a discussion of the implications of the new aid relationships for gender equality see Alami and Goetz (2006). For more information on the principles of the new aid relationships, see the Paris Declaration on Aid Effectiveness (ibid.), and the Rome Declaration on Harmonization, <www. aidharmonization.org/ah-overview/secondary-pages/why-RomeDeclaration>.

## References

Alami, N. and A. M. Goetz (2006) 'Promoting Gender Equality in New Aid Modalities and Relationships', mimeo (New York: UNIFEM).

Rao, A., R. Stuart and D. Kelleher (1999) *Gender at Work: Organizational Change for Equality* (West Hartford, CT: Kumarian Press).

Sandler, J. (2004) 'Whither Gender Mainstreaming?', in *Gender Mainstreaming: Can It Work for Women's Economic Rights* (Toronto: Association for Women's Rights in Development).

United Nations (UN) (2005) *World Summit Outcome*, <http://daccessdds. un.org/doc/UNDOC/GEN/N05/487/60/PDF/N0548760.pdf?OpenElement>, accessed 13 March 2006.

Vlachova, M. and L. Biason (eds) (2005) *Women in an Insecure World: Violence Against Women – Facts, Figures and Analysis* (Geneva: Geneva Centre for the Democratic Control of Armed Forces).

Wade, R. (1997) 'Greening the Bank: The Struggle Over the Environment, 1970–1995', in D. Kapur, J. P. Lewis and R. Webb (eds), *The World Bank: Its First Half-Century, Vol. 2* (Washington, DC: Brookings Institution).

THREE | **Looking to the future: challenges for feminist engagement**

# 14 | The NGO-ization of Arab women's movements[1]

## ISLAH JAD

One of the dominant trends in the evolution of the Arab women's movements is a steady increase in the number of women's non-governmental organizations (NGOs) dealing with aspects of women's lives such as health, education, legal literacy, income generation and rights advocacy. This can be seen as a sign of the failure of centralized Arab states to bring about social change and development. The expansion of NGOs is widely viewed as constituting the development of an Arab 'civil society' that can contain the authoritarian state and as a healthy sign of real, 'bottom-up' democracy in the region; it may also be viewed as a new and growing form of dependency on the West. Debates abound concerning the ideology of NGOs, their links both to their own states and to the states that fund them, and their utility for development and social change. These debates have been given a new edge by current American government attention to 'democratization' and 'modernization' of Arab societies and Arab regimes and its increased funding for civil society organizations. The US administration sees the role of women as vital in this respect.

This article traces the development of the Arab women's movements, paying special attention to what I call their 'NGO-ization'. I use this term to denote the process through which issues of collective concern are transformed into projects in isolation from the general context in which they are applied and without taking due consideration of the economic, social and political factors affecting them. NGO-ization has a cultural dimension, spreading values that favour dependency, lack of self-reliance and new modes of consumption. In advertisements in Palestinian newspapers, for example, it is common to read about collective community actions organized by groups of youth, such as cleaning the streets, planting trees, painting on the walls, followed by a little icon indicating the name of the donors who funded these 'projects'. It is also noticeable that many of the NGO events are held in expensive hotels, serving fancy food, distributing glossy material and hiring 'presentable' local youth. All this is leading to the gradual disappearance of the 'old' image of the casual activist with the peasant accent and look.

NGO-ization can also introduce changes in the composition of the women's movement elites (Goetz 1997), which results in a shift in power relations. Radtke and Stam define power as the 'capacity to have an impact or produce an effect' so that 'power is both the source of oppression in its abuse and the source of emancipation in its use' (1994: 8). Like Rowlands (1998), they differentiate between two types of power: 'power over' as controlling power, which may be responded to with compliance or resistance, and 'power to' as generative or productive power, which creates new possibilities and actions without domination. This power can be what enables the individual to hold to a position or activity in the face of overwhelming opposition, or to take a serious risk.

Professionalism, and what I term 'project logic', can provide a new power base for NGO elites which determine which women's issues should be brought to public attention. They can also allow a shift from 'power to' women in the grassroots to 'power over' them by the new elite. Driven by project logic, NGO professionals often lack awareness of the forces active in civil society and the public sphere and their objectives, and risk weakening calls for more equitable gender relations and empowering more conservative actors in civil society. To shed some light on this trend among Arab NGOs, I examine the changing structures and discourses of Arab women's movements, in the context of a development discourse based in binaries such as West/East and state/civil society. The growing number of Arab NGOs in general, and women's NGOs in particular, must be seen in the context of a broader development trend that views NGOs as a vital vehicle for social change and democratization. I will argue that the NGO as a form of organization is different in critical ways from another kind of organization aimed at social change, namely the social movement. Analysing this difference is useful in revealing the limitations of NGOs in introducing genuine, comprehensive and sustainable development, and the social changes desired by local populations. In doing so, I argue that NGOs should be subjected to historical and empirical analysis so that equating them with 'healthy' socio-political development is problematized and not assumed.

### Arab women's organizations in historical context

Many discussions about the proliferation and efficacy of Arab women's NGOs are contextualized in the dichotomy of West versus East. The West is seen by fundamentalist groups as a power which wants to impose its cultural values – especially individual freedom, materialism and secularism – on the world. Arab nationalists and leftists view the West as colonial and corrupting, buying the loyalties of the local elites, and bringing to the foreground what Leila Ahmed calls 'colonial feminism' (Ahmed 1992: 163).

Others set the proliferation of NGOs in a context of ongoing expansion of neo-liberalism, and the formation of a 'globalized elite' (Hanafi and Tabar 2002: 32–6; see also Hann and Dunn 1996; Petras 1997), or as 'mitigating the class conflict, diluting class identities and culture, blurring the class borders and blunting the class struggle within nations and between them' (Qassoum 2002: 44–56).

With the region experiencing increasing Western economic and political intrusion, Arab women's movements emerged in the first half of the twentieth century amid two major political projects, independence and modernization, stemming from secular nationalism and Islamic modernism respectively. While Islamic modernism aimed to rescue religion from narrow or erroneous interpretations, opening up Islam as a vital force in women's and men's daily lives, secular nationalism, articulated in the wake of colonial occupation, involved collective self-review as part of a project of national reinvigoration to win independence (Badran 1995; Baron 1994; Radwan 1998; Lazreg 1994).

Women were seen by the secular nationalists as an integral part of the 'new nation'; and women themselves saw the realization of their social rights as linked to future independent Arab states. In this context, Arab women formed organizations to enhance women's participation in the battles for independence, to defend their people and work to 'advance' women in the realms of education, political participation and cultural life. Their organizations and unions were strongly supported by the emerging national and religious elite striving for independence and the advancement of their countries. The heroic role played by Algerian and Palestinian women in the battles to liberate their countries was one outcome of this phase in the growth of women's organizations.

Arab women's movements at that time were not isolated from the emerging international women's movements. Egyptian women, for example, were closely involved in the International Women's Suffrage Alliance, and the Egyptian Feminist Union (EFU) produced a journal in French, *L'Egyptienne*, aimed in part at altering the national image of Egypt abroad. Egyptian feminists also called in the international feminist forum for attention to the violation of the national rights of Palestinian Arabs, as well as convening an early international conference in 1938 to support Palestinian women in their struggle against Zionism. This conference, 'Women of the Orient', attracted delegations from all over the Arab world and abroad, as well as a large Palestinian women's delegation (Zu'aytir 1980). International feminists were confronted with issues of imperialism that they may have preferred to ignore (Badran 1995).

In Egypt, Algeria, Palestine and many other Arab countries, the 'new woman' was deployed, and deployed herself, against the colonizer. 'Authentic' dress and veiling did not constitute worrying issues at this time, and were not adopted by nationalist women as pressing strategies (Ahmed 1992; Badran 1995; Fleischmann 1999). Influenced by Arab socialism, many newly independent nations – Egypt, Algeria, Iraq, Syria and Yemen – installed 'state feminism', introducing economic and social policies aimed at integrating women in the labour market and the new nation (Kandiyoti 1991; Molyneux 1991; Moghadam 1993; El-Kholy 1998). Many women, especially those from poorer social strata, benefited from social rights such as free education, health and maternity services.

In contrast to the situation before independence, however, the newly emerging states showed strong hostility towards independent women's organizations, especially during the 1960s, which led to their banning (Egypt, Jordan), or their cooptation (Syria, Iraq, Algeria, Tunisia). The legacy of 'populist authoritarianism' as an elite strategy for maintaining hegemony (Brumberg 1995: 230) endured despite the broad-based nature of independence struggles.

Arab women's experiences with their states vary from one nation to another. In most of the Gulf area, women's movements are still struggling to obtain basic political rights. In the states that claimed to be nationalist, socialist or progressive, women suffered from the 'Algerian syndrome': disappointment with state policies which did little or nothing to change women's status as 'dependants' on male citizens. The state in most of these countries did little to change laws and penal codes that did not reflect changes in the situation and status of women, especially well-educated, professional women from the middle and lower middle classes. New restrictions on women's organizations were imposed, and women who participated in opposition political parties were 'equally' targeted by state persecution and punishment. This led to the destruction or weakening of all forms of political and social participation, including political parties, workers', peasants', students' and women's unions. Some feminist voices arose in this period to denounce 'Arab patriarchy' as the main obstacle to women's advancement.

From the mid-1970s, with most Arab states failing to achieve a sustainable level of development, or to absorb the increasing number of young people seeking employment, structural adjustment policies were widely adopted. This resulted in the almost complete withdrawal of the state from investment in the public sector, which led in turn to a severe deterioration of social and economic rights, manifest in rising rates of unemployment and declining social welfare support from the state. In the longer term, this deterioration had a strong impact on women's status, illustrated by the

UNDP's *Arab Human Development Report 2002*, which showed increases in women's illiteracy, unemployment, poverty and political marginalization.

By the 1980s, when many Arab states were shaken by economic and social crises, most leaders successfully continued to evade domestic challenges, making only minimal response to demands for economic and political change. The collapse of the 'communist bloc', a traditional ally of many Arab states, contributed further to the retreat of progressive nationalism, at the same time as the Iranian revolution put an end to the regime of the Shah, bringing an Islamist religious leadership to power. Development within the region has also been held back by the increasingly aggressive policy of the state of Israel and the devastating destruction it has inflicted on countries like Lebanon and Palestine, and the consequent effects on ethnic separatist groups whether in Iraq, Sudan, Lebanon or elsewhere (Jawad 2003). Against an increasingly bleak background of internal stagnation, external pressure increased on Arab countries to introduce more change, this time under the banner of a new development policy, 'good governance', supported by the World Bank, the IMF, the USA and many European donors.

This external pressure has ratcheted up in the wake of September 11, with the increasingly aggressive policy of the USA and its demonization of Muslims in general and Arabs in particular. This has had negative effects of putting the whole region on the defensive and forcing its peoples to adhere even more to a decaying status quo. The discourse of 'good governance' has became particularly important in underpinning US interventions in the region, with the military aggression to force regime change in Iraq being justified by a rhetoric of the need to 'democratize'. The current US administration views the many ills in Arab society, including the inferior status of Arab women, as due to lack of democracy. US officials have said that their focus on democracy-building projects and the redirection of aid money to grassroots efforts can accomplish two things. One is to build the desire and ability to reform authoritarian governments, great and small. The other is to soften the image of the USA as a malign power whose only concern in the region is defending Israel on the Arab street and thus preserving its access to cheap oil. After infrastructure and free trade, 'democracy' tops the United States Agency for International Development's (USAID) regional agenda (*Washington Post*, 4 November 2002). The promotion of democracy and the rule of law includes activities intended to strengthen 'civil society' and significant support to NGOs.

The USA's professed concern with democracy arouses the scepticism of many in the Arab world. Mustapha Kamel Al Sayyid, director of the Center for Developing Countries Studies at Cairo University, argues it would not be in US interests to promote true democracy in Egypt, since the only viable alternative to the present government is the Islamist opposition – a group known for its dislike of American policy. 'If the result of democratization is that Islamists gain more voice in politics, then no doubt the US government will not, in practice, do much in the way of the real promotion of democracy' (cited in Lussier 2002). Important for women activists is that support for women's organizations by international actors, particularly the US government, and more generally for building up 'civil society', serves to add yet more fuel to an already burning debate in the Arab world on the role envisioned and played by Arab NGOs, and women's NGOs in particular, in the process of development, democratization and social change.

## Development and feminism: echoes of the colonial encounter

These debates have to be examined with care and it must be taken into consideration that external aid, whether from UN agencies or foreign governments, is seen in many Third World countries as a small portion of what was historically stolen from them in the colonial encounter. The problem therefore is not in the aid itself, but rather in the way it is offered and invested and how it can be brought under more democratic control.

Some Arab feminists suggest that 'what the colonists sought was to undermine the local culture' through 'colonial feminism' (Ahmed 1992). Like Lazreg, Ahmed is disturbed by the resemblance she perceives between colonial discourses and that of some contemporary Western feminists. She perceives them as devaluing local cultures and assuming that there is only one path to the emancipation of women, namely the path of 'adopting Western models' (Ahmed 1992; Lazreg 1994). Badran (1995) rejects such a position, arguing that 'attempts to discredit or to legitimise feminism on cultural grounds ... are political projects'. For her, the origins of feminism cannot be found in any culturally 'pure' location: 'External elements – external to class, region, country – are appropriated and woven into the fabric of the "indigenous" or local. Egypt, for example, has historically appropriated and absorbed "alien elements" into a highly vital indigenous culture' (Badran 1995: 31–2). She implies that Egyptian feminism is part of such an indigenous culture, underlining how women such as Hoda Sharawi and Ceza Nabarawi were more nationalist and uncompromising regarding British colonialism than men of their class. In spite of meeting with European feminists, and developing their ideas in relationship to European feminist organizations, Egyptian feminists were politically independent, expressing criticism of European support for Zionism. Further, their deepest concern was with the conditions of Egyptian and Arab women. Thus Egyptian feminists were very much part of, and concerned with, their own societies, and cannot be dismissed as Western (hence somehow inauthentic) agents.

It is important to study the contexts in which women's groups and organizations are working empirically. Their strategies, their form of organizations, their links to other social and political groups, to the state, and to powerful external agencies and their models of development cannot be analysed in a framework of the cultural dichotomies of East and West, especially, as Abu-Lughod has noted, because 'notions of separate cultures have themselves been produced by the colonial encounter':

> This leads to different possibilities for analysing the politics of East and West in the debates about women, ones that do not take the form of narratives of cultural domination versus resistance, cultural loyalty versus betrayal, or cultural loss versus preservation. It also opens up the possibility of exploring, in all their specificities, the actual cultural dynamics of the colonial encounter and its aftermath. (Abu-Lughod 1998: 16)

The rapid proliferation in the Arab world of issue-oriented groups, which is one way of defining an NGO, obliges us to ask how the struggle for these issues (mostly related to social rights) is linked to a wider political, social and economic context. This is particularly important with respect to women's issues so as to identify what other social groups might join the struggle for change on any specific issue. What we are seeing so far is that most Arab women's NGOs do not attempt a thorough analysis of, for example, the role of the state in allowing specific issues to persist; nor do they ask about its project for social change, or what the role of a wider women's and social constituency should be to achieve this change.

The Latin American experience supports the necessity for such analysis. Latin American women's movements have demonstrated that women's rights cannot be realized by pleading with an authoritarian state, nor by isolating women in women's organizations. By having their own organizations, then enlarging their constituencies, allying with political parties, and participating in the struggle for democratization and political transition, Latin American women managed to mainstream their demands within state and society (Alvarez 1990; Molyneux 1996; Waylen 1996). These scholars have shown that women's organizations did not follow one path or strategy in their conflict with the state, but rather a multifaceted approach that included many options.

An important point stressed by Waylen is that, in order to form political power, women's organizations need to link poor women's needs and interests with middle-class women's interests. The concept of citizenship implies some commitment to the principle of equality, and to universal principles, but without assuming an undifferentiated public with identical needs and interests (Molyneux 1998). These challenges of reconciling different class interests face Arab women's movements. The way that these challenges are met will depend partly on organizational structure. It is here that a differentiated and nuanced approach to the concept of 'civil society' becomes necessary.

## The NGO-ization of Arab women's movements

The formation of women's NGOs with particular social aims marks a very different form and structure for Arab women's activism than in earlier periods. The early years of the twentieth century were characterized by the spread of women's literary salons, mainly for highly cultured and educated upper-middle-class women. Urban middle- and upper-class women also ran charitable societies and later women's political unions, based on open membership for women. In Palestine, for example, charitable societies recruited hundreds of women in their administrative bodies and general assemblies, while women's unions had large memberships extending to women in villages, and after 1948 in refugee camps. Contemporary NGOs reach far fewer women.

The prevailing structure of today's NGOs is that of a board of between seven and twenty members and a highly qualified professional and administrative staff whose number is generally small, depending on the number and character of projects being dealt with. The power of decisions is often not, as it is supposed to be, in the hands of the board, but usually in those of the director, who sometimes has the power to change board members, without their knowledge. The power of the director stems from his or her ability to fund-raise, be convincing, presentable and able to deliver the well-written reports that donors require: communication and English-language skills become essential. The highly professional qualities required of administrative staff for better communications with donors may not directly affect the links between an NGO and local constituencies, but most of the time they do.

In the Palestinian experience, the qualities of cadres in the 'grassroots organizations' – the women's committees that were branches of political formations that sustained the first Palestinian Intifada – differed considerably from those required in NGO staff. The success of the cadres lay in *organizing* and *mobilizing* the masses, and was based on their skills in building relations with people. They succeeded in this because they had a 'cause' to defend, a mission to implement and because they had a strong belief in the political formations to which they belonged. It was important for the cadre to be known and trusted by people, to have easy access to them, to care about them, and to help them when needed. The task needed daily, tiring, time-consuming effort in networking and organizing. These cadres knew their constituency on a personal level and communication depended on face-to-face human contact.

NGOs, by contrast, depend mainly on modern communication methods such as media, workshops and conferences – globalized tools, rather than local ones. These methods are mainly used to 'advocate' or 'educate' a 'target group', usually defined for the period needed to implement the 'project'. Here the constituency is not a natural social group; rather it is abstract, receptive rather interactive. The temporality of the project and the constituency makes it difficult to measure the impact of the intervention. The 'targeting' policy is thus always limited and implemented by professionals hired by the organizations to do the 'job'. This differentiates it from a 'mission' based on conviction and voluntarism. In addition, most NGOs do not set organization or mobilization as goals and they do not act to initiate them.

As for the internal governance of NGOs, a study of more than sixty Palestinian NGOs found that besides the marginal role played by their boards, most of their employees do not participate in the decision-making due to 'their passivity or their lack of competence' (Shalabi 2001: 152). The 'target' groups do not participate in decision-making or drawing up policy either. In many women's NGOs, the staff had nothing to do with the general budget of their organization and did not know how it was distributed. According to Shalabi, the internal governance of the surveyed NGOs was 'a mirror reflection of the Palestinian political system based on individual decision making, patronage and clientelism' and the lack of rules organizing internal relations (Shalabi 2001: 154).

It is important to notice these differences to help clarify the prevailing confusion between social movements and NGOs. In order to have weight or, in political terms, power, a social movement has to be based in large numbers. According to Tarrow, what constitutes social movements is that 'at their base are the social networks and cultural symbols through which social relations are organized. The denser the former and the more familiar the latter, the more likely movements are to spread and be sustained' (1998: 2). He adds that 'contentious collective action is the basis of social movements; not because movements are always violent or extreme, but because it is the main, and often the only recourse that most people possess against better-equipped opponents' (ibid.).

The same can be said of women's movements. There are contrasting views as to what a women's movement is. One kind of movement is that which mobilizes to demand women's suffrage, has a leadership, a membership, and diffuse forms of political activity, as distinct from other forms of solidarity such as those based on networks, clubs or groups. According to Molyneux (1998), a movement also implies a social or political phenomenon of some significance, due both to its numerical size, and to its capacity to effect change in some way or another whether in the legal, cultural, social or political domains. A women's movement does not have to have a single organizational expression and may be characterized by a diversity of interests, forms of expression and spatial location; it can be made up of a substantial majority of women, when not exclusively made up of women (Molyneux 1998). It seems preferable to reserve the term 'movement' for something larger and more effective than small-scale associations. Yet it is important to note that a large number of small associations, even with very diverse agendas, can in cumulative terms come to constitute a women's movement. In that case, it has no central coordinating body nor agreed agenda, although there will be common goals.

The typical structure of NGOs, described above, means that however much they proliferate they cannot sustain and expand a constituency, and find it difficult directly to tackle issues related to social, political or economic rights on a macro or national level. The cases of Sa'ad el-Dine Ibrahim, a seasoned defender of Egyptian 'civil society', and of Eyad Sarraj, a prominent defender of Palestinian human rights, illustrate this difficulty. Both ran NGOs which used the media to raise contentious issues of election fraud and corruption. Both were jailed by their governments. Further analysis of these cases may shed light on the limitations of NGOs as political forces. Big issues such as those they raised need an organized constituency to carry them, otherwise their actions are likely to be seen as stepping beyond legitimate action, and draw authoritarian punishment.

Their single-issue focus of women's NGOs makes it difficult, and perhaps not feasible, to assemble a number together to work towards a common goal – the minimum requirement for the definition of 'women in movement'. The NGO structure appears to create actors with parallel powers based on their recognition at the international level, and on their access to important national and international figures. But this international recognition is not translated into recognition or legitimacy at local and national levels. This creates a competitiveness between NGO directors which makes it hard to compromise or agree on common goals. Although coordination is sometimes possible between NGOs with similar aims, it seems more difficult for NGOs to achieve coordination with women's organizations such as charitable societies and grassroots organizations. NGO leaders, empowered by high levels of education, professional qualifications, and the international development 'lingo', also have a tendency to patronize the others.

These observations are supported by NGO studies in other Third World countries, where proponents of a 'bottom-up' approach argue that the organization of popular pressure and participation from below is a necessary prerequisite for political change and economic progress. They are also extremely sceptical about the ability and willingness of any regime truly to reform itself. Under such conditions, the 'top-down' approach may simply be ineffective, as official donors have to work mainly through the governments of recipient countries. However, under such conditions, the 'bottom-up' approach is also likely to fail, though for different reasons.

Empowering the powerless from below is a time-consuming process. Most importantly, though, it is naïve to assume that participatory development at the grassroots level can be significantly promoted in developing countries whose governments are notoriously unwilling to reform their political and economic systems. If governments are not reform-minded, they will suppress participatory developments wherever they emerge as soon as such developments threaten to undermine the power base of the ruling elites. The experience of NGOs in various countries offers ample evidence to this effect. The 'bottom-up' approach obviously relies on supportive measures by government authorities (Nunnenkamp 1995: 14–15). The evidence from Iraq, Egypt, Palestine, Saudi Arabia and other Arab countries suggests that Arab governments are not willing to introduce reforms and do not. Rather than evidence of a willingness to reform, the recruitment of the wives of presidents and rulers, princesses and prominent women into certain women's NGOs implies that women's single issue rights and claims are seen as apolitical and politically unthreatening, unlikely to touch the political, economic and social foundations of the Arab regimes.

The potential of NGOs to foster participatory developments beyond the grassroots level is fairly small, given the transitory nature of projects. The activities of NGOs are typically project-focused; coordination between NGOs pursuing different aims is weak; and the potential to create change beyond narrowly defined target groups is uncertain at best. All this is in marked contrast to the way that many NGOs have come to adopt 'rights-based approaches' (RBAs) in recent years. Universal women's rights approaches, of which RBAs are an example, are open to the charge that they 'ignore local feminisms and the historical realities of colonialism, but also makes untenable and essentialist assumptions about the sameness of the position of women worldwide' (Nesiah 1996).[2] While we may agree with Coomaraswamy that 'the discourse of women's rights assumes a free, independent woman, an image that may be less powerful in protecting women's rights than other ideologies, such as "women as mothers"' (Coomaraswamy 1994: 55), it is in the weaknesses of the politics of NGOs that the main limitations lie.

NGOs generally lack a sufficiently robust power base to support claims for all women's rights. Adopting a rights-based approach in this context might backfire, providing important grounds for the Islamists, as a powerful social and political movement in the region, to discredit and delegitimize these claims. In a context of unachieved national independence, as in the case of Palestine, for example, separating women's rights from collective national rights might inadvertently lead to the marginalization of women as a social group and subsequently to the fragmentation of the group. The approach adopted by many Arab women's NGOs, based on individual and universal women's rights, worked on the assumption that social power rests with the state and not in other social and political groups opposing and competing with it (i.e. the Islamists). This approach, based on international conventions, usually ignores to a great extent home-grown, locally developed feminisms and the historical realities of different layers of colonialism and Occupation and the roles imposed upon, or accepted by, women (Nesiah 1996).

## Conclusion

In this chapter, I have argued that the role attributed by UN agencies and international development organizations to Arab women's NGOs as a vehicle for democratization and participatory-based development needs to be reassessed through empirical studies, and not pursued on the basis of the old dichotomies of West versus East. Arab women's NGOs might be able to play a role in advocating Arab women's rights in the international arena, provide services for certain needy groups, propose new policies and visions, and generate and disseminate information. But, in order to effect a comprehensive, sustainable development and democratization, a different form of organization is needed with a different, locally grounded vision, and a more sustainable power base for social change.

## Notes

1 The analysis in this chapter draws on an empirical study of different forms of social organizations in Palestine and elsewhere in the Arab World required for my PhD thesis submitted to the University of London (SOAS) in August 2004.

2 See Phillips (1993), Voet (1998), Charlesworth and Chinkin (2000) for other discussions of the problems of universal women's rights approaches.

## References

Abu-Lughod, L. (1998) *Remaking Women – Feminism and Modernity in the Middle East* (Princeton, NJ: Princeton University Press).

Ahmed, L. (1992) *Women and Gender in Islam* (New Haven, CT and London: Yale University Press).

Alvarez, S. E. (1990) *Engendering Democracy in Brazil: Women's Movements in Transition Politics* (Princeton, NJ: Princeton University Press).

Badran, M. (1995) *Feminists, Islam, and Nation: Gender and the Making of Modern Egypt* (Princeton, NJ: Princeton University Press).

Baron, B. (1994) *The Women's Awakening in Egypt – Culture, Society and the Press* (New Haven, CT and London: Yale University Press).

Brumberg, D. (1995) 'Authoritarian Legacies and Reform Strategies in the Arab World', in R. Brynen, B. Korany and P. Noble (eds), *Political Liberalization and Democratization in the Arab World* (London: Lynne Rienner).

Charlesworth, H. and C. Chinkin (2000) *The Boundaries of International Law: A Feminist Analysis* (Manchester: Juris Publishing, Manchester University Press).

Coomaraswamy, R. (1994) 'To Bellow Like a Cow: Women, Ethnicity, and the Discourse of Rights' in R. Cook (ed.), *Human Rights of Women: National and International Perspective* (Philadelphia: University of Pennsylvania Press).

El-Kholy, H. A. (1998) 'Defiance and Compliance: Negotiating Gender in Low-income Cairo', unpublished PhD thesis, School of Oriental and African Studies, London.

Fleischmann, E. (1999) 'The Other "Awakening": The Emergence of Women's Movements in the Modern Middle East, 1900–1940', in M. Meriwether and J. Tucker (eds), *A Social History of Women and Gender in the Modern Middle East* (Boulder, CO: Westview Press).

Goetz, A. M. (ed.) (1997) *Getting Institutions Right for Women in Development* (London: Zed Books).

Hanafi, S. and L. Tabar (2002) 'NGOs, Elite Formation and the Second Intifada', *Between the Lines*, Vol. 2, no. 18: October (Jerusalem), <www.between-lines.org>, accessed 20 March 2003.

Hann, C. and E. Dunn (1996) *Civil Society: Challenging Western Models* (London: Routledge).

Jawad, A. S. (2003) 'Why Israel Pushes for the Strike Against Iraq', *Between the Lines*, Vol. 3, no. 21: March (Jerusalem).

Kandiyoti, D. (1991) *Women, Islam and The State* (London: Macmillan Press).

Lazreg, M. (1994) *The Eloquence of Silence: Algerian Women in Question* (New York: Routledge).

Lussier, A. M. (2002) 'Aid to Trade to Democracy?', *Cairo Times*, Vol. 6, no. 37 (November): 21–7.

Moghadam, V. (1993) *Modernizing Women: Gender and Social Change in the Middle East* (Boulder, CO: Lynne Rienner).

Molyneux, M. (1998) 'Analyzing Women's Movements', in C. Jackson and R. Pearson (eds), *Feminist Visions of Development: Gender Analysis and Policy* (London and New York: Routledge).

— (1996) 'Women's Rights and the International Context in the Post-communist States', in M. Threlfall (ed.), *Mapping the Women's Movement: Feminist Politics and Social Transformation in the North* (London: Verso).

— (1991) 'The Law, the State and Socialist Policies with Regard to Women:

The Case of the People's Democratic Republic of Yemen 1967–1990', in D. Kandiyoti (ed.), *Women, Islam and the State* (London: Macmillan).

Nesiah V. (1996) 'Towards a Feminist Internationality: A Critique of US Feminist Legal Scholarship', in R. Kapur (ed.), *Feminist Terrains in Legal Domains: Interdisciplinary Essays on Woman and Law in India* (New Delhi: Kali for Women).

Nunnenkamp, P. (1995) 'What Donors Mean by Good Governance: Heroic Ends, Limited Means, and Traditional Dilemmas of Development Cooperation', *IDS Bulletin*, Vol. 26, no. 2: 9–16.

Petras, J. (1997) 'Imperialism and NGOs in Latin America', *Monthly Review*, Vol. 49, no. 7, December <www.monthlyreview.org/1297petr.htm[a1]>, accessed on 12/5/2003.

Phillips, A. (1993) *Democracy and Difference* (Cambridge: Polity Press).

Qassoum, M. (2002) 'Imperial Agendas, "Civil Society" and Global Manipulation of the Intifada', *Between the Lines*, Vol. 3, no. 19, December (Jerusalem), <www.between-lines.org>, accessed 20 May 2003.

Radtke, H. L and H. J. Stam (1994) 'Introduction', in H. L Radtke and H. J. Stam (eds), *Power/Gender: Social Relations in Theory and Practice* (London: Sage).

Radwan, E. S. (1998) 'Jurisprudence and Women: Reformist and Traditional', *Bahithat, Lebanese Association of Women Researchers, Fourth Issue: 1997–1998*, Beirut, Lebanon.

Rowlands, J. (1998) 'A Word of the Times, but What does It Mean? Discourse and Practice of Development', in H. Afshar (ed.), *Women and Empowerment, Illustration from the Third World* (London: Macmillan).

Shalabi, Y. (2001) 'Al-ta'thirat al-dawleya 'ala tahdid ro'aa al-monathmat ghayr al-hokomeyya al-felastineyya wa-adwareha' [International and local impacts on the visions and roles of Palestinian NGOs], MA thesis, Bir Zeit University, Palestine.

Tarrow, S. (1998) *Power in Movement: Social Movements and Contentious Politics*, Cambridge Studies in Comparative Politics (Cambridge: Cambridge University Press).

UNDP (2002) *Arab Human Development Report 2002* (New York: UNDP).

Voet, R. (1998) *Feminism and Citizenship* (London: Sage Publications).

Waylen, G. (1996) *Gender in Third World Politics* (Milton Keynes: Open University Press).

Zu'aytir, A. (1980) *Yawmiyyat Akram Zu'aytir: al-haraka al-wataniyya al-Filastiniyya 1935–1939* (Beirut: Palestine Studies Association).

# 15 | Political fiction meets gender myth: post-conflict reconstruction, 'democratization' and women's rights

DENIZ KANDIYOTI

It is possible to identify at least two distinct clusters of concerns in feminist engagement with development. The first contains a vigorous internal critique of how the concepts, tools and frameworks generated through scholarly and policy engagement with gender have fared in the real world of development practice.

The second cluster of concerns centres on the process of development itself and the ways in which changes in global economic and political conjunctures modify the very terms of the debates we engage in. Starting in the 1980s with the DAWN initiative, there has been an enduring preoccupation with issues of global inequality and the limits these place on human flourishing – for both women and men. What types of agenda for gender justice are we to adopt in the face of glaring global disparities in wealth and power? Are the gains implicit in standard-setting instruments and gender equality guidelines, however imperfect their implementation, secure in a global climate of conservatism and social and religious polarization? What precisely does 'empowerment' mean in the context of neo-liberal policies that restrict access to basic services and social safety-nets? This strand of critique is evident in feminist interrogations of the gendered effects of macro-economic policies (UNRISD 2005) and in more recent scholarship on democratization and the 'good governance' agenda. We must add another important question to these concerns: what happens in contexts where development and humanitarian aid have been reconceptualized as tools for the promotion of global security (Duffield 2001)?

An area that presents us with persistent challenges of both a conceptual and practical nature is the attempts to accommodate a women's rights agenda in conflict and post-conflict situations. Many cases have entered our political lexicon under the somewhat misleading label of 'failed states' to refer to countries torn by war and internal strife with collapsed, decayed or vestigial apparatuses of governance and political economies that are often driven by illicit trade in arms, narcotics and primary commodities. These challenges are augmented, in the case of Iraq, by the potential casualties of a policy of armed 'democratization' and regime change.

Gender issues are becoming politicized in novel and often counter-productive ways in a geo-political context where armed interventions usher in new blueprints for governance underwritten by international donors – and where gender mainstreaming and women's rights are folded into a package of donor-driven prescriptions. The difficulties of developing a principled feminist response (and an appropriate politics of solidarity) in the face of these developments must be self-evident. Indeed, debates within transnational feminist constituencies about the plight of women in Afghanistan proved to be divisive.[1] These exchanges followed the familiar tropes of women's rights as universal human rights vs 'feminism-as-imperialism', reflected in a spate of articles both in the popular press and in academic journals (Abu-Lughod 2002; Arat-Koc 2002; Moghadam 2002; Viner 2002; Hirschkind and Mahmood 2002). While some denounced intervention in the name of Muslim women's rights as an extension of imperial meddling, others highlighted the hypocrisy inherent in sanctioning oppression in the name of cultural relativism. There was, however, broad consensus over the effects of policies that channelled massive support to *mujahidin* groups, often to the most extremist among them, as part of the United States' Cold War strategy. The fact that gross abuses of human rights, including extreme forms of gender-based violence, under the *mujahidin* were barely noted (Niland 2004), and that aid agencies and NGOs were themselves complicit in this strategic silence (Goodhand 2002), inevitably enhanced perceptions of self-serving instrumentalism when an outcry about women's rights accompanied Operation Enduring Freedom. When women's rights become implicated in the geo-political manoeuvring of powerful global actors, it is small wonder that they elicit a degree of scepticism.

In Afghanistan, attempts at post-conflict institution-building and peace consolidation are taking place against the background of unstable political settlements between competing factions, some of which explicitly target women's rights as an area over which they are in no mood for compromise. Security and the rule of law are signally lacking: alongside continuing armed attacks by insurgents, schools go up in flames in many parts of the country and NGO personnel and women face substantial risks (Oates and Solon Helal 2004). How does gender advocacy play out in instances where the gap between the technical solutions offered by gender mainstreaming and the social and political preconditions for an expansion of women's rights remains alarmingly wide? Does it open up new spaces and empower actors whose voices would otherwise remain muted? Is it simply ignored or marginalized? Do gender advocacy and the 'real world' of politics coexist in parallel universes? Or does the very existence of such a gap create its own dynamic with unpredictable consequences? Although a great deal of detailed work is necessary to obtain precise, context-specific answers to these questions, some preliminary observations may assist further debate and dialogue.

## Parallel universes? Gender mainstreaming and the 'real world' of politics

If we take seriously the proposition that the state must be a central instrument for the protection of rights (Molyneux and Razavi 2002), contexts where primary state functions such as the provision of basic social services are offloaded on to humanitarian and international aid organizations certainly present specific challenges. In a fragmented polity, where the central government does not have a monopoly over the means of violence and in the absence of a functioning judiciary system, the concept of 'mainstreaming' may beg the question unless it is narrowly understood as a practice embraced by donors in their own programming. These programming priorities have significant implications in countries where international assistance accounts for a substantial part of licit national revenue, although it is widely acknowledged that informal flows (from remittances and illicit cross-border trade) play an even larger role. New types of humanitarian assistance and peacekeeping operations have created a demand for operational procedures that include a recognition of the gender-differentiated outcomes of war and humanitarian crises (Rehn and Sirleaf 2002). This recognition was enshrined in UN Security Council Resolution 1325 (October 2000), stressing the need to address gender issues in peace-building and peacekeeping efforts. Agencies have accordingly developed their own 'toolkit' for the integration of a gender perspective into humanitarian and recovery interventions at the project level (UNDP 2001). More ambitious efforts at institutional reform and state-building have also involved prescriptions for gender mainstreaming.[2]

However, donor-led gender mainstreaming efforts and the institutional architecture they attempt to put in place comes up against the world of 'real' politics. In Afghanistan, institutions of global governance, the UN system in particular, demand compliance with the various international conventions and standard-setting instruments that underwrite women's human rights. Gender advisers in bilateral and multilateral agencies work with government ministries and NGOs offering training, technical assistance and working on 'capacity-building' more generally. This expenditure of financial and organizational resources is taking place against the background of extreme poverty in a war-ravaged country where donor activity inevitably raises popular expectations of rapid betterment and relief.

While international agencies compete for their share of the 'gender' market, drawing upon limited local capacity to staff their own projects, politicians are more interested in producing rapid results that bolster their ability to extend patronage and secure a following. Ministerial and government personnel are likewise prone to 'talk the talk' in matters pertaining to gender and in their interactions with international staff, while pursuing their own agendas.[3] Some focus on a fundamental lack of understanding of Afghan 'culture' on the part of outsiders as the major stumbling block for gender-focused international aid (Abirafeh 2005). There is, however, a great deal more to these interactions than an inability on the part of international agencies to strike the right 'cultural' note. They are also indicative of the limitations of top-down managerial blueprints (which also include the blueprints for 'bottom-up' participatory approaches) in the absence of substantive local ownership in a complex and fluid situation. The managerial objectives pursued by international aid agencies – with their limited timeframes and specification of outputs – and the strategies of political actors on the ground may produce genuine contradictions and reveal profound differences in understanding about the means and meaning of ownership and empowerment. There is little room for recognition and negotiation of these differences. A strong argument has been made to the effect that the aid system in Afghanistan undermines rather than supports state effectiveness (Ghani et al. 2005) but a genuine dialogue on these matters is yet to start. Meanwhile, some of the most powerful internal political actors remain uncompromising on the interpretation of Islamic laws and have been vocally opposed to introducing changes in women's status. Mindful of these tensions, the *National Development Framework* (Government of Afghanistan 2002: 96) treated the paragraph on 'gender' with extreme caution: 'all programs must pay special attention to gender, and not include it as an afterthought. We have to engage in a societal dialogue to enhance the opportunities of women and improve cooperation between men and women on the basis of *our culture, the experience of other Islamic countries, and the global norms of human rights*' (emphasis added).

These qualifications carefully frame the terms of the societal dialogue, while glossing over potential contradictions between them. Donor-supported attempts to secure and expand women's rights in the absence of a stable political settlement between an aid-dependent government and fractious opposition groups, including *jihadi* factions that invoke the primacy of the Shar'ia (Islamic religious law), have resulted in a delicate balancing act in the drafting of the constitution ratified in January 2004. Article 7 requires that the state of Afghanistan 'abide by the UN Charter, international treaties, international conventions that Afghanistan has signed, and the Universal Declaration of Human Rights'. These conventions include CEDAW (the Convention for All Forms of Discrimination Against Women) which was ratified without reservations in March 2003. Article 22 on 'Basic Rights and Non-discrimination' makes explicit reference to full equality of men and women before the law. (This wording was introduced as an important amendment to the original draft which referred to 'citizens' without specifying gender.) Article 83, which offers an important constitutional guarantee for the political participation of women by reserving a quota of 25 per cent of the seats in the Wolesi Jirga (lower house of Parliament) and 17 per cent in the upper house, was hailed as a major step forward.

On the other hand, Article 3 on 'Islam and Constitutionality' states that 'no law can be contrary to the beliefs and the provisions of the sacred religion of Islam'. This article, along with its affiliate which declares Afghanistan an Islamic state, is not subject to amendment. The constitution gives the Supreme Court the authority to determine whether laws and treaties made by the government are in accordance with the constitution, giving it the power to reject any law or treaty deemed un-Islamic.[4]

Comparisons with the constitutional process in Iraq are instructive. These suggest that the process of 'democratization' may result in an erosion of women's existing legal rights. Women's demands for representation and for quotas were consistently rejected by the US administration and a 'target' of 25 per cent of parliamentary seats being occupied by women was stipulated by the Transitional Administrative law, falling far short of the original demands of women's groups. Although Resolution 137 passed by the Interim Governing Coalition in December 2003 (and proposing a return to pre-1959 legislation) did not enter into force, it polarized opinions between women's rights activists vehemently opposed to retreating from the secular code of 1959 and religiously-oriented Shi'ite and Sunni women favouring a return to Shar'ia law. The provision that no law may be passed that contradicts the rules of Islam and the role of the Supreme Federal Court in overseeing the constitutionality of legislation mirrors the provisions of the constitution of Afghanistan. In both cases, the tight relationship between religious doctrine and the judiciary potentially opens the way to 'hard-line' interpretations of Shar'ia law.

The 'federalization' of the Iraqi political system, and the fact that women's rights within the family are not elaborated in the constitution, may lead to Lebanese-style implementation of different personal status legislation in different regions. This gives rise to legitimate concerns over the effects of the 'communalization' of politics on women's citizenship rights (Pratt 2005). The increasing social conservatism affecting women's attire and mobility, while a partial result of the deteriorating security environment and concern for women's safety, is also part of a backlash against occupying forces. Women's rights initiatives promoted by external actors in this context are, if anything, more likely to delegitimize and undermine rather than support locally initiated women's organizations (Al-Ali 2005).

The question of legal reforms affecting women's rights is also a thorny issue in Afghanistan. Three competing components of the legal system – the state legal codes, Shar'ia law and local customary law – have coexisted here. The relative weights of these components have waxed and waned through time, with the Taliban's rejection of statutory laws in favour of the Shar'ia marking a violent swing of the pendulum in favour of Islamic clerical influence. In practice, customary laws have a more direct bearing on women's rights and are the source of many practices that have attracted comment as particularly iniquitous. However, the reform of customary law presents significant political dilemmas. On the one hand, overlooking tribal law and informal dispute resolution mechanisms may threaten the very legitimacy of the legal reform process and appear top-down and undemocratic at a critical political juncture when the political centre needs to consolidate its rule. Some argue that the formal justice system has, in any case, always been elitist and corrupt and that the majority of Afghans resorted to institutions of informal justice that must be recognized and incorporated in a post-war justice system (Wardak 2004). On the other hand, without reforms at the national level this may give an indefinite lease of life to some of the most discriminatory practices against women, such as the custom of *bad* (which involves offering women as brides as a means of reparation to an aggrieved party in cases of criminal offences) (Azarbaijani-Moghaddam 2003). Attempts at legal reform during the rule of the Soviet-backed People's Democratic Party of Afghanistan (PDPA), which included legislation banning under-age and forced marriage and the practice of brideprice, backfired spectacularly as a case of unwanted social engineering by an intrusive state. Indeed, Roy contends that the uprisings against the communist regime which broke out from 1978 were directed 'as much against the state itself as against the Marxist government' (1986: 10). Little political will appears to exist outside a small group of technocrats, left-leaning politicians and women to venture on to this dangerous territory. The strongest case that can legitimately be made is that such customary practices contravene Shar'ia law.

In both Afghanistan and Iraq, ethnic and sectarian constituencies have been locked in struggles of representation in defence of their collective rights and seeking a voice in governance. In both cases elections have entrenched and legitimized social forces that are more likely to resist an expansion of women's rights along the lines mandated by standard-setting instruments such as CEDAW. In Afghanistan, a sizeable proportion of the Wolesi Jirga belongs to parties that could be classified as conservative/ fundamentalist or Islamist, and *jihadis* are expected to be the best organized legislative force in Parliament. The likelihood is high that the National Assembly will push a more conservative social agenda than the government, which since the Bonn Agreement in 2001 has been heavily influenced by Western donor agendas. Female members who hold 27 per cent of the seats are not necessarily expected to function as a coherent political group since they are affiliated with parties across the political spectrum (Wilder 2005).

In short, the notion that 'democratization' under the conditions obtaining in Afghanistan and Iraq need be coterminous with an expansion of women's rights requires close scrutiny. More importantly, the promise of democratic consolidation is itself compromised in contexts where security remains the key issue. An expansion of women's formal rights cannot be expected to translate into actual gains in the absence of security and the rule of law. In Afghanistan, the pace of disarmament of factional militia and the creation of a national army was necessarily influenced by the military objectives of Operation Enduring Freedom that continued to distribute arms and money to militia armies to assist them in their ongoing battle against Al Qaeda and the Taliban. The hold of regional strongmen and military commanders, some implicated in the lucrative trade in narcotics, continues to haunt the Afghan polity. The fact that some militia commanders, drug smugglers and criminals slipped through the net of the candidate vetting system for the parliamentary elections of September 2005 has created disillusionment among voters.[5] These social forces form part of a corrosive dynamic that leads to the loss of personal and community autonomy through a system of patronage that enmeshes clients in bonds of indebtedness and dependence. This increases vulnerability to abuses of all kinds, including grave abuses of women's most fundamental rights. I have argued elsewhere that to understand the nature of abuses against women in Afghanistan we may do well to turn to detailed analyses of the ways in which the war economy has affected existing patterns of gender inequality rather than simply assume these patterns are unmediated expressions of local culture (Kandiyoti 2005). In addition to inequalities embedded in kinship practices and local customs, poverty and displacement have eroded some of the cushioning effects of family ties and obligations and increased female vulnerability. The consequences of years of protracted conflict are plainly evident in some of the worst human development indicators for women in the world.[6]

The intrinsic limitations of the tools of gender training, mainstreaming and capacity-building as a means of promoting empowerment and redressing inequalities in Afghanistan must be self-evident. These remain largely confined to a parallel universe that has relatively little direct bearing on shaping the political landscape on which women's actual prospects for empowerment will ultimately depend. In a context where the vast majority of women have limited contact with the institutions of the state, market or civil society, donor-assisted gender projects can easily either miss their target or give rise to unrealistic – and often thwarted – expectations of immediate betterment.[7] A more creative engagement with the complexities of the politics of gender, which is laden here as elsewhere with its own historical baggage, would mandate a contextual, non-technocratic approach which requires temporal horizons, levels of commitment and types of coalition-building (including cross-gender coalitions) and collaboration that far exceed the bureaucratic blueprints of international aid. Women activists who have been fighting for their rights for a long time both in exile abroad and in Afghanistan deserve nothing less.

## Notes

1 This is not to suggest that global feminist mobilization has been totally without effect, but its results were mixed. Feminist Majority's 'Campaign to Stop Gender Apartheid in Afghanistan' is a case in point. Through a series of petitions and lobbying activities this organization played a significant role in 1998 in the refusal by the UN and the USA to grant formal recognition to the Taliban. It also exerted pressure to push the US energy company Unocal out of a US $3 billion venture to put a pipeline through Afghanistan, which would have given the Taliban US $100 million royalties. On the other hand, at a point in time when the Feminist Majority was in alliance with the Revolutionary Association of the Women of Afghanistan (RAWA), the unveiling of a burqa-clad young representative of the organization in the midst of a reading by Oprah Winfrey of Ensler's *The Vagina Monologues* during a performance in New York, represented precisely the type of sensationalism and objectification which women struggling for their rights inside Afghanistan could do without.

2 In Afghanistan, the Ministry of Women's Affairs (MoWA) was tasked with the advancement of women. Its intended aim is to coordinate inter-ministerial gender policy and strategy development through Gender Focal Points and deputing members from its Advisory Group on Gender (AGG) – a rather unwieldy group with representations from donors, UN agencies and civil society organizations – to the national programme of consultative groups (CGs) which coordinate planning and strategy. Assessments of the capacity of MoWA to fulfil its mandate are generally lukewarm (World Bank 2005; Sultan 2005).

3 I am grateful to Rachel Wareham, Principal Gender Adviser with GTZ, for sharing her observations on 'fake ownership'. Gender mainstreaming is primarily internationally understood and led. It is not clear whether the gen-

der mainstreaming mandate of MoWA elicits engagement or uptake among nationals.

4 The test case for this type of concern came ten days after the ratification of the constitution when the performance of a female pop singer on Kabul television was deemed un-Islamic and therefore illegal by the Supreme Court. On this occasion, both the Ministers of Culture and Women's Affairs pointed out that the actions of the Supreme Court were not in conformity with its legal mandate and state television flouted this injunction.

5 The unexpected popularity of female candidates was interpreted by some as a protest vote on the part of an electorate looking for candidates with an unsullied past (Wilder 2005).

6 A comparison across a range of female well-being indicators with other Muslim countries indicates that women in Afghanistan are clearly disadvantaged (World Bank 2005).

7 This is not to deny the important contributions to more secure livelihoods and humanitarian assistance made by donors, often through the activities of NGOs operating at the local level. What is at issue here are some of the claims made concerning women's empowerment and the instruments used to achieve this goal.

## References

Abirafeh, L. (2005) 'Lessons from Gender-focused International Aid in Post-Conflict Afghanistan ... Learned?', *Gender in International Cooperation 7* (Friedrich Ebert Stiftung).

Abu-Lughod, L. (2002) 'Do Muslim Women Really Need Saving? Anthropological Reflections on Cultural Relativism and Its Others', *American Anthropologist*, Vol. 104, no. 3: 1–8.

Al-Ali, N. (2005) 'Reconstructing Gender: Iraqi Women Between Dictatorship, War, Sanctions and Occupation', *Third World Quarterly*, Vol. 26, nos 4–5: 739–58.

Arat-Koc, S. (2002) 'Imperial Wars or Benevolent Interventions? Reflections on "Global Feminism" Post September 11th', *Atlantis*, Vol. 26, no. 2; <www.mun.ca/fkn/Journals/atlantis/satlantisissue26.2.htm> accessed 21 November 2002.

Azarbaijani-Mhogaddam, S. (2003) 'Including Marginalized Groups in the Legal System, State Reconstruction and International Engagement in Afghanistan', paper presented at the Symposium on State Reconstruction and International Engagement in Afghanistan, Centre for Development Research, Bonn, 30 May–1 June.

Duffield, M. (2001) *Global Governance and the New Wars: The Merging of Development and Security* (London: Zed Books).

Ghani, A., C. Lockhart and M. Carnahan (2005) 'Closing the Sovereignty Gap: An Approach to State-Building', Working Paper 253, Overseas Development Institute.

Goodhand, J. (2002) 'Avoiding Violence or Building Peace? The Role of International Aid in Afghanistan', *Third World Quarterly*, Vol. 23, no. 5: 837–59.

Government of Afghanistan (2002) *National Development Framework* (Kabul).

Hirschkind, C. and S. Mahmood (2002) 'Feminism, the Taliban, and Politics of Counter-insurgency', *Anthropological Quarterly*, Vol. 75, no. 2: 339–54.

Kandiyoti, D. (2005) *The Politics of Gender and Reconstruction in Afghanistan*, Occasional paper 4 (Geneva: UNRISD).

Moghadam, V. (2002) 'Patriarchy, the Taleban and Politics of Public Space in Afghanistan', *Women's Studies International Forum*, Vol. 25, no. 1: 19–31.

Molyneux, M. and S. Razavi (2002) 'Introduction', in M. Molyneux and S. Razavi (eds), *Gender Justice, Development and Rights* (Oxford: Oxford University Press), pp. 1–44.

Niland, N. (2004) 'Justice Postponed: The Marginalization of Human Rights in Afghanistan', in A. Donini, N. Niland and K. Wermester (eds), *Nation-Building Unraveled? Aid, Peace and Justice* (Bloomfield, CT: Kumarian Press), pp. 61–82.

Oates, L. and I. Solon Helal (2004) 'At the Cross-Roads of Conflict and Democracy: Women and Afghanistan's Constitutional Loya Jirga', *Rights and Democracy*, 1 May; <www.dd-rd.ca/site/publications/index.php?lang=en&subsection=catalogue&id=1372>.

Pratt, N. (2005) 'Reconstructing Citizenship in Post-invasion Iraq: The Battle Over Women's Rights', Paper presented at MESA, Washington, DC, 19–22 November.

Rehn, E. and E. Johnson Sirleaf (2002) *Women, War and Peace. The Independent Experts' Assessment on the Impact of Armed Conflict on Women and Women's Role in Peace-building* (New York: UNIFEM).

Roy, O. (1986) *Islam and Resistance in Afghanistan* (Cambridge: Cambridge University Press).

Sultan, M. (2005) 'From Rhetoric to Reality: Afghan Women on the Agenda for Peace'; <www.womenwagingpeace.net/content/articles/AfghanistanFullCasestudy.pdf>, accessed 25 September 2005.

Viner, K. (2002) 'Feminism as Imperialism', *Guardian*, 21 September.

Wardak, A. (2004) 'Building a Post-war Justice System in Afghanistan', *Crime Law and Social Change*, Vol. 41, no. 4: 319–41.

Wilder, A. (2005) *A House Divided? Analysing the 2005 Afghan Elections* (Kabul: AREU).

World Bank (2005) 'Afghanistan: National Reconstruction and Poverty Reduction – the Role of Women in Afghanistan's Future' (Washington, DC: World Bank).

UNDP (2001) *Gender Approaches in Conflict and Post-Conflict Situations* (Rome: UNDP).

UNRISD (2005) *Gender Equality: Striving for Justice in an Unequal World* (Geneva: UNRISD).

# 16 | Reassessing paid work and women's empowerment: lessons from the global economy

RUTH PEARSON

In an era of increasingly global production and trading systems, contradictions in how we think about women and work are becoming steadily more evident. Very often, our concern with women's poverty, with women's status and with women's autonomy rests on implicit and unexamined assumptions about the relationship between paid work and women's empowerment. This chapter will seek to explore these assumptions, and to interrogate precisely what it is that we are seeking in terms of women's engagement with paid work and employment.

There are two strands of assumptions that we need to consider. The first is what I have termed 'the Engelian myth' which persists in spite of our increasing acknowledgement of both the ongoing 'informalization' of production in the global economy, and the recognition that for the overwhelming majority of women workers in the global labour force, paid work has never been located within the formal economy. The second is the importance of understanding the nature and dynamics of intra-household and community-level gender relations, particularly concerning any assumed relationship between women's paid work and their empowerment. This is important for theorizing, and designing policy interventions on employment and work, both for women working in factories and collective workplaces and for those women engaged in what have become known as 'micro-enterprises', linked to the extensive practice of providing micro-credit for poor women.

This chapter argues that it is important to dismantle the analytical and policy-framing separation between the formal and informal sectors of the economy, a separation which has allowed the major part of women's paid (and unpaid) work to remain outside the remit of public policy. It is also time to connect up to hitherto separate debates about the empowerment of women though employment in export production and the empowerment which is assumed to result from women being involved in credit-supported micro-enterprises. In recognizing that women's growing income-generating work in the market is often a response to the increased demand for cash which is needed to fulfil gendered responsibilities in social reproduction, we need to challenge the assumption that women can become empowered solely by selling their labour or their products for money.

## The 'Engelian myth' meets the informal economy

By the 'Engelian myth' I mean the view that women's empowerment, or emancipation as it used to be called, lies in their incorporation into the paid workforce; the position that reflects Joan Robinson's oft repeated observation that 'the only thing worse than being exploited by capital is not being exploited by capital'. Certainly the Marxist tradition has long emphasized that identity, and thus political strategy, should be led by the vanguard 'working class' and that women's political interests lie in being incorporated, on an equal basis, into that vanguard (Pearson 1994).

Many feminists have for some time emphasized the importance of women's paid employment. Within a socialist feminist tradition, the conditions under which women worked were also highlighted. Particular concern has been paid to equal pay, opportunities for promotion, training and progression through the hierarchy, and that women's priorities – such as flexible hours and leave, protection of reproductive health, freedom from harassment and appropriate non-wage benefits – be recognized by both trade unions and management.

However, viewed from the perspective of the twenty-first century, it is increasingly clear that these concerns, while universal, need to be contextualized within the changing global economy. For a start, the bulk of the female labour force in the majority world do not labour within a formal economy regulated by national laws concerning pay, working hours, leave, or indeed have any access to work-related social protection. ILO data (2002) indicate that in Latin America, Asia and sub-Saharan Africa the informal economy continues to be the location of recorded employment for the vast majority of women in the non-agricultural sectors.[1] Indeed, it is probable that such figures are underestimated, since there are difficulties in capturing the full range of informal work, particularly since most employment surveys are still based on the notion of a main occupation, whereas the reality of women's work demands engagement in a whole portfolio of income-generating activities. Rather than informal employment being a transitional activity that will be superseded by development or incorporation into the global economy, there is considerable statistical, empirical and analytical evidence that there has been an increase in the *informalization* of production in countries of both the global South and the North.

This term refers to several factors which operate simultaneously, with different factors being of more importance in different contexts. Very often the term refers to the way in which activities which had once taken place within a formal sector environment, regulated by state labour protection and taxation norms, have been reorganized in enterprises that no longer conform to those rules – as happened in the electronics assembly industry (Chhachhi 2004). But much of informal sector activity comprises work in informal workshops, home-based production and petty trading, all dominated by women workers. While difficult to capture accurately, available data point to the importance of women in home-based work and street vending – with women comprising 30–90 per cent of street vendors, 35–80 per cent of home-based workers (including both self-employed enterprises and home-based workers), and 80 per cent of industrial sub-contracted homeworkers (ILO 2002: 6–8). Not only is it the case that informal work is the main source of cash earnings for the majority of economically active women, but it is clear that the very patterns of globalization of the economy are fuelling the trend towards informalization. In some cases the drive to ensure lowest costs and maximum flexibility has taken serial subcontracting beyond the factory gates to the small workshops and home workers to ensure lowest costs and maximum flexibility (Pearson 2004); in other cases global advertising and brand marketing have fuelled demand for the local production of 'fake' items which are manufactured outside the formal regulated economy (Kothari and Laurie 2004). In all sectors, whether they involve export or produce for a purely domestic market, the capacity of the state to regulate the complex systems of subcontracting of production or distribution is generally inadequate, even where there is the political willingness to do this.

Informalization can also be used to capture another phenomenon that requires us to rethink our assumptions about women's formal sector employment. As is well documented, factories located in Export Processing Zones and other situations where women work in labour-intensive assembly lines, turning out garments, sportswear, trainers, micro-electronic components and consumer goods for the world market, were often assumed to be offering opportunities for Third World women to have a stake in the higher-paid, regulated and protected industrial sector, previously reserved for a labour aristocracy of male workers. Instead, what has happened over the last forty years is that women have been recruited to these factories but under conditions that are increasingly remote from any general understanding of formal sector working conditions and employment. In many situations, even where there is a nominal minimum wage and statutory non-wage benefits, such as pension contributions, health insurance, housing benefits and sick pay, it is very rare for women working in assembly plants to access such benefits. Even when, in the initial years of export factory growth, there was an assumption that women workers would have a remuneration and benefit package which compared favourably with alternative occupations (working for domestic companies and/or the domestic market, or working in the informal economy), this situation has not been maintained. While export processing, assembly and even upgraded production have proliferated to many countries and, no longer confined to designated industrial estates, have spread to locations throughout whole national territories, any even partial systems of employment protection for women working in these sectors have been steadily eroded (Razavi and Pearson 2004). Even in cases where a small number of what has been described as 'the first tier' of export workers can be said to be in the formal economy, they are the tiny minority of those employed in the sector and, as the Bangladeshi case illustrates, even the 'elite' workers have never enjoyed the full range of social protection that might be expected (Kabeer 2004). In the 'new' booming export sectors of China, or elsewhere in East and South-Asia, where routinely issues of excessive working hours, low wages, and the absence of employment security and social protection have become commonplace, the conditions of work for the mainly rural migrants in those factories bear little resemblance to the regulated protected ideal of the formal economy (Chan 2003).

If this is the situation, we clearly need to revise our assumptions about the ways in which paid employment for women delivers empowerment, higher status and parity with men, since, as the statistics indicate, women are still more likely to be working in the unprotected informal economy than men (ILO 2002). This does not mean that women derive no benefits from such employment – indeed, as has been argued cogently by Kabeer (2000) and others, any kind of paid work enhances women's capacity to exercise choices and gain some control over the different aspects of their lives. Women universally welcome opportunities to earn cash incomes from engaging in manufacturing employment, however small their wages might be in terms of international comparisons, or indeed compared with some male occupational equivalent.[2] Therefore, assumptions about political strategy and policy derived from Northern-centric generalizations about women's labour force engagement can be rather misplaced because there are complicated issues arising when we try and understand the ways in which paid work might promote the empowerment of women and contribute towards the goal of gender equity.

Women's increasing role in global production is taking place in a growing range of sectors, including globally traded garments and electronics, the 'supermarket' trade in seasonal fruit and vegetables from more temperate climes, in the out-sourcing of computer-related services such as data entry and call centre operations. Debates about women's employment in export sectors have raged since the 1970s: does the employment of women in world market factories offer opportunities or exploitation for women in growing numbers of countries in the developing world (Lim 1990; Pearson 1998)? There are sharp exchanges between different positionalities. Some argue that factory employment offers women a chance to be independent of their families, and to have more say in household decision-making. Others return to the image of the 'global sweatshop', or even a modern-day version of Foucault's electronic panopticon to insist that the work is underpaid, degrading and exploitative (see Basi 2005 for an account of this debate). The earlier analysis Diane Elson and I made in the 1980s (Elson and Pearson 1981) that women's subordination could be intensified, decomposed or recomposed by the construction of a new nimble-fingered female labour force is often sidelined as particular cases studies or standpoints provide contrasting evidence, and are frequently elevated to general conclusions.

But interestingly, with a few noble exceptions, such as Diane Wolf's (1992) study of 'factory daughters' in Indonesia, there have been limited efforts to test empirically theoretical assumptions about the implications of factory work for different groups of women workers in terms of status and power within households and communities. The debates have largely been centred round the access to wage earning employment – as against no access – reflecting the 'public/private divide' which characterized both Marxist discussions of the 'Woman Question' in the nineteenth century and socialist feminist debates about women and work up to the late twentieth century (Evans 1982). But the reality faced by the majority of the female labour force in the twenty-first century is the normalization of market activity; total exclusion from earned income is becoming the exception rather than the rule for women in different situations. This is a reality which is dictated not only by the need for cash to purchase consumption items for day-to-day survival; it is also a consequence of the ways in which access to basic social reproductive services have been reorganized – partly as the result of the Washington consensus which underlay the new economic policies and structural adjustment – which led to the imposition of user charges for primary and other health services and the (re)imposition of school fees and other parental contributions for basic education.

## Women remain 'cheap' workers

In these circumstances, more eurocentric concerns about equality and assumptions that labour market engagement eroded gender subordination appear increasingly irrelevant. First, in most situations in which women work, whether in large-scale formally organized factories or indeed in small workshops or home-based production, the norm is for a very flat occupational structure with no possibility of promotion to more skilled or managerial positions. Indeed, it is very often the case that in spite of an overwhelming predominance of women workers, the management remains firmly male (Pearson 1995). Second, although women have long been recognized as the archetypical 'cheap' workforce, new categories of cheap labour are now emerging – migrant labour in West European agriculture or domestic services for example, or young men in the case of export sectors such as sports footwear in Mexico, where gender is not the only relation through which a profitable and flexible labour force can be constructed. And thirdly, even when women's paid work does increase, there is very little evidence that there is a corresponding adjustment in the burden of (unpaid) domestic labour within the home or the community (Pearson 2000).

## Women's paid work and intra-household gender relations

In addition to work on opportunities, rewards and conditions for women's work in the paid labour force, there is another strand of feminist economics which has a bearing on the relationship between women's income-generating activity and empowerment. I refer here to the analysis of processes of intra-household relations and decision-making, which has interrogated the variations in (mis)-match between the amount of paid and unpaid work women do, and how – and by whom – income gets spent by and on behalf of different household members. Nancy Folbre's (1986) significant observation that both Marxist and neo-classical economics treated the household as a 'black box' ruled by a benevolent dictator underlined the importance of understanding the link between women's paid work and the implications for gender relations in the private as well as the public sphere.

This is a key issue underlying assumptions that empowerment of women is a consequence of engagement in paid employment. A major contribution was made by the work of the development welfare economist Amartya Sen (1990), who reconceptualized the process of intra-household bargaining as 'cooperative conflict', which rightly challenges the notion that a woman's well-being can be read directly from her positioning as an autonomous individual, regardless of her affective and economic relationships with her family or household. Instead he demonstrated that women's material and social status derives in part from how (scarce) resources are distributed within households and communities, a distribution that will be affected both by the status of women and by the acknowledgement of her paid (and unpaid) contributions to the household. Sen bases his arguments on extensive research which demonstrates that women's well-being – in terms of self-perception, but also in terms of external measures – is inextricably linked with that of their family, and also that a high proportion of a woman's earnings contributes directly to meeting the basic needs of household members including children as well as her own. This more nuanced approach to understanding the link between women's paid work and notions of 'empowerment' is helpful because it challenges the assumptions that women's earning capacity automatically translates into empowerment as well as questioning the extent to which women's empowerment can be conceptualized in isolation from family, kin and community relations. Instead, it highlights the ways in which earning money may extend women's options, but may also intensify their workload and responsibilities without necessarily increasing their autonomy.

## Micro-credit and women's empowerment?

Nowhere is the assumption that market engagement leads to women's empowerment more widespread – and least theorized – than in the literature and practice on micro-credit and micro-enterprise. The literature abounds with assertions and refutations about the extent to which borrowing money, being responsible for putting it to a hopefully productive use, repaying it and making some profit, constitute a path for empowerment of poor women (Pitt et al. 2003; Kabeer 2005). Very often these conclusions are not based on any systematic effort to interrogate the processes involved or to situate them within specific contexts, or even to examine the nature of the income-generating activity that credit might, or might not, give rise to. Instead there is often an unspoken hypothesis that credit – and by extension market-based economic activity – must represent a challenge to existing household norms of decision-making and status. The idea persists, particularly in the world of development organizations, that money in women's hands will directly facilitate women into productive economic activity, which in itself will alter the power dimensions within the household and the family.

There are several problems with this view. First, it frequently relies on unconscious assumptions about autonomy and empowerment, which, as I have argued above, are inappropriate in many contexts. Much of the literature is focused on experiences in South Asia since this is where micro-credit has been most extensively applied, though little of it is based on a reliable analysis of the nature of household budgeting and decision-making processes. Inevitably, there are contrasting conclusions: that micro-credit increases women's power; that it further reduces women's autonomy, making women responsible for debts while their husbands actually control the activities related to the credit payments; and/or that it increases or decreases domestic violence.[3] But the point being made here is that, in the case of micro-credit and micro-enterprise, the relationship between women's economic activity and empowerment is as complicated and context specific as it is in the case of waged work in manufacturing and services.

In some of the literature there is a recognition of the complexities of these relationships. Mayoux (2001), among others, suggests that in the case of micro-finance (which includes savings as well as credit activities), it is in fact the collective activity carried out in groups which leads to the 'empowerment' claimed by observers. Indeed, many micro-credit schemes in the early years were organized through 'group' collateral. The whole basis of Mohammed Yunis's model for the Grameen bank was that social collateral in the form of group underwriting of loans should replace individual collateral in 'banking for the poor', since by definition the poor do not have the regular income or financial or capital assets that would provide surety to a would-be financial lender (Yunus and Jolis 1999). So organizing borrowing groups was a key tool in the spread of micro-credit to poor households. Other providers have adapted this model and, in doing so, extended credit to those who have utilized it to ensure household subsistence and survival rather than to invest it in an enterprise with growth potential from a business perspective. But the group collateral approach has also formed the basis for linking a range of related and non-related activities – literacy, community development and family planning, and political empowerment – with a range of top-down as well as bottom-up techniques (CEZONTLE 1999). Where such activities are part of programmes directly aimed at challenging some of the dimensions of women's subordination, such as in supporting women to take on leadership roles within the organization or the community, to speak and be heard, to challenge harmful practices such as female genital mutilation, dowry or female infanticide, then the links between the financial services projects and women's empowerment can be positively traced. But it remains difficult to evaluate the direct correlation between women taking out loans and trying to start micro-businesses, and any short-term change in their status or autonomy within the household or in the wider society.

Of course there are many examples of women entrepreneurs who can genuinely claim that their business success was facilitated by access to credit in situations where traditional financial institutions were not available to them. But most micro-credit borrowers are in fact the same women as those involved in subsistence activities within the informal economy. They borrow to facilitate their petty trading, or even their home-based production – to buy stock, raw materials, pay off other creditors or loans etc. – and the return on their activities is low. There is no systematic evidence that it is actually involvement with loans and repayments that changes women's subordination or makes them independent traders or businesswomen. Where business success is achieved, women are of course in a stronger position to renegotiate intra-household relations, but the connection with accessing credit is context-specific rather than generalizable. It may well be, however, that there is an inter-generational effect whereby daughters of women who are involved in activities involving loans and other services might be in a stronger position to challenge traditional forms of gender subordination.

### Women, work and money: contradictory implications

Whether women are working in export factories or in credit-financed micro-enterprises, they are generally adding to their domestic responsibilities the task of earning money to support their households. Effectively, women's traditional responsibility for the well-being of household members has been monetized by changes such as the introduction of user charges for medical services as well as the general commoditization of different aspects of local economies. Women have to earn money to meet their gendered household responsibilities. Their work burden is often intensified by their income-generating activities, and there is little evidence that there has been a widespread renegotiation of gendered unpaid reproductive work responsibilities as the result of increased economic engagement.

So – how do we respond politically to this situation? On the one hand, like Oxfam (2002), we can protest about inequality of wages and bad working conditions for poor women workers in different parts of the world. Undoubtedly this continues to be a central issue. We can insist that remuneration and working conditions comply with internationally agreed standards or codes of conduct, as has been done in the vegetable and fruit sector (Barrientos et al. 2000) as well as in manufacturing, and that these codes reflect the priorities of women workers (Pearson and Seyfang 2002). We can also examine how women's contribution to foreign exchange earnings and economic growth can be reflected in the ways in which labour regulation and social policies are organized, rejecting the view that participation in the global economy denies nation-states, and thus women's movements in particular countries, the possibility of locally negotiated settlements about social protection, workplace norms and non-wage benefits (Razavi and Pearson 2004).

But we also need a more radical rethink that will connect the two up-to-now separate debates about the empowerment of women in export production and in credit-supported micro-enterprises. Instead of assuming that women in low-income countries should aspire to an (assumed male) norm of protected and regulated employment, with all the concomitant benefits and social protection which such employment signals, we should begin from the recognition of a different reality. The norm for women in the majority world is economic engagement without regulation or protection, regardless of whether it takes place in large-scale workplaces, small or family-based workshops or within women's own houses or compounds. Women provide 'cheap' labour, which is part of the so-called 'informal' economy, and also part of the way in which the global economy operates in out-sourcing not just globally traded products, but the social reproduction of labour at the lowest cost to international capital. The informal economy is not the exception in most developing countries – it is the norm, and by all statistical accounts it is growing both because the formal sector is becoming informalized, and because the range of market-oriented informal economic activities is expanding to meet the requirements of poor households for cash. Women are playing a bigger and bigger role in this economy, and policies and demands which might improve their position should be based on this reality.

We also need to acknowledge that the Engelian myth is based on a conceptualization of work which somehow has remained independent from the extensive analysis in the 1970s, which we then called the 'Domestic Labour Debate' (Molyneux 1979). Although wages for housework was dismissed as an essentialist and radical feminist fantasy, it is time to extract from this something important. Women's participation in the money economy – whether through factory employment, home-based production for nationally and internationally traded goods such as fashion wear or sports shoes, or small-scale trading and services which provide money for daily survival – is not on its own going to achieve women's equality or empowerment. Over the last three decades, the labour force participation of women has doubled worldwide; and if we add to this women's involvement in all kinds of market-oriented activities, it would be hard to find any group of women who could not be said to be economically active.

Poor women, like men, strive to earn incomes which represent an adequate return on their labour. But whether this includes access to all the resources, both monetary and publicly provided, which are necessary to ensure that they can cover their responsibilities to their children and other household members is increasingly uncertain. Economic participation by women is increasing rapidly but our concern should not be limited to the ways in which money income can be increased. Poor women need money, but increases in wages will not on their own make women either less poor or more powerful. Improvements in the conditions and returns from work must be coupled with expectations that the state will ensure that they achieve a minimum income; that they have access to affordable and high-quality education; health and transport services; and that their environment is healthy and their lives are not blighted by community and domestic violence.

Being exploited by capital is the fate of virtually all women in today's global economy, but the exchange value of their labour will not on its own provide the basis for women's empowerment. If we challenge the separation between factory work and home-based work, between the formal and informal sector, we will have a clearer perception of what women's economic and social rights might cover. If we challenge the myth that poor women have endless resources of time and energy to dedicate to improving the return on their labour in the marginal economies of the informal sector, the role for public policy will become clearer. Demands for international support to improve the working conditions and wages earned by poor women must be linked to explorations of universal entitlements in terms of minimum income and services. It is not reasonable to assume that the improvements required for the genuine empowerment of poor women can come solely from selling their labour without resourcing collective provision of services and rewarding women's responsibilities in reproductive activities.

## Notes

1 Figures for 1994–2000 (see Charmes 2002) indicated that the figures were 58 per cent for Latin America, 65 per cent for Asia (though this atypically includes Syria but not the rest of North Africa) and 84 per cent for sub-Saharan Africa.

2 It is often pointless to make a comparison with male wages, because in many sectors where women are concentrated there are no comparable male occupations and no possibility of legislation to achieve 'equal pay for work of equal value'.

3 The incidence of domestic violence is one of the most difficult indicators to quantify, and many of the studies attempting this are based on very small samples that have no statistical significance (Goetz and Gupta 1996; Hashemi et al. 1996). However, many researchers take this to be a significant indicator of (economic) empowerment, since, as explained in terms of Sen's cooperative conflict model, a woman's ability to leave a violent household (the breakdown point) is largely determined by their degree of self-generated income. However, this may be an over-simplistic formulation since decades of research on domestic violence indicates that such decisions are not just based on alternative incomes, but on housing, children, community and personal notions of status and inclusion/exclusion as well as complicated issues of duty and affection.

# References

Barrientos, S., S. McClenaghan and L. Orton (2000) 'Ethical Trade and South African Deciduous Fruit Exporters – Addressing Gender Sensitivity', *European Journal of Development Research*, Vol. 12, no. 1: 140–58.

Basi, T. J. K. T. (2005) *Globalisation and Transnational Indian Call Centres: Constructing Women's Identities*, unpublished PhD thesis, School of Sociology and Social Policy, University of Leeds.

CEZONTLE (Centro Para la Participacion Democratica y el Desarrollo) (1999) 'Strengthening Women's Political and Economic Participation: A Training and Education Project in Nicaragua', <www.cedpa.org/publications/PROWID/LA/cenzontle_rib.pdf>.

Chan, A. (2003) 'A "Race to the Bottom": Globalization and China's Labour Standards', *China Perspectives*, Vol. 46: 41–9.

Charmes, J. (2002) 'Women and Men in the Informal Economy: A Statistical Picture', ILO Employment Sector, Geneva; available at <www.ilo.org/public/english/employment/gems>.

Chhachhi, A. (2004) *Eroding Citizenship: Gender and Labour in Contemporary India*, PhD thesis, University of Amsterdam.

Elson, D. and R. Pearson (1981) ' "Nimble Fingers Make Cheap Workers": An Analysis of Women's Employment in Third World Export Manufacturing', *Feminist Review*, Vol. 7: 87–107.

Evans, M. (ed.) (1982) *The Woman Questions: Readings on the Subordination of Women* (London: Fontana).

Folbre, N. (1986) 'Hearts and Spades: Paradigms of Household Economics', *World Development*, Vol. 14, no. 2: 245–55.

Goetz, A. M. and R. S. Gupta (1996) 'Who Takes the Credit? Gender, Power and Control Over Loan Use in Rural Credit Programmes in Bangladesh', *World Development*, Vol. 24, no. 1: 45–63.

Hashmeni, S. M., S. R. Schuler and A. P. Riley (1996) 'Rural Credit Programs and Women's Empowerment in Bangladesh', *World Development*, Vol. 24, no. 4: 635–53.

ILO (2002) 'Women and Men in the Informal Economy: A Statistical Picture', ILO Employment Sector, Geneva; available at <www.ilo.org/public/english/employment/gems>.

Kabeer, N. (2005) 'Is Microfinance a "Magic Bullet" for Women's Empowerment?: Analysis of Findings from South Asia', *Economic and Political Weekly*, 26 October, pp. 4709–18; available at <www.eldisorg>.

— (2004) 'Globalization, Labor Standards and Women's Rights: Dilemmas of Collective (In)action in an Inter-Dependent World', *Feminist Review*, Vol. 10, no. 1: 3–35.

— (2000) *The Power to Choose: Bangladeshi Women and Labour Market Decisions in London and Dhaka* (London: Verso).

Kothari, U. and N. Laurie (2004) 'Different Bodies, Same Clothes: An Agenda for Local Consumption and Global Identities', *Area*, Vol. 37, no. 2: 223–7.

Lim, L. (1990) 'Women's Work in Export Factories: The Politics of a Cause', in

I. Tinker (ed.), *Persistent Inequalities: Women and World Development* (New York and Oxford: Oxford University Press).

Mayoux, L. (2001) 'Women's Empowerment Versus Sustainability? Towards a New Paradigm in Micro Finance Programmes', in B. Lemire, R. Pearson and G. Campbell (eds), *Women and Credit: Researching the Past: Refiguring the Future* (Oxford and New York: Berg).

Molyneux, M. (1979) 'Beyond the Domestic Labour Debate', *New Left Review*, no. 115 (July/August): 3–28.

Oxfam (2002) 'Rigged Rules and Double Standards: Trade, Globalisation and the Fight against Poverty'; available from <www.oxfam.org.uk/waht_we_do_/issues/trde/trade_report.htm>.

Pearson, R. (2004) 'Organising Home-based Workers in the Global Economy: An Action-Research Approach', *Development in Practice,* Vol. 14, nos 1–2: 136–48.

— (2000) 'All Change? Men, Women and Reproductive Work in the Global Economy', *European Journal of Development Research*, Vol. 12, no. 2: 219–37.

— (1998) 'Nimble Fingers Re-Visited', in C. Jackson and R. Pearson (eds), *Feminist Visions of Development: Gender Analysis and Policy* (London: Routledge).

— (1995) 'Male Bias and Women's Work in Mexico's Border Industries', in D. Elson (ed.), *Male Bias in the Development Process* (Manchester: Manchester University Press).

— (1994) 'Gender Relations, Capitalism and Third World Industrialization', in L. Sklair (ed.), *Capitalism and Development* (London: Routledge).

Pearson, R. and G. Seyfang (2002) '"I'll Tell You What I Want ...": Women Workers and Codes of Conduct', in R. Jenkins, R. Pearson and G. Seyfang (eds), *Corporate Responsibility and Labour Rights: Codes of Conduct in the Global Economy* (London: Earthscan).

Pitt, M. M., S. R. Khandker and J. Cartwright (2003) 'Does Micro-Credit Empower Women? Evidence from Bangladesh', *Policy Research Working Paper*, WPS2998, World Bank, Development Research Group; available from <http://econ/worldbank.org>.

Razavi, S. and R. Pearson (2004) 'Globalization, Export-oriented Employment and Social Policy: Gendered Connections', in R. Pearson, S. Razavi and C. Danloy (eds), *Globalization, Export-oriented Employment and Social Policy* (Basingstoke: Palgrave Macmillan).

Sen, A. (1990) 'Gender and Cooperative Conflicts', in I. Tinker (ed.), P*ersistent Inequalities: Women and World Development* (New York and Oxford: Oxford University Press).

Yunus, M. and A. Jolis (1999) *Banker to the Poor: The Autobiography of Mohammad Yunus* (London: Aurum Press).

Wolf, D. (1992) *Factory Daughters: Gender, Household Dynamics and Rural Industrialization in Java* (Berkeley: University of California Press).

# 17 | Announcing a new dawn prematurely? Human rights feminists and the rights-based approaches to development

DZODZI TSIKATA

The adoption of rights-based approaches (RBAs) by various UN agencies, bilateral development agencies and international development NGOs[1] has allowed human rights language to enter the world of development programming as a welcome and legitimate friend. Not surprisingly, this has generated vigorous debates. Sceptical voices are arguing that the development industry has simply adopted the language of rights without any substantive changes in policies or programmes (Uvin 2002).

While the literature reveals more endorsements of the RBAs than disagreements with them, the critique of the RBAs is strikingly similar to feminists' concerns about how the development industry has taken up and digested their analyses and prescriptions in unpredictable ways and often with unhappy outcomes. Since the 1970s when gender issues became part of the development industry, different approaches to gender inequalities have become dominant and then waned under the critical gaze of feminists within and outside the industry.

There are several explanations for why the RBAs are on the ascendancy, but are generating so much debate in the development industry at this time. Two aspects of this story interest us here. One is why governments and some NGOs of developing countries have given such a lukewarm response to the RBAs. It is curious that the same governments who championed the Right to Development within the context of a New International Economic Order (NIEO) would rather not work with an approach to development said to be based on the resulting Declaration that they fought hard to have adopted by the UN General Assembly in 1986. A second question is why a section of the women's movement, specifically its human rights wing, welcomes the new-found popularity of the RBAs. Are they rushing to judgement or is this really a new and interesting development? What, if anything, has changed and what does it mean for the old ways of doing development in general, and gender and development in particular?

In this chapter, I begin with an account of the debates about the RBAs' policy and programmatic implications, arguing that differences in interpretation signal the need for caution. As Pratt (2003) has argued, in a critique of the unquestioning attitudes of much of the literature, the RBAs need the same scrutiny as any other development approach. I then discuss how gender has been treated within certain RBAs and relate this to the claims being made for the RBAs by women's rights organizations. I conclude that many of their hopes for the RBAs are not likely to be realized given their processes and contexts.

## The case for the RBAs

There is no one RBA. Marks (2003) has identified seven approaches through which human rights thinking is applied to development.[2] Whether or not one accepts this classification, it points to certain differences in ways of linking human rights and development. However, the RBAs also have important commonalities: their legal basis; their normative framework; and the principle that the process of realizing them is a goal in itself (Ljungman and Forti, forthcoming). The legal basis refers to their roots in international and regional human rights instruments.[3] The normative framework relates to the emerging consensus on their basic elements, including an explicit linkage to human rights; greater accountability on the part of states and international actors; a stress on empowerment, participation and non-discrimination; and attention to vulnerable groups (OHCHR 2004).

According to its proponents, the RBAs have several advantages. These include:

- the identification of rights, and duties to respect, protect and fulfil them, as well as the holders of such rights and duties, thereby enhancing accountability
- strategies directed at redressing injustice rather than relieving suffering
- a normative stance on the side of the oppressed and excluded, thus compelling a focus on vulnerable groups such as women
- the position that rights are inalienable, universal, non-negotiable, indivisible and interdependent
- starting point that people have agency, can drive change and are not passive recipients of development aid
- a point of reference inherent in the violation of rights which promotes systematic analysis
- efforts directed at the roots of structural injustices rather than their effects
- the promotion of institutional change rather than charity because of a change in discourse from needs to rights
- the promotion of collective rather than individual actions and alliances

215

- legitimacy because governments have signed agreements which remain independent of the interests of a single government
- precise, grounded and realistic language which can be an advantage in negotiations and making demands. (Kerr 2001; Archer 2005; Brouwer 2005)

In relation to poverty reduction, the RBAs' core principles of account-ability, universality, non-discrimination and equality, participatory decision-making processes, and the inter-dependence of rights are all important (Brouwer 2005). Some observers also highlight the congruence between the RBAs and social policy and social protection, the former said to strengthen the normative case for the latter by offering standards and principles, analy-tical tools and operational guidance (Piron 2005).

Many of these 'advantages' are actually aims and objectives with which few would take issue. Rights discourse is certainly a welcome counter-balance to prevailing functionalist and instrumentalist development approaches, and RBAs may also help develop healthier cultures of citizen-ship among communities and their members. At the UN, rights have clearly been useful to gender equality activists, and in public interest law cases, such as those brought on behalf of communities affected by development projects or natural resource extraction, rights have also been a useful basis for legal arguments.

The disagreements about RBAs have rarely been about the importance of human rights and the right to development. Rather, critics question whether aims such as accountability, participation and people-centredness, which have long been fought for in development circles, are now realizable simply because of the adoption of the RBAs. Do the RBAs really have the ability to transform development practice? Are the RBAs' advantages really new? After all, several pre-RBA approaches have in their time claimed some of the advantages listed above. These issues are taken up in the next section.

### Critiquing the RBAs: what the sceptics are saying

Questions about the RBAs can be divided into three broad categories: conceptual, political and issues of practical application and outcomes. A recent conference organized by the University of Manchester on the 'Winners and Losers from the Rights-based Approaches to Development' allowed many of these questions to be aired in the same space (see Refer-ences to this chapter for conference papers).

Conceptual problems include lack of clarity caused by the existence of many different RBAs: what are the precise differences between Marks's seven RBA approaches; or in Ljungman and Forti's distinction between a human rights perspective to development assistance and a full-scale rights-based approach? (Marks 2003; Ljungman and Forti, forthcoming). Other questions concern the lack of clarity about the implications of the RBAs for the older ways of doing development (identified as the needs or service-based approaches); the gaps in mutual understanding about concepts, motivations and approaches between RBA approaches and other development paradigms (Archer 2005); and lack of agreement about what duties exist and who has the obligations (Brouwer 2005).

Political issues concern: (1) the observation that the RBAs lean more towards political and civil rights and have a relatively weak appreciation of social and economic rights; (2) the danger of privileging elite interests in the context of liberal constructions of citizenship (Green 2005); (3) the erroneous identification of the state as the primary site of accountability when more and more economic decisions are not in the control of nation-states; (4) the contradictions between the market principles of the neo-liberal paradigm and the RBAs (Tsikata 2004; Gledhill, 2005); and (5) the implication of the limitations of accountability and participatory decision-making for the RBAs (Tsikata 2004). A further issue is how the RBAs meet the challenges of universality and sovereignty in different and particular social and cultural contexts (Morvaridi 2005). The RBAs have also been criticized for moral grandstanding; a refusal to be pragmatic or to identify development priorities at any point in time; and for an insistent individualism which ignores the social relations at the heart of development (Archer 2005; Sheehy 2005). They have also been charged with being donor-driven, imposed often indirectly by funding strictures (Tsikata 2004; Pettit and Wheeler 2005).

In terms of application and outcomes, concerns persist that some of the narrower interpretations of the RBAs can result in the neglect of the interests of the poorest and a devaluation of work at the grassroots (Chapman et al. 2005). The 'absolutist' tendencies of RBAs may not be compatible with strategic project-level planning and may therefore weaken programming quality (Munro 2005). Much of this aspect of the critique has been generated by case studies, for example on the failure to implement a rights-based approach in decentralization in Ghana (Crawford 2005); and on the failure of the RBA to enable most representatives of marginalized groups in a Nepali village to exercise their rights because of their situation as underlings, the precariousness of their livelihoods and their lack of command of the language of public meetings (Masaki 2005).

What follows is a brief discussion of a few of these issues. These include the contradictions between the RBAs and the right to development; the challenges of implementing the RBAs in the context of International Financial Institution (IFI)-driven Poverty Reduction Strategy Papers (PRSPs); problems with the conception of accountability and participation; and the roles of donors, the nation-state and citizens in the implementation of the RBAs.

*Conceptual questions about the RBAs* The Right to Development (RTD) on which the RBAs are based is itself being vigorously debated within the UN (Sengupta 2000a and b; Piron 2002; Marks 2003). While many Third World governments have argued that it is a new right, Western governments have argued that it crystallizes social, economic and cultural rights. The roles of nation-states and international actors in ensuring rights are also being debated. Northern governments disagree with the position that they have a duty to provide resources to address the problems of developing countries.

Disagreements persist over whether the RTD is a group or an individual right and whether it has the force of law or is mainly in the realm of values. The independent expert on the Right to Development, Arjun Sengupta, has tried to address some of these debates by arguing controversially that the RTD is about the right to a particular process of development which allows all fundamental freedoms and rights to be realized and which expands capabilities. The RTD in his interpretation cannot be equated with the right to the outcomes of development or the sum of all existing human rights (Piron 2002).

These debates about RBAs point to the legal paraphernalia needed to work within a rights paradigm, raising serious doubts that the powerless would take centre-stage within them. Instead, the RBAs may be prone to deepening the technicization and depoliticization of gender and development work which many have justly criticized. Meanwhile, the expectations of legal institutions and the legal and para-legal professions may be overstated given their poor record as champions of the rights of the poor and social groups such as women. The complicated relationship between women, the state and the law makes rights at best an arena of struggle. Rights may also not be the best analytical tool for understanding the challenges of class, gender, race, kinship and other social relations. Rights discourses have been unable successfully to address human rights abuses against women taking place in the private sphere in relation to sexuality, marriage, reproduction, inheritance and the custody of children (CCEIA 2000). Not surprisingly, the majority of African women do not resort to legal action in pursuit of their rights despite years of legal literacy programmes all over the continent. Optimism for RBAs seems to have obscured a wealth of analysis about the state, the law and rights generated over many years.

*The context of IFI-driven PRSPs* Rights may also not be the best analytical tools for understanding the challenges of globalization, militarism, the rise of the transnational corporations, or impacts of neo-liberal policies. Much of the scepticism about the RBAs arises from an impression that little more than the language of development changes in many organizations which espouse them. This impression is fed by claims such as the World Bank's statement that much of its work since its formation has been to create the environment in which human rights can flourish. Fundamental changes in how organizations operate and which economic policy directions they pursue seem not to be guaranteed by the adoption of a RBA. Within the RBAs, the economic liberalization agenda of the IFIs is not up for discussion and will continue to be the context in which rights have to be realized (Piron 2002; Uvin 2002). Activists had argued that the privatization of essential services such as water, education and health along with extensive cost recovery under SAPs are a violation of the rights of poor people because these policies have resulted in their loss of access and in increasing levels of poverty. In the words of Uvin (2002: 1), with RBAs 'the powerful and the rich have voluntarily set out to collaborate and redefine the conditions of misery and exploitation for the rest of the world'.

*The nation-state and the RBAs: unjustified great expectations?* One of the problems raised by RBAs lies in the role claimed for nation-states as duty bearers, who need to improve accountability for ensuring the fulfilment of rights. Indeed, this clear identification of the nation-state as the bearer of obligations is seen by many as one of the strengths of the RBAs. But in practical terms, three decades of structural adjustment have dismantled and disabled many states in important ways, rendering them poor performers of this role. On the other hand, little accountability is demanded by RBAs of the IFIs and other multilateral agencies, bilateral agencies, transnational corporations, Western governments or international NGOs, who to various degrees are the ones in the driving seat of development policy-making, particularly in Africa. If the site of development policy-making has shifted to the international arena, then the RBAs' focus on national actors – citizens and governments – to the exclusion of the corporate sector, foreign governments and the IFIs, is diversionary.

Some also note the irony that while the RBAs are a response by the UN, Northern governments and the IFIs to demands by countries from the South that the right to development be taken seriously, many RBA provisions are directed at Southern governments to implement. The lukewarm reception given to the RBAs in capitals of the developing world has been attributed to fears that they represent another round of donor conditionalities which continue in the tradition of protecting donors and the IFIs from having to take equal responsibility for policy errors.

*The role of the multilateral and bilateral agencies and international NGOs* The manner in which powerful players within the economic policy establishment have adopted RBAs and are pushing them within various constituencies has meant that a programme touted as ensuring grassroots participation is being imposed top-down on governments, civil society organizations and communities in much the same way as the Results Based Management approach was. Given the history of donor faddism, it is anyone's guess how long it will take for a new development approach to take over the current 'holy grail' status of the RBAs. Continuing confusion over what the RBAs are and are not, and the fact that what is being claimed for them has been advocated within the development circles for decades, may precipitate this process.

An example of donor faddism is the prominence being enjoyed by the Millennium Development Goals (MDGs) in development programming. MDG goals have been tagged on to the RBAs and use rights language. Feminists and other NGO activists are arguing that the achievements represented by the documents adopted by the various 1990s conferences are being threatened by the MDGs because they represent a ruthless distillation of undertakings, taking the essence out of the rich analysis and detailed commitments of the various platforms. The eight goals, fifteen targets and forty-eight indicators of the MDG document are so selective that achieving them would not take either the development or the gender and development agenda significantly forward.

Demands for the full participation of disadvantaged social groups in policy and programme decision-making to promote local ownership, and for bottom-up and people-centred approaches to development, have been the staple of development literature since the late 1970s. Chambers (1983) and others have long advocated participatory approaches to development without claiming it for human rights. Policy advocacy among NGOs which has involved making demands on governments, transnational corporations or the IFIs certainly predated the RBAs. The use of targets and indicators to measure the outcomes of development efforts is also not new, even if these particular MDG indicators are now couched in rights terms. AWID (2002) concedes this indirectly when it argues that the RBAs are not a rejection of former development models, but have evolved from lessons learned from the development experiences of many countries.

*The role of citizens: formal or substantive participation?* The RBAs guarantee citizens' participation in development policy-making and programming. While the scope and purpose of participation vary in different versions of the RBAs, certain common standards apply. These include timely notification and access to information, access to support groups and legal resources, freedom to communicate concerns, access to the media, relevant officials and agencies and a fair hearing for people to present their case, access to institutions that can redress harms and impose accountability (Paul 1992). As Paul argues, the human rights concept of participation is 'much more tough and explicit than the soft notion often propounded by development experts who discuss participation as if it was some sort of discretionary policy to be determined by those who control projects' (Paul 1992: 7).

In today's policy-making context, citizens and their organizations are hemmed in by the donors and national governments. The experience of the production of Poverty Reduction Strategy Papers in several countries shows how the standards, processes and scope of participation are not properly clarified and fall far below those established in the Universal Declaration and other instruments. What passes for participation in the policy arena is often anaemic, unclear and heavily circumscribed. Relevant policy documents are hard to access. Written by technocrats under the supervision of the IFIs, they often rely mainly on foreign consultants. Citizens are engaged in perfunctory consultations, sometimes even without the benefit of documents. There is no clear process for incorporating the outcomes of such consultations into policy. Given this scenario, it is not clear how the RBAs would enhance citizens' participation and what kind of participation they can deliver.

All these issues raise fundamental questions about the development paradigm of the RBAs. Given that RBAs are said to have special relevance for gender and development, and are heralded as capable of achieving what women failed to achieve under other gender and development approaches, interrogating the gender dimensions of the RBAs is a critical task.

*RBAs and gender* If the RBAs raise so many questions, why are women's human rights activists so positive about its prospects? There are several reasons for this. One is the observation that the norm of gender equality is central, rather than an 'add on', to the RBAs because 'equality and non discrimination are central tenets of human rights and are included in most conventions'. Second, since RBAs focus on the most marginalized in society, women are one of their natural constituencies (AWID 2002: 3). But even if the above observations are correct, they do not necessarily translate into the superiority of RBAs over other gender and development approaches. Moreover, that such views about RBAs are not necessarily shared by the main actors in development programming in capitals around the developing world is of some concern.

Interestingly, there is no agreement about the fate of gender mainstreaming under the RBAs. While some have argued that the RBAs will enhance gender mainstreaming, others suggest that the RBAs will end mainstreaming's dubious agenda, or at the very least modify its aims and objectives (Kerr 2001). Even more worrying, the space devoted to gender inequality in some RBAs is quite small. For example, OXFAM International's RBA articulates five rights: (1) to sustainable livelihoods; (2) to basic services; (3) to life and security; (4) to be heard; and (5) to an identity. In a matrix that explains the RBA approach by identifying which human rights instruments speak to which rights, it is stated that CEDAW speaks to the right to an identity, the optional protocol to CEDAW speaks to the right to be heard and the declaration on violence speaks to the right to life and security.[4] The gender strategy therefore has two tracks: gender mainstreaming and support for women's organizations and networks. Gender mainstreaming as a strategy has not been very successful in addressing gender inequalities, a situation attributed to analytical weaknesses, lack of political commitment, inadequate funding and a lack of clarity about the its ends (Kerr 2001). Without fundamental change, the RBAs do not make a convincing case tackling gender inequalities.

The approach of human rights activists to RBAs could be an issue of position and history. They are no novices to struggles within the mainstream human rights movement, have a well deserved reputation for fighting long and hard and have been successful in injecting women's rights into the discourse of human rights. However, with a few exceptions, their contribution to gender and development advocacy, particularly on questions of economic, social and cultural justice has been less significant. Many of their allies in African countries are human rights lawyers' organizations which have tended to work with specific women's rights issues such as violence against women, discrimination under customary laws of marriage and inheritance and, more recently, women's land rights. They are less known for their work on the broader issues of the direction and orientation of development policies. Thus, human rights feminisms continue to be dominated by forces not particularly worried about the development paradigm and its implications for women. This situation does not augur well for the promotion of socio-economic rights within the RBAs.

The optimism of gender activists about the RBAs may also be overplayed in the current geo-political situation where security questions override concerns about development and where conservative forces are on the ascendancy. That the RBAs' dissemination is UN-led means that it comes with the UN's strengths and weaknesses. In relation to women's rights, the demobilizing effects of the UN's uptake of the gender equality agenda of second-wave feminism has gone hand-in-hand with the greater visibility and legitimacy it has given to these issues at the national and international levels. The UN continues to be an important player in top-down agenda-setting and while it is today one of the few progressive but increasingly wobbly voices in discussions about development and women's rights, its current political weakness and its desperate alliances with transnational corporations and powerful governments make it an unreliable ally in the fight for gender equality and development.

## What challenges are posed for feminists by the RBAs?

The main challenges posed by RBAs is that they represent another instalment of contestation within gender and development. This is not helped by the multiplicity of RBAs and the confusion about what they represent. The RBAs have been touted as representing a convergence of two strands of feminism – the women's human rights and gender and development perspectives – which have had distinct terminologies, different experts, specialized methodologies, separate agencies and different institutional actors. Kerr (2001) has argued that this divide, which was not good for the women's movement because it caused duplicated efforts and a lack of holistic understandings, is now undergoing change because of a convergence on issues related to globalization. The nature of the convergence is that the development constituency is recognizing a link between laws and institutions and the outcomes of development schemes and programmes. On the other hand, rights activists are increasingly focusing on economic and social well-being, cultural practices, traditions and state economic policy.

This convergence, if it is real, will be a fragile one in the light of the foregoing critique of the RBAs. The array of forces on the different sides of the RBA divide – with Northern governments and their development agencies, the World Bank, the UN and Northern NGOs promoting RBAs, and Southern governments and certain southern NGOs and other civil society organizations remaining sceptical about them – makes the danger of fragmentation within the international women's movement real. It is time to debate the RBAs and what they represent more fully, and this time voices from developing countries need to take the lead.

Without such interrogation, we may be seeing myth-making in progress. At the very least, all the elements are there: claims based on high moral principles backed by selective evidence; a large army of convinced proponents;

eloquent and elegant defences; and tall claims when the myth is questioned. As things stand, the claim that RBAs will deliver gender equality and development is premature, notwithstanding its heavy endorsement by a respected section of the women's movement. Even if the RBAs help to reposition gender and give gender equity work a new lease of life as some have argued, in what directions would this lead and what ends would it serve?

## Notes

1 Bilateral agencies that have adopted an RBA include those from Canada, the United Kingdom, Australia, Norway, Sweden and Denmark; international NGOs include Action-Aid, Oxfam, CARE, Danish Church Aid and Save the Children (Interaction 2003).

2 These are the holistic approach, the rights-based approach, the social justice approach, the capabilities approach, the right to development approach, the responsibilities approach and the human rights education approach. The UNDP's approach is holistic, the approach of other UN agencies is rights-based, Oxfam's approach is the social justice approach, Amartya Sen and Nussbaum's analysis is classified as capabilities while the right to development approach is attributed to the non-aligned movement, and so on. (Marks 2003).

3 Such as the UN Declaration on the Right to Development (1986), the UN Declaration on Human Rights, the International Covenant on Civil and Political Rights and the International Covenant on Economic, Social and Cultural Rights. In relation to gender equality, three instruments – the CEDAW, the optional protocol to the CEDAW and the Declaration on Violence Against women – are also relevant (AWID 2002).

4 As a member of Oxfam International explained, gender is part of the right to identity, but will also be mainstreamed.

## References

Archer, R. (2005) 'What Might be Gained and What Might be Lost Through Adopting a Rights-based Approach to Pro-poor Development?', paper presented at 'The Winners and Losers from Rights-based Approaches to Development' conference, Manchester, 21–22 February.

AWID (2002) 'A Rights-based Approach to Development' Facts and Issues, *Women's Rights and Economic Change*, no. 1 (Toronto: Association for Women's Rights in Development [AWID]).

Brouwer, M. (2005) 'RBA: A Duty to Co-operate?', paper presented at 'The Winners and Losers from Rights-based Approaches to Development' conference, Manchester, 21–22 February.

Carnegie Council on Ethics and International Affairs (CCEIA) (2000) 'Silence Breaking: The Women's Dimension of the Human Rights Box', *Human Rights Dialogue*, Series 2, no. 3.

Chambers, R. (1983) *Rural Development: Putting the Last First* (London: Longman).

Chapman, J., V. Miller, A. Soares and J. Samuel (2005) 'Rights-based Development: The Challenge of Change and Power', paper presented at 'The Winners and Losers from Rights-based Approaches to Development' conference, Manchester, 21–22 February.

Crawford, G. (2005) 'Linking Decentralisation and a Rights-based Approach: Opportunities and Constraints in Ghana', paper presented at 'The Winners and Losers from Rights-based Approaches to Development' conference, Manchester, 21–22 February.

Gledhill, J. (2005) 'The Rights of the Rich Versus the Rights of the Poor', paper presented at 'The Winners and Losers from Rights-based Approaches to Development' conference, Manchester, 21–22 February .

Green, M. (2005) 'Private Goods and Public Bads. Human Rights and Social Differentiation in Southern Tanzania', paper presented at 'The Winners and Losers from Rights-based Approaches to Development' conference, Manchester, 21–22 February.

Interaction (2003) *Definitions of a Rights-Based Approach to Development* (Washington, DC: Interaction).

Kerr, J. (2001) 'International Trends in Gender Equality Work: A Discussion Paper for the Gender Review Workshop at NOVIB', Den Haag, November.

Ljungman, C. and S. Forti (forthcoming) 'Applying a Rights-Based Approach to Development: Concepts and Principles', in B. Mikkelsen (ed.), *Methods for Development Work and Research – A New Guide for Practitioners* (New Delhi: Sage).

Marks, S. P. (2003) 'The Human Rights Framework for Development: Seven Approaches', Working Paper no. 18 (Cambridge, MA: François-Xavier Bagnoud Center for Health and Human Rights, Harvard University).

Masaki K. (2005) 'A Paradox of "Rights-Based Approaches to Development": How Should We Address the "Dialectics of Universality?"', paper presented at 'The Winners and Losers from Rights-based Approaches to Development' conference, Manchester, 21–22 February.

Morvaridi, B. (2005) 'Rights to Development: Constraints and Opportunities', paper presented at 'The Winners and Losers from Rights-based Approaches to Development' conference, Manchester, 21–22 February.

Munro, L. (2005) 'The "Human Rights-Based Approach to Programming": A Contradiction in Terms?', Paper presented at 'The Winners and Losers from Rights-based Approaches to Development' conference, Manchester, 21–22 February.

OHCHR (2004) *Human Rights and Poverty Reduction: A Conceptual Framework* (Geneva: OHCHR).

Paul, J. C. N. (1992) 'Law and Development into the 90s: Using International Law to Impose Accountability to People on International Development Actors', *Third World Legal Studies*, pp. 1–16.

Pettit, J. and J. Wheeler (2005) 'Whose Rights? Examining the Discourse, Context and Practice of Rights-based Approaches to Development', paper presented at 'The Winners and Losers from Rights-based Approaches to Development' conference, Manchester, 21–22 February.

Piron, L.-H. (2005) 'Rights-based Approach to Social Protection', paper presented at 'The Winners and Losers from Rights-based Approaches to Development' conference, Manchester, 21–22 February.

— (2002) *The Right to Development: A Review of the Current State of the Debate for the Department of International Development* (London: Overseas Development Institute).

Pratt, B. (2003) 'Rights or Values?' *ONTRAC, the Newsletter of the International NGO Training and Research Centre (INTRAC)*, no. 23 (January).

Sengupta, A. (2000a) 'Realizing the Right to Development', *Development and Change*, Vol. 31: 553–78

— (2000b) 'The Right to Development as a Human Right', *Working Paper* no. 7 (Cambridge, MA: François Xavier Bagnoud Center for Health and Human Rights, Harvard University).

Sheehy, O. (2005) 'The Discourse of Human Rights and Aid Policy: Facilitating or Challenging Development?', paper presented at 'The Winners and Losers from Rights-based Approaches to Development' conference, Manchester, 21–22 February.

Slim, H. (2002) 'A Response to Peter Uvin. Making Moral Low Ground: Rights as the Struggle for Justice and the Abolition of Development', *PRAXIS: The Fletcher Journal of Development Studies*, Vol. XVII: 1–5.

Tsikata, D. (2004) 'The Rights-based Approach to Development: Potential for Change or More of the Same?', *IDS Bulletin*, Vol. 35, no. 4: 130–3.

Uvin, P. (2002) 'On High Moral Ground: The Incorporation of Human Rights by the Development Enterprise', *PRAXIS: The Fletcher Journal of Development Studies*, Vol. XVII: 1–11.

# 18 | The chimera of success: gender *ennui* and the changed international policy environment

MAXINE MOLYNEUX

Among the many myths that populate the field of gender and development is the one that claims that gender has been so successfully mainstreamed into development policy that there is now little need for women's projects and programmes, or indeed for women's policy units. The job of creating 'gender awareness' is done. After all, the argument goes, the major development agencies and donors have all incorporated clear commitments to ensuring that women are adequately taken into account at all stages of development policy.[1] The view that gender awareness has become part of the common sense of development policy is now so widespread that some NGOs report a growing *ennui*, a 'gender fatigue'[2] in metropolitan policy arenas with women's programmes increasingly being seen as *passé*.[3]

At least one of these claims is hard to refute. No reputable international non-governmental organization (NGO) has been without its gender-sensitive guidelines for some decades and the power centres of development policy have followed suit. The UN was, not surprisingly given the dynamic of the Beijing process, among the first to mainstream gender across its many agencies. The World Bank, after initial hesitation, also incorporated gender diagnostics into its various guidelines; in the late 1980s its principal rationale for 'investing in women' was that it could be a 'cost effective' way to promote economic efficiency. However, a decade later, the World Development Report (WDR) 2000/01 went as far as to state that gender *inequality* is 'of such pervasive significance that it deserves *extra emphasis*' (World Bank 2001a: 9).[4] The Organization for Economic Cooperation and Development/ Development Assistance Committee's (OECD/DAC) Guidelines on Poverty Reduction (2001) also seem to offer proof of this institutionalized gender awareness; here gender inequality is cited as a 'major cause' of poverty and impediment to development.[5] The Millennium Development Goals, to which all nations subscribe, also incorporate gender: the third MDG is 'to promote gender equality and empower women'.

Such policy commitments are hard won, and not easily dismissed as being without any significance. They can influence policy direction and programme design, and they can provide those pressing for positive policy outcomes with some leverage. On the other hand, they are fragile gains, and they can remain ineffective, purely formal, without teeth or support for implementation. Hostile lobbies at home and abroad resist and ignore them, selectively adopt them, or interpret them in ways that are cynically instrumental or simply counter-productive. Political, cultural and religious resistance, sometimes in deadly combination, can militate against their application in contexts where gender relations and liberal rights discourses have become politicized through external intervention or secular dictatorship. The conditions under which these commitments find a supportive environment are rarely optimal and there is much scope for interpretation of the letter of the law. Who has interpretative power when it comes to the implementation stage ultimately affects the impact such commitments are likely to have on gender relations.

For their part, and despite their encouraging rhetoric, the main development institutions have a mixed record in applying gender-sensitive recommendations. The evidence indicates a significant gap between the gender equality guidelines and the practice. This is not surprising considering that guidelines issued by development agencies such as the World Bank are simply advisory and there are few, or most often, no penalties for failing to comply. Evaluations of World Bank programmes are but one indicator of the gap between word and deed. A report by the Gender Unit of the World Bank entitled *The Gender Dimension of Bank Assistance* analysed Bank assistance in twelve countries covering 180 projects. It found that while satisfactory results were achieved in health and education, 'the Bank has been weak in promoting the economic participation of women and in improving the Borrower's institutional framework for gender, thereby reducing the overall development effectiveness of its assistance' (World Bank 2002a: 1).[6] The report further noted that despite the fact that the Bank is required to monitor the gender impact of its assistance, its efforts in this regard were found to be 'negligible'. This echoed the disappointing result of another gender-focused evaluation of 100 World Bank projects which concluded that gender issues were in fact 'widely neglected' in their design and implementation (Frances 2001: 86).

One might have expected that Poverty Reduction Strategy Papers (PRSPs) would have a better record on gender sensitivity since gender is identified as a key to project success along with participatory methods in the design of projects. However, progress has been slow here too (Whitehead and Lockwood 1999). A review by the World Bank's Gender Division of fifteen PRSPs completed by 2001 found that less than half discussed gender issues in any detail in their diagnosis of poverty. Even fewer incorporated a gender analysis into their implementation and evaluation sections (Kabeer 2003). Another investigation into PRSPs supported by the World Bank among others, found that issues of gender equality, and women's and men's differential access to resources and opportunities, were not taken into account in most analyses and policy proposals.[7] Three PRSPs – from Bolivia, Vietnam and Zambia – were found to be negligent in regard to gender, that of Bolivia emerging as the least gender-sensitive of them all. The author reported that even the poverty diagnoses were 'astonishingly gender-blind, genuine mainstreaming [was] quite limited and many key chapters in all three reports [were] void of any reference to gender' (de Vylder 2003: 20). Further findings were that women were frequently lumped together with other vulnerable and disempowered groups, notably children and the disabled whose needs were very different. In general, the report concluded, gender analysis was 'either absent or highly unsatisfactory, and the policy actions suggestion are often exceedingly vague (viz: improve conditions for women). In short, lip service is paid to "gender mainstreaming" ... but not to what to do or how to do it' (de Vylder 2003: 20). A later report on PRSPs in four countries also voiced similar concerns (Whitehead 2003).

These disappointing findings may have prompted the further development of diagnostic tools, found in *Integrating Gender into the World Bank's work: A Strategy for Action* (World Bank 2002b), which identifies four dimensions of gender and poverty that are proposed for assisting in the planning of PRSPs: opportunities, capabilities, security and empowerment. At the same time the Bank recommended that each country with an active lending project now had to prepare a periodic Gender Assessment, and assigned more resources to support operational interventions. In its 2004 report on progress, the Bank found that only a minority had produced a Gender Assessment, although there was 'some greater attention to gender issues in project design and supervision' (Prügl and Lustgarten 2006: 63). However, the indications are that even where there is some improvement in project design, there is little take-up of these ideas on the ground.[8] Bradshaw and Linneker, for example, who analysed two PRSPs, one in Nicaragua, the other in Honduras, found that there was no attempt to deal with the specificity of women's poverty; in the participation process, women were not considered a specific interest group, and where they were included in participatory exercises it was 'in their capacity as civil society actors rather than as "gendered" beings' (2003: 16).

Development agencies might claim, with varying degrees of justification, that they do not bear sole responsibility for these outcomes since programmes are usually developed and implemented by governments or in collaboration with them. Governments naturally vary in the support they give to gender equality and women's projects, and in how far such support is backed up by adequate institutionalization and funding. Lamentably, we face a shortage of publicly available studies of how governments design and manage development programmes. With some notable exceptions this is strikingly true in regard to the growing numbers of poverty relief programmes which have appeared in the wake of the World Bank's New Poverty Agenda (NPA), launched in 1990.[9] The founding principle of the NPA is 'social risk management' as outlined in the 2000/01 WDR *Attacking Poverty*, wherein sustainable poverty alleviation entails measures to increase the security of the poor, through developing their capacity to 'cope, mitigate or reduce' their risks (World Bank 2001a: 1). To this is added some ideas that originated on the creative margins of development practice, summed up in the triad of 'empowerment, voice and presence', along with a belated recognition that poverty is multidimensional. Yet if such ideas permeate the official publications, they are still only vaguely or partially reflected in policy design and implementation, as grassroots accounts and an extensive literature attests (see Cornwall 2003; Cooke and Kothari 2001).

Meanwhile, poverty reduction programmes remain in many cases badly managed, highly clientelized and inefficiently administered with responsibility spread across different government departments leading to a lack of coordination and consistency in approach. Poor statistical collection and evaluation procedures add to the lack of reliable data for policy feedback processes. Despite the efforts of UNIFEM and other lobbies, and some small advances, measurements and indicators used to assess the scope and magnitude of poverty are still rarely disaggregated to show sex difference.[10] Women's organizations find it hard to make an impact in such circumstances, especially on social policy provision and anti-poverty programmes, and many do not even try, preferring to remain 'outside power'. A history of cooption and clientelization of women's movements by political parties tends to deepen the divisions between those who work 'in the state' and 'against the state', limiting the scope for cooperation in this vital area for feminist intervention.[11]

Feminist NGOs have often pioneered creative and successful projects that incorporate principles of gender justice. They have been assisted in this by having been able to develop their own research capacity in recent years allowing closer attention to women's needs. Yet in today's fast-proliferating poverty relief schemes, such influence as they may have is largely confined to local or small-scale project design. It is not unknown for policy-makers to argue that there is no need to incorporate a gender dimension in their poverty programmes since policies that benefit the poor 'necessarily benefit women', eliding women with poverty in a simple reduction that exports gender analysis altogether. This problem reportedly surfaced even in Brazilian President Lula's anti-poverty programmes, which is surprising given the strength of the women's movement in Brazil and its historic association with the ruling party.[12]

Given this scenario it would not be overstating the case to conclude that despite the formal recognition of the gender–poverty link, anti-poverty programmes have remained for the most part either innocent of gender analysis or markedly selective in their understanding of its implications. As a result they both ignore women's particular circumstances and rarely problematize gender relations, remaining locked into dated conceptions of 'gender roles' which fail to correspond to the realities of most poor women's lives and therefore fail to meet their needs. This is starkly exemplified in the design of the new child-centred anti-poverty programmes that are being adopted in Latin America following the success of Progresa/Oportunidades in Mexico. These are conditional cash transfer schemes, where a stipend is paid to mothers subject to their ensuring children's attendance at school and at health clinics. The recipients are typically expected to fulfil a range of additional obligations from cleaning clinics and schools, being available to attend programme meetings and serving as unpaid programme auxiliaries (*promotoras*). If their children fail to reach the requisite number of attendances at school or clinic, they (the mothers) risk being fined or ejected from the programme. Yet most low-income households are dependent on women's capacity to contribute money incomes and the demands of these programmes risk further weakening their tenuous hold on the labour market.[13] Such efforts at 'capacity building' as these projects offer confer few marketable skills.

It goes without saying that these programmes not only depend on normative assumptions about women's 'natural roles', but actively reinforce and re-traditionalize gender divisions, marginalizing men even further from parenting, and arguably also from financial responsibility for the household. In effect they use women as a conduit of policy, deepening the gender divide and overloading already burdened women with even more responsibilities (Molyneux 2006). As Chant has argued, there has occurred through these programmes a 'feminization of responsibility and obligation' for managing poverty with women being made to do even more to ensure household survival, when men are increasingly doing less (2006). So much, one might say, for national governments signing up to the international covenants on gender equality (CEDAW) and shared parenting (CRC). For all the talk of participation and citizenship, supposedly integral to these programmes' rationale, few do much to incorporate the beneficiary-mothers into the various stages of their planning and implementation. Moreover, as training in useful skills is weak or non-existent in many of these programmes, participants lack the means to achieve a sustainable exit route from poverty – the ultimate goal of the programme. This latter point goes to the heart of the problem with the anti-poverty agenda.

The current emphasis on poverty relief in development policy is worrying enough, in that it stands for the failure of macro-economic and development policy to generate adequate levels of growth and effective redistribution. Poverty relief programmes have proved no palliative in dealing with the adverse effects of adjustment and have offered little to the poor in a context of persistent, even deepening inequality. Effective poverty relief can come about only when linked to sustainable development strategies, which are currently thin on the ground. But there is a failure of another kind, evident in the token, partial and selective incorporation of gender and gender equality principles into public/international policy. Macro-economic policy has remained highly resistant to gender critique, notwithstanding the well-documented evidence of the negative impacts it can have on women's employment, well-being and livelihoods (Elson 1995; Rai 2002). The World Bank's Millennium contribution, *Engendering Development* (2001b), which provides a panoramic overview of the state of the world's women, offers a policy approach which remains closely identified with market-led growth and makes few concessions to the gender critique of neo-liberal policies.[14] The mass entry of women into low-paid, informalized and insecure employment over recent decades can hardly be counted as a sign of economic policy success. Neither is the targeting of women in anti-poverty programmes necessarily a step forwards when they are only 'visibilized' in their roles as mothers and unpaid 'volunteer' workers. Here the gender blindness at the 'top' of the policy pyramid is only replicated, and its effects multiplied on those at the sharp end.

All this is not to deny that women worldwide, on all the standard indicators, appear to have made some progress over the last half century. As discussed in more detail elsewhere (Molyneux and Razavi 2005), there have been notable advances in education with female illiteracy declining, and the gender gap in girls' enrolment in both primary and secondary education falling, shrinking and in some cases reversing. More women are gaining access to tertiary education, and to political life; they are living longer, having fewer children, and their health indicators continue to improve. However, there are several important qualifications regarding these indicators of progress. There is considerable variation among countries in the progress achieved, and, overall, it has been slower than expected in both the public and private domains. For instance, while the number of women parliamentary representatives doubled between 1995 and 2004 partly as a result of quotas, they still make up only 17 per cent of the total.

In the private sphere, change is even slower; survey after survey shows that the domestic division of labour has either not altered or has altered only slightly in favour of women in the last fifty years. The fact that the fastest-growing proportion of HIV/AIDS victims are female is also striking testimony to the lack of female power and autonomy in the most intimate realm of all. Women may be able to claim more autonomy through entering the labour force as they have in substantial numbers, but despite changes in their occupational and educational status, the gender gap in income remains as much as 40 per cent in some cases, with between 20 per cent or 30 per cent being standard.

A different but related problem is that the positive trends that are shown by the data are also in many cases accompanied by *negative* ones, some of these being unanticipated consequences of the broader processes of change. Rapid fertility decline has resulted from increased use of contraception, but sex ratio imbalances have deepened in societies with marked 'son preference', as infant daughters are subjected to maltreatment, neglect and abandonment, and new technologies allow sex-selective biases against females.[15] China and India (fast growing economies *nota bene*), account for nearly 80 per cent of all 'missing women' in the world (ibid.: 990). Violence against women (and violence in general) appears to be on the increase, with new phenomena such as serial murders of young women workers as in Mexico and Guatemala adding to this grim litany. Taken together, these factors make assessments of progress for women a far from straightforward exercise (ibid.). Considerable caution therefore needs to be exercised in any assessment of the impact of gender mainstreaming in international policy guidelines.[16] Gender mainstreaming may have been coopted, as some have argued, thereby turning 'a radical movement idea into a strategy of public management' (Prügl and Lustgarten 2006: 62), but it has been a *selective and partial* cooptation. Yet, if, as I argue, the spread of gender awareness and the impact of mainstreaming is exaggerated, how do we explain the current gender *ennui* when so much is still at stake? One thing is clear: it has less to do with a surplus of success and more to do with a changed *zeitgeist* brought about by the post-2000 darkening international political climate, more effective strategizing and alliance building by conservative forces – popular, governmental and faith-based – and last but not least, the less than women-friendly policy mission of the most powerful nation in the world.[17] But there has also occurred a troubling loss of vitality and direction of some feminist movements, the specific causes of which vary from region to region. While there are still vital movements in Latin America and parts of Africa and South Asia, all regions report some loss of dynamism.[18]

One indicator of this was the passing without notice of the Beijing Plus Ten (B+10) events in March 2005. These were decidedly low key in contrast to the 1995 World Conference on Women which was attended by more than 30,000 participants. No large international conference was contemplated for B+10 for fear of risking the gains won in Beijing and defended in the Plus 5 negotiations in 2000. In the event, B+10 was confined to an intergovernmental meeting where the mood was defensive rather than confidently optimistic, and the main achievement was to reaffirm the consensus encoded in the Platform ten years earlier (Molyneux and Razavi 2005).

This changed *zeitgeist* has proceeded in tandem with a critical re-assessment of the Beijing process itself, with doubts variously expressed as to its representativity, the content of its proposals, and the universalist pretensions of the overall project. Even among those who can be counted as broadly sympathetic to the aims of Beijing, opinion is divided over how to evaluate the gains that were made from the 'globalization of feminism'. For sceptics, the glass is half-empty rather than half-full. Their concern is that the transformative agenda has been captured by power, coopted and instru-mentalized, and its political vision has been neutralized, where not excised. Some worry that feminism's original and critical aim – to eradicate social inequalities and to create new forms of social life and political practice – has been abandoned. Others doubt if an international women's movement can now be said to exist: the editors of one collection of articles by activists and scholars reflecting on Beijing express a concern that women's movements and feminism may have become 'an expression of women's integration into hegemonic patriarchal institutions where they are reduced to a lobbying group, an appendix without influence' (Braig and Wolte 2002: 6).

This scepticism has two aspects. One, often found among policy prac-titioners, is based on an evaluation of the policy record of three decades of activism, domestically and internationally. Here, concerns about bureau-cratization, NGO-ization, and 'technification' of the women's movement and its analytic insights are foregrounded. The other is of a somewhat different kind, deriving as it does from a theoretical position that sees integration into or even negotiation with governments and international institutions as, *in itself*, an abandonment of the broader, 'critical' and, at least implicitly, revolutionary goals of much second-wave feminism.[19]

No amount of national policy initiatives, quotas or international norms and conventions will assuage this latter concern. However, in viewing the feminist influence on international legal instruments as primarily cosmetic, there is a tendency to underplay the positive impact that this legislation has had on national law and policy. Those who prefer to see the glass as half-full stress that legal gains are significant, and cite the example of CEDAW, the most important piece of international legislation encoding women's rights, which commits 171 signing governments to respect a range of principles that have in some regions (notably Latin America, and parts of Africa and South Asia) led to positive reforms in constitutions and civil codes. Much of course depends on the will of governments and the energies of women's movements to put flesh on these bones, and there are wide regional disparities in what has been, and can be, done with these instruments. CEDAW, after all, had the distinction among international conventions of having the most reservations or 'bracketed clauses'. Yet as the history of working-class and female suffrage demonstrates, reform processes are, by their very nature, slow. They encounter enormous institutional (and often overtly political) resistance, as is evident in the energetic mobilization at the UN level of opportunistic conservative coalitions (US–Vatican–Islamist) against women's reproductive rights, one that is contributing to the devastating spread of the HIV/AIDS pandemic across the world.

Any consideration of Beijing necessarily problematizes the significance of the advances made possible by human rights legislation. The human rights instruments and discourse helped to transnationalize women's movement activism, combining advocacy in international arenas with national, regional and local initiatives. Some Asian and African, and most Latin American and Caribbean women's movements have based their struggles for economic and social rights on international human rights instruments. Which rights *matter* is the key question for those women's movements which have often situated their demands increasingly within a framework which counterposes an ethic of justice expressed in socio-economic rights to the prevailing 'thin' utilitarian version of rights. Human rights instruments have enabled women's movements to provide a normative and analytic framework for fighting against discrimination, reframing socio-economic injustices against women as human rights violations.[20] The examples of education, quota laws, violence against women, and health show how rights discourses can be deployed to legitimize women's demands for the improvement of their legal status, social rights, political representation and well-being.

Convenient though it may be for some governments (and some identity-based political movements) to oppose human rights legislation on the grounds that it is an alien Western imposition, ideas of rights and justice are not the sole property of 'the West' and, in an increasingly transnationalized world, they have acquired both local and regional resonance. Concepts of rights and justice have a complex and diverse genealogy, and even liberal conceptions of rights, with their origins in the West, have been contested, radicalized, extended and pluralized over the course of their history. But if these ideas are to be part of a genuine global conversation, they require some translation and adaptation to local contexts. The transnationalization of a debate about gender justice has accompanied the growth and diversification of the global women's movement and has established the idea of feminisms in the plural. At the same time, debates over women's rights have become more intensely regionalized in recent years, demanding closer scrutiny to the particular context within which they are framed and fought for. There is some greater awareness of the political and ethical dimensions of the interface between global instruments and local settings than at the onset of the Beijing process and this might turn out to be an area where the glass appears more full than empty. Respect for difference, *but anchored within a movement essentially concerned with equality and justice*, and in a world of ever deepening social and economic inequalities and political conflict, still has its place.

To those who think that gender equality is *passé*, it is worth remembering one final point, that women are not a 'social problem' to be solved or a minoritarian constituency. Whatever the current priority in development policy is deemed to be, and however these priorities change, women remain half the population and gender analysis will remain an indispensable adjunct to any programme or policy development process. But if gender analysis and mainstreaming are to be more than another policy tool, they need to be accompanied by some strategy for achieving gender *justice* as part of a broader commitment to greater social and economic equality. That is unlikely to happen without the political will, vision and strategy provided by collective action. This, perhaps is the main lesson of Beijing – and of its muted aftermath.

## Notes

Thanks are due to the United Nations Research Institute of Social Development (UNRISD) for helping to support some of the research on which these reflections are based. A particular debt of gratitude is owed to Shahra Razavi, head of the gender programme at UNRISD, with whom I have collaborated on some of the publications drawn upon and cited here.

1 The Dutch government's rationale for cutting financial support to the United Nations Development Fund for Women (UNIFEM) in 2003 was reportedly along these lines.

2 See also Jaquette and Summerfield who echo this observation. They worry that a 'GAD [gender and development] fatigue' is setting in (2006: 5).

3 This was the fate of the pioneering Nicaraguan feminist NGO Puntos de Encuentro which had to close most of its programmes due to dwindling donor commitment (discussed in Molyneux and Lazar 2003).

4 The surrounding text is noteworthy, viz: 'Unequal gender relations are part of the broader issue of social inequities based on societal norms and values … While patterns of gender inequity vary greatly across societies, in almost all countries a majority of women and girls are disadvantaged in terms of their relative power and control over material resources … and they often face more severe insecurities … Poor women are thus doubly disadvantaged. Moreover, the lack of autonomy of women has significant negative consequences for the education and health of children' (World Bank 2001a: 9).

5 This document indeed offers what is, in effect, a gender analysis of poverty with which most feminists might agree. An illustration: 'Gender inequality concerns all dimensions of poverty because poverty is not gender neutral … Female poverty is more prevalent and typically more severe than male poverty. Women and girls in poor households get less than their fair share of private consumption and public services. They suffer violence by men on a large scale … gender related "time poverty" refers to the lack of time for all the tasks imposed on women, for rest and for economic and social activities.'

6 See also commentary by Wood (2003).

7 Commissioned by the Swedish Ministry of Foreign Affairs, see de Vylder (2003).

8 Based on author's interviews with fieldworkers in Latin America in 2005.

9 The Mexican and Chilean social welfare ministries can be included among the exceptions in Latin America to this general rule.

10 See Chant (2006) for further elaboration.

11 See chapters by Goetz and Blondet in Molyneux and Razavi (2003) for discussion of women's organization cooptation.

12 Progresa was relaunched in 2002 under the name of Oportunidades, and has some 5 million beneficiaries, making it the second largest programme in Latin America after the Brazilian Bolsa Familia scheme which had between 7 and 8 million beneficiaries by early 2006.

13 Escobar Latapí's and González de la Rocha's evaluation of Oportunidades (2004) found that households were increasingly depending on women's income contribution from work, and that the demands of the programme were incompatible with their efforts at income generation.

14 For an alternative view, sympathetic to more heterodox economic approaches, see UNRISD's (2005) report prepared for Beijing +10: *Gender Equality: Striving for Justice in an Unequal World*.

15 Since females tend to be more robust, there is normally a higher ratio of women to men in any population. However, in certain societies where son preference is marked, social practices (e.g. in the form of girl neglect) favours the survival of males. The most recent estimates of 'missing women' (Sen 1999) – those missing as a result of the unequal treatment of males and females – show that the number has increased in absolute terms, even though it has fallen as a share of the number of women alive (Klasen and Wink 2003, cited in Molyneux and Razavi 2005: 990).

16 See also Hirschmann (2006) for a critical 'insider's view' of this issue.

17 Sexual and reproductive rights are a particular and predictable focus of

this conservative trend. In the UN machinery, states with conservative agendas have been actively supporting the accreditation of anti-choice NGOs whose numbers and influence have been growing in recent years.

18 This theme appears with regularity in global feminist events; it was, for instance, discussed in many of the workshops of the 'Feminist Dialogues' conference at the World Social Forum in Porto Alegre 2005.

19 A view strengthened by the association of the US with imposed agendas, especially in post- or ongoing conflict situations.

20 See Molyneux and Razavi (2003) for case studies that explore these issues.

## References

Bradshaw, S. and B. Linneker (2003) *Challenging Women's Poverty: Perspectives on Gender and Poverty Reduction Strategies from Nicaragua and Honduras* (London: Catholic Institute for International Relations).

Braig, M. and S. Wolte (2002) *Common Ground or Mutual Exclusion. Women's Movements and International Relations* (London and New York: Zed Books).

Chant, S. (2006) 'The "Feminization of Poverty" and the "Feminization of Anti-Poverty": A Case for Revision?', forthcoming.

— (2003) 'New Contributions to the Analysis of Poverty: Methodological and Conceptual Challenges to Understanding Poverty from a Gender Perspective', Santiago de Chile, Comisión Económica para América Latina (CEPAL), Unidad Mujer y Desarrollo, Serie 47, available at <www.cepal.org>.

Cooke, B. and U. Kothari (eds) (2001) *Participation: The New Tyranny?* (London and New York: Zed Books).

Cornwall, A. (2003) 'Whose Voices? Whose Choices? Reflections on Gender and Participatory Development', *World Development*, Vol. 31, no. 8: 1325–42.

de Vylder, S. (2003) 'Gender Equality and Poverty Reduction Strategies', discussion paper, mimeo, commissioned by Swedish Ministry for Foreign Affairs, Stockholm, June.

Elson, D. (ed.) (1995) *Male Bias in Macro Economics: The Case of Structural Adjustment* (Manchester: Manchester University Press).

Escobar Latapí, A. and M. González de la Rocha (2004) 'Evaluación Cualitative del Programe Oportunidades', Centro de Investigación y Estudios Superiores en Antropología Social, México.

Frances, P. (2001) 'Participatory Development at the World Bank: The Primacy of Process', in B. Cooke and U. Kothari (eds), *Participation: the New Tyranny?* (London and New York: Zed Books).

Hirschmann, D. (2006) 'From Home Economics to Microfinance: Gender Rhetoric and Bureaucratic Resistance', in J. Jaquette and G. Summerfield (eds), *Gender Equity in Development Theory and Practice: Institutions, Resources, and Mobilization* (Durham, NC and London: Duke University Press).

Jaquette, J. and G. Summerfield (eds) (2006) *Gender Equity in Development*

*Theory and Practice: Institutions, Resources, and Mobilization* (Durham, NC and London: Duke University Press).

Kabeer, N. (2003) *Gender Mainstreaming in Poverty Eradication and the MDGs* (London: Commonwealth Secretariat).

Klasen, S. and C. Wink (2003) 'Missing Women: Revisiting the Debate', *Feminist Economics*, Vol. 9, nos 2–3: 263–99.

Molyneux, M. (2006) 'Mothers at the Service of the New Poverty Agenda: Mexico's Cash Transfer Programme, the PROGRESA/Oportunidades Programme in Mexico', *Social Policy and Administration*, Special Issue on Latin America, Vol. 40, nos 2–3.

— (2002) 'Gender and the Silences of Social Capital: Lessons from Latin America', *Development and Change*, Vol. 33, no. 2: 167–88.

Molyneux, M. and S. Lazar (2003) *Doing the Rights Thing: Rights-Based Development and Latin American NGOs* (London: Intermediate Technology Publishing Group).

Molyneux, M. and S. Razavi (2005) 'Beijing Plus Ten: An Ambivalent Record on Gender Justice', *Development and Change*, Vol. 36, no. 6: 983–1010.

— (eds) (2003) *Gender Justice, Development and Rights* (Oxford: Oxford University Press).

Moser, C. (1996) 'Confronting Crisis: A Comparative Study of Household Responses to Poverty and Vulnerability in Four Urban Communities' (Washington, DC: World Bank).

OECD/DAC (2001) 'The OECD/DAC Guidelines on Poverty Reduction', Paris; available at <www.oecd.org/dataoecd/47/14/2672735.pdf>, accessed 16 May 2005.

Prügl, E. and A. Lustgarten (2006) 'Mainstreaming Gender in International Organizations', in J. Jaquette and G. Summerfield (eds), *Gender Equity in Development Theory and Practice: Institutions, Resources, and Mobilization* (Durham, NC and London: Duke University Press).

Rai, S. (2002) *Gender and the Political Economy of Development* (Oxford and Malden, USA: Polity Press and Blackwell).

Sen, A. (1999) *Poverty and Famines: An Essay on Entitlement and Deprivation* (Oxford and London: Oxford University Press).

UNRISD (2005) *Gender Equality: Striving for Justice in an Unequal World* (Geneva: UNRISD).

Waylen, G. (1997) *Gender in Third World Politics* (Milton Keynes: Open University Press).

Whitehead, A. (2003) *Failing Women, Sustaining Poverty: Gender in Poverty Reduction Strategy Papers* (London: Gender and Development Network, Christian Aid).

Whitehead, A. and M. Lockwood (1999) 'Gendering Poverty: A Review of Six World Bank Poverty Assessments', *Development and Change*, Vol. 30: 525–55.

Wood, C. (2003) 'Adjustment with a Woman's Face: Gender and Macroeconomic Policy at the World Bank', in S. Eckstein and T. Wickham-

Crowley (eds), *Struggles for Social Rights in Latin America* (New York and London: Routledge).

World Bank (2001a) *World Development Report 2000/2001: Attacking Poverty* (Washington, DC: World Bank).

— (2001b) *Engendering Development through Gender Equality in Rights, Resources and Voice* (Washington, DC: World Bank).

— (2002a) *The Gender Dimension of Bank Assistance: An Evaluation of Results* (Washington, DC: World Bank).

— (2002b) *Integrating Gender into the World Bank's work: A Strategy for Action* (Washington, DC: World Bank).

# Notes on contributors

*Nandinee Bandyopadhyay* is an independent consultant, researcher and trainer on development issues with particular focus on gender, class, sexuality and social movements. She is closely associated with the shop workers' and sexual minorities' movements in India and is now also working with domestic workers. Between 1995 and 2002 she was an adviser to Durbar. Her passion is reading crime fiction and, of course, talking about sex.

*Srilatha Batliwala* is an India-based Civil Society Research Fellow at the Hauser Center for Nonprofit Organizations, Harvard University, where her work focuses on transnational civil society, particularly on transnational grassroots movements, and on bridging the divide between practitioners and scholars. She has over twenty-five years' experience as a grassroots activist, gender equality advocate, and women's studies teacher and researcher, and has written extensively on gender, empowerment and grassroots movements. Her most recent work is *Transnational Civil Society: An Introduction* (co-edited with L. David Brown, Kumarian Press, 2006).

*Sylvia Chant* is Professor of Development Geography at the London School of Economics and Political Science, UK. She has carried out research on gender and development in Mexico, Costa Rica, the Philippines and The Gambia. Her publications include *Women-headed Households: Diversity and Dynamics in the Developing World* (Macmillan, 1997), *Three Generations, Two Genders, One World: Women and Men in a Changing Century* (with Cathy McIlwaine, Zed Books, 1998), *Mainstreaming Men into Gender and Development: Debates, Reflections and Experiences* (with Matthew Gutmann, Oxfam, 2000), and *Gender in Latin America* (in association with Nikki Craske, Latin America Bureau/Rutgers University Press, 2003). She is currently undertaking comparative research on gendered and generational aspects of poverty in Africa, Asia and Latin America.

*Andrea Cornwall* is a Research Fellow at the Institute of Development Studies, University of Sussex. Her work on gender includes ethnographic research and writing on gender identities and relationships, on men and masculinities, and on gender and participatory development. She is co-editor of *Dislocating Masculinity: Comparative Ethnographies* (with Nancy

Lindisfarne, Routledge, 1994), *Realizing Rights: Transforming Sexual and Reproductive Wellbeing* (with Alice Welbourn, Zed Books, 2002) and editor of *Readings in Gender in Africa* (James Currey/Indiana University Press, 2004).

*Deepa Dhanraj* is a feminist filmmaker, and director of D&N Productions. She is best known for documentary films that explore the struggles of poor women in India to negotiate the social, economic and political processes that affect them. Her most noted documentary, *Something Like a War*, outlining the excesses committed on poor women by the government's family planning programme, won several international awards. The in-depth field research she carries out when making her films enables her to present a nuanced perspective and insights on the impact of public policies on poor women's lives.

*Rosalind Eyben* is a social scientist with a career in international development policy and practice including in Africa, India and, most recently, Latin America. She resigned from the UK Department for International Development in 2002 – where, among other matters, she had responsibility for DFID's gender equality work – to become a Fellow of the Institute of Development Studies at the University of Sussex where she convenes the Power, Participation and Change programme. Current interests include rights-based approaches, women's empowerment, the politics of policy-making, organizational learning and change, and the sociology of donor–recipient relations.

*Anne-Marie Goetz* is Chief Adviser, Governance Peace and Security at UNIFEM. Prior to joining UNIFEM in 2005, she worked as a feminist political scientist at the Institute of Development Studies, University of Sussex, specializing in the study of gender and governance in development. She has also worked on pro-poor and gender-sensitive approaches to public sector reforms, anti-corruption initiatives, and decentralization, and has also studied ways of supporting political liberalization and state-building in fragile states and post-conflict situations. She is the author of five books on gender and politics in developing countries, and on accountability reforms, most recently *Reinventing Accountability: Making Democracy Work for Human Development* (with Rob Jenkins, Palgrave, 2005).

*Elizabeth Harrison* is a Senior Lecturer in Anthropology at the University of Sussex. She has undertaken research in Southern Africa, Ethiopia, Sri Lanka and Bangladesh. Her research has focused on the anthropology of development, with a particular interest in understandings of gender and development from different positions in the development process. She has been co-director of the MA in Gender and Development at the University of Sussex for several years and is the co-author of *Whose Development? An Ethnography of Aid* (with Emma Crewe, Zed Books, 1998).

*Islah Jad* is Assistant Professor of Gender and Political Science at Bir Zeit University. She is one of the founders of the Women's Studies Institute at Bir Zeit University and of the Women's Affairs Committee, a national coalition for women. The author of a number of articles on Palestinian and Arab women's political participation, she is co-editor of the forthcoming *Arab Human Development Report* on the empowerment of Arab women (2006).

*Deniz Kandiyoti* is Reader in the Department of Development Studies, School of Oriental and African Studies, and former chair (2001–04) of the Centre of Contemporary Central Asia and the Caucasus, University of London. She is the author of *Concubines, Sisters and Citizens: Identities and Social Transformation* (Metis Yayinlari, 1997, in Turkish) and the editor of *Fragments of Culture: The Everyday of Modern Turkey* (with Ayse Saktanber, Rutgers University Press, 2002), *Gendering the Middle East* (Syracuse University Press, 1996), *Women, Islam and the State* (Temple University Press, 1991) and numerous articles on gender, Islam, development and state policies. Her current work includes post-Soviet transitions in Central Asia and gender and post-conflict reconstruction in Afghanistan.

*Amina Mama* is the chair in Gender Studies at the African Gender Institute (AGI), University of Cape Town. Her intellectual interests centre round bringing feminist theory to bear on post-colonial subjectivities, social relations and politics. Her research has addressed gender, governance and politics in a variety of African contexts, including the gender politics of militarism in Nigeria, and African higher education development. Her publications include: *Beyond the Masks: Race, Gender and Subjectivity* (Routledge, 1995), *The Hidden Struggle: Statutory and Voluntary Sector Responses to Violence Against Black Women* and *Women's Studies and Studies of Women in Africa* (Whiting and Birch, 1996). She has devoted much of the last five years working with colleagues to establish the AGI as a regional resource dedicated to strengthening teaching and research in the trans-disciplinary field of Gender Studies in African universities.

*Maxine Molyneux* is Professor of Sociology at the Institute for the Study of the Americas at the University of London where she directs an MSc on Globalization and Development in Latin America. She is the author of

*Women's Movements in International Perspective: Latin America and Beyond* (Palgrave, 2000); co-author of *Doing the Rights Thing: Rights-based Development and Latin American NGOs* (with Sian Lazar, Intermediate Technology Publications, 2003), *The Ethiopian Revolution* (with Fred Halliday, Verso, 1980), *Gender Justice, Development and Rights* (with Shahra Razavi, Oxford University Press, 2002), *The Hidden Histories of Gender and the State in Latin America* (with E. Dore, Duke University Press, 2000), and *Gender and the Politics of Rights and Democracy in Latin America* (with N. Craske, Palgrave, 2001). Among her current research projects is the New Poverty Agenda in Latin America, commissioned by UNRISD.

*Maitrayee Mukhopadhyay* is the area leader for Social Development and Gender Equity in the Department of Development Policy and Practice at the Royal Tropical Institute, Amsterdam. Maitrayee has worked on rural and urban development policy and programming in Asia and Africa for the last twenty years, specializing in gender issues in development. Her current work focuses on citizenship and participatory governance and its relevance to development policy and practice, and she has led an inter-regional action research programme on Gender, Citizenship and Governance. She has published extensively on gender and development. Her recent publication, *Creating Voice and Carving Space* (KIT Publishers, 2004), profiles women's struggles for citizenship.

*Ruth Pearson* is Professor of Development Studies at the University of Leeds where she directs the Centre for Development Studies. She has been researching in the area of 'gender and development' since the mid-1970s, mainly around employment, the internationalization of production and new technology. More recently she has focused on gender issues in economic transition economies and on gender and economic rights, particularly for informal and home-based workers.

*Joanne Sandler* is the Deputy Executive Director for Programmes of the United Nations Development Fund for Women (UNIFEM). She has worked with international organizations and women's groups worldwide for the past 25 years, with a focus on organizational development, strategic planning and economic justice. She has also served on the Board of Directors of a number of international and domestic organizations, including the Breakthrough, Association for Women's Rights in Development, Gender at Work, and Women Make Movies. In her role as Deputy Director, Joanne guides UNIFEM's efforts to implement rights-based, results-based programmes in support of women's empowerment and rights in Africa, Asia-Pacific, Latin America and the Caribbean and Central and Eastern

Europe and the Commonwealth of Independent States. Prior to her work with UNIFEM, Joanne worked as a consultant to international and US-focused women's rights organizations, including many UN organizations, the Ms. Foundation for Women, the Global Fund for Women, the National Council for Research on Women, the International Planned Parenthood Federation – Western Hemisphere, and the US Department of Agriculture. She also worked, for 11 years, for the International Women's Tribune Centre, concentrating on special projects and producing training manuals and workshops related to marketing, economic development and economic justice, and fundraising for women's organizations.

*Cecília M. B. Sardenberg* is a feminist who holds a PhD in Anthropology from Boston University and has been a member of the Faculty of Philosophy and Human Sciences of the Federal University of Bahia (UFBa), in Salvador, Bahia, Brazil, since 1982. She was one of the 'founding mothers' of UFBa's Women's Studies Research Centre (NEIM-UFBa), and is its present director. She is executive coordinator of the Feminist Network of Women's Studies Centers in the North and Northeastern Regions of Brazil (REDOR), and has served in the coordinating committee of the Brazilian Network of Feminist Studies (Redefem) and as a member of the State Council for Women's Rights of Bahia, Brazil. She has edited several books and published articles in Brazil as well as abroad.

*Hilary Standing* is a Research Fellow at the Institute of Development Studies, University of Sussex. Trained originally as a social anthropologist, she worked extensively in South Asia. She has a broad interest in the political economy of social transformation, including gender relations in low-income and transition countries. She now specializes in health and development with a particular interest in gender and health. She was formerly a Senior Lecturer at the University of Sussex, where she was a co-founder of the University of Sussex/IDS MA programme in Gender and Development.

*Ramya Subrahmanian* is a Research Fellow at the Institute of Development Studies, University of Sussex. Her research and work interests include education policy and service delivery, with a special focus on gender and other forms of social exclusion, and child labour and social policy. She is the co-editor of *Institutions, Relations and Outcomes: A Framework and Case Studies for Gender-aware Planning* (with Naila Kabeer, Kali for Women, 1999) and *Child Labour and the Right to Education in South Asia: Needs versus Rights?* (with Naila Kabeer and Geetha Nambissan, Sage, 2003).

*Dzodzi Tsikata* is a Senior Research Fellow at the Institute of Statistical, Social and Economic Research (ISSER) of the University of Ghana, where she has worked for the last twelve years. Her research interests and writing in the last ten years have been in the areas of gender and livelihoods, land tenure policies and state and society in Ghana. She is the editor of the book *Gender Training in Ghana: Politics, Issues and Tools* (Woeli Publishing, 2001). Dzodzi is the convenor of the Network for Women's Rights in Ghana (NETRIGHT). She is also convening the drafting committee of a women's manifesto for Ghana.

*Ann Whitehead* is Professor of Anthropology at the University of Sussex. She was one of a small group of feminists who initiated research and teaching on gender and feminist anthropology at the university and, with feminist colleagues, at IDS. She has conducted field research in the UK and in Northern Ghana, where she has written extensively on socio-economic and agrarian change, poverty and changes in gender relations. She is best known for her contributions to feminist debates on the social relations of gender and the gender division of labour and intrahousehold relations. Recent work explores gender issues in relation to land tenure policy in sub-Saharan Africa, gender in Poverty Assessments and PRSPs and gender and liberalization in trade and agriculture in Africa.

*Everjoice J. Win* is a Zimbabwean feminist. She has spent her working life in the women's movement in Africa, and particularly Zimbabwe. She was editor of the popular education publication *Speak Out/Taurai/Khulumani*, with the Women's Action Group, and headed the Zimbabwe programme for Women in Law and Development in Africa (WiLDAF), spearheading the organization's participation in a number of international conferences that put African women's rights issues on the map. She also served as a Commonwealth Adviser to the Commission on Gender Equality of South Africa. Currently, as the International Head of Women's Rights for Action-Aid International, she leads their work on women's rights globally.

*Prudence Woodford-Berger* has an MA in Social Anthropology from Stockholm University, Sweden, with ethnographic field research experience in West Africa, primarily in Ghana. She has worked as a consultant and policy adviser in Swedish international development work since 1978 and is presently a special adviser on social and gender equality issues at the Ministry for Foreign Affairs, Department for Global Development.

# Index

Index

# SPACES FOR CHANGE?
## The Politics of Citizen Participation in New Democratic Arenas
### *Edited by Andrea Cornwall and Vera Schattan Coelho*

In recent years, innovations in governance have created a plethora
of new democratic spaces in many countries. Yet there remains a gap
between the legal and technical apparatus that has been created to
institutionalize participation and the reality of the effective exclusion
of poorer and more marginalized citizens. Through diverse case studies
this book examines what the expansion of the participatory sphere
has to offer processes of democratization and equitable development.
They explore how the democratic potential of these new spaces might
be enhanced. And they reflect on what it might take for those who
have often been excluded from participation to gain opportunities to
influence the decisions and institutions that affect their lives.

'New democratic spaces at the intersection of the state and public
sphere provide important opportunities for the more effective
democratization of political life. This book constitutes a thorough and
stimulating guide to the prospects for this emerging participatory sphere.
It combines theoretical sophistication with incisive case analysis of
deliberative spaces, with a much-needed focus on the developing world.'
- *Professor John Dryzek, Australian National University*

'Democratic theorists and development practitioners will learn and cite
from this volume for years to come.'
- *Professor Neera Chandhoke, University of Delhi*

Hb ISBN 978 1 84277 552 3
Pb ISBN 978 1 84277 553 0

## CLAIMING CITIZENSHIP SERIES
Rights, Participation and Accountability
*Series Editor: John Gaventa, Institute of Development Studies, UK*

# RIGHTS, RESOURCES AND THE POLITICS
## OF ACCOUNTABILITY
*Edited by Peter Newell and Joanna Wheeler*

Many conflicts in development are about struggles by the poor to hold the powerful to account and the rights and responsibilities of each. They reflect conflicts between the promotion of rights-based and market-based approaches to development which have enormous implications for efforts to tackle poverty. This book explores the range of ways in which the poor mobilize to claim their rights and demand accountability, and the exciting and imaginative strategies they use towards the state, the private sector, international institutions and within civil society itself. Overarching themes and key questions emerge about how and when the poor can improve the accountability of powerful actors in development for their actions and inactions.

'*Rights, Resources and the Politics of Accountability* is the first study to seriously explore how the poor claim, contest and secure rights and how the rights of the powerful are deployed to defend their privileges and to control resources and access to power. Drawing upon exemplary case studies - spanning the globe from Mexico to Nigeria to India to the US - Newell and Wheeler have laid out a provocative new agenda ... A state-of-the-art book: theoretically rich, empirically compelling and irresistibly forward-looking.'
- *Michael Watts, Director of African Studies, UC Berkeley*

'This book is fascinating ... because it tells stories about how the poor and the marginalized come together to negotiate and claim their rights to resources from the rich and the powerful.'
- *Chandra Bhushan, Associate Director of the Centre for Science and Environment, New Delhi*

Hb ISBN 978 1 84277 554 7
Pb ISBN 978 1 84277 555 4

## CLAIMING CITIZENSHIP SERIES
Rights, Participation and Accountability
*Series Editor: John Gaventa, Institute of Development Studies, UK*

# SCIENCE AND CITIZENS
## Globalization and the Challenge of Engagement
*Edited by Melissa Leach, Ian Scoones and Brian Wynne*

Rapid advances and new technologies in the life sciences - such as biotechnologies in health, agricultural and environmental arenas - pose a range of pressing challenges to questions of citizenship. This volume brings together for the first time authors from diverse experiences and analytical traditions, encouraging a conversation between science and technology and development studies around issues of science, citizenship and globalization. It reflects on the nature of expertise; the framing of knowledge; processes of public engagement; and issues of rights, justice and democracy. A wide variety of pressing issues is explored, such as medical genetics, agricultural biotechnology, occupational health and HIV/AIDS. Drawing upon rich case studies from Asia, Africa, Latin America and Europe, *Science and Citizens* asks: Do new perspectives on science, expertise and citizenship emerge from comparing cases across different issues and settings? What difference does globalization make? What does this tell us about approaches to risk, regulation and public participation? How might the notion of 'cognitive justice' help to further debate and practice?

'This is a very timely and well-focussed collection of articles and insights. The global scope of the case studies, and of its theoretical and normative perspectives is particularly novel and a uniquely valuable contribution.'
– *Professor Ulrich Beck, University of Munich*

'A unique blend of two, hitherto separate, streams of work - science and technology studies and development studies ... The Southern perspective provides a timely warning that, far from being a panacea, escalating demands for public participation have paradoxical potential to disempower.'
– *Professor Steve Rayner, University of Oxford*

Hb ISBN 978 1 84277 550 9
Pb ISBN 978 1 84277 551 6

## CLAIMING CITIZENSHIP SERIES
Rights, Participation and Accountability
*Series Editor: John Gaventa, Institute of Development Studies, UK*

# INCLUSIVE CITIZENSHIP
## Meanings and Expressions
*Edited by Naila Kabeer*

This volume seeks to go beyond the intellectual debates of recent years on democratization and participation to explore a related set of issues around changing conceptions of citizenship. People's understandings of what it means to be a citizen go to the heart of the various meanings of identity, including national identity, political and electoral participation, and rights. The researchers in this volume come from a wide variety of societies, including the industrial countries in the North, and they seek to explore these difficult questions from various angles. Themes include:

citizenship and rights; citizenship and identity; citizenship and political struggle; The policy implications of substantive notions of citizenship

Particular contributions throw light on the variety of ways in which people are excluded from full citizenship; the identities that matter to people and their compatibility with dominant notions of citizenship; the tensions between individual and collective rights in definitions of citizenship; struggles to realize and expand citizens' rights; and the challenges these questions entail for development policy.

'This is important, cutting edge work in the new discussions around rights, responsibilities, subjectivity and agency.
Very highly recommended.'
*- Professor Gita Sen, Centre for Public Policy, Indian Institute of Management*

'Naila Kabeer is to be congratulated for bringing together this collection of essays that give us a comparative perspective on citizenship in everyday life.'
*- Professor Mahmood Mamdani, Department of Anthropology, University of Columbia*

Hb ISBN 978 1 84277 548 6
Pb ISBN 978 1 84277 549 3

## CLAIMING CITIZENSHIP SERIES
Rights, Participation and Accountability
*Series Editor: John Gaventa, Institute of Development Studies, UK*

# REINVENTING DEVELOPMENT?
Translating Rights-based Approaches
from Theory into Practice
*Edited by Paul Gready and Jonathan Ensor*

'This is a timely and important contribution to the rights and
development literature. The moral appeal of what have become
known as "rights-based approaches" is irrefutable on a superficial
gloss, accompanied in recent years by a burgeoning volume of policy
statements, programming guidelines and scholarly analyses. But the
virtuousness of the rhetoric masks a great many hard questions as to
how such putatively transformational approaches can be applied in
practice, and more fundamentally still, how far these approaches must
themselves be examined for consistency with the ideals they purport to
embody, and how far they can go in attacking the complex and varied
"root causes" of poverty and injustice in any given situation. While
shunning pretences at easy answers, this book frames these dilemmas
coherently and articulately, based on practitioners' own experiences,
against an engaging account of the philosophical underpinnings and
history of human rights and rights-based approaches. The result is a
critical and nuanced analysis that will appeal to practitioners, academics
and policy-makers alike.'
– *Mac Darrow, Coordinator, Human Rights Strengthening (HURIST)*
*programme, UN Office of the High Commissioner for Human Rights, Geneva*

'At last a book that digs deeply into what it means in practice for
humanitarian and development agencies to adopt a political philosophy
of rights as they respond to people suffering from poverty, war and
disaster. The case studies are clear and revealing. The advantages and the
risks of a rights-based approach are openly discussed'
– *Dr. Hugo Slim, Chief Scholar,*
*Centre for Humanitarian Dialogue, Geneva.*

Hb ISBN 978 1 84277 648 3
Pb ISBN 978 1 84277 649 0

# A RADICAL HISTORY
## OF DEVELOPMENT STUDIES
### Individuals, Institutions and Ideologies
*Edited by Uma Kothari*

In this book, leading thinkers in development studies trace the history of the subject from the late colonial period to contemporary concerns with poverty reduction. They present a critical genealogy of development and challenge simplistic, unilinear periodizations of its evolution. In particular, they draw attention to ongoing critiques of development studies, including Marxism, feminism and postcolonialism, which have been marginalized in mainstream development discourse. Personal and institutional reflections are combined with an examination of key themes, including gender and development, NGOs, and natural resource management. A more complex and nuanced understanding of development is elucidated, revealing common themes and trends, and repositioning development studies along a more critical trajectory.

The volume is intended to stimulate new thinking on where the discipline may be moving. It ought also to be of great use to students coming to grips with the historical continuities and divergences in the theory and practice of development.

Contributors: Henry Bernstein, John Cameron, Robert Chambers, Admos Chimhowu, John Harriss, Teresa Hayter, Uma Kothari, David Lewis, Ruth Pearson, Phil Woodhouse.

Hb ISBN 978 1 84277 524 0
Pb ISBN 978 1 84277 525 7

# THE GLOBAL WOMEN'S MOVEMENT
## Origins, Issues and Strategies
### *Peggy Antrobus*

The spread and consolidation of the women's movement in North and South over the past 30 years looks set to shape the course of social progress over the next generation. Peggy Antrobus asks: Where are women now in the struggle against gender inequality? What are the common issues that they face around the world? What challenges confront the women's movements? And what strategies are needed to meet them? The author draws on her long experience of feminist activism to set women's movements in their changing national and global context. Her analysis will be an invaluable aid to reflection and action for the next generation of women as they carry through the unfinished business of women's emancipation.

'This is a fascinating book where the researcher and the activist come together to tell the history of a revolutionary movement that changed the way we think about gender and sexuality, social justice and human rights, the political economy and power. The author has the authority of someone who was an active participant in many major events of that history.'
– *Carmen Barroso, Regional Director, International Planned Parenthood Federation, Western Hemisphere Region*

'This reflection on the international women's movement by one of its most important leaders is both timely and stimulating. Locating its origins in the quest for broader social justice, Peggy Antrobus examines this movement over three decades. ... She makes the case that if our movement is to continue to find solutions to the problems of human security and well-being, we must deal as seriously with issues of race and class as we do with patriarchy.'
– *Noeleen Heyzer, Executive Director, UNIFEM*

Hb ISBN 978 1 84277 016 0
Pb ISBN 978 1 84277 017 7

# FEMINIST POST-DEVELOPMENT THOUGHT
Rethinking Modernity, Post-Colonialism
and Representation
*Edited by Kriemild Saunders*

'This is such an up-to-the-feminist-minute book. If one ever imagines
that radical feminist thinkers or feminist cultural studies scholars can
leave "women in development" to those who know about digging wells
and sampling soil, think again. Kriemild Saunders and her savvy, worldly
contributors make one realize that "development" is about the gendered
constructions of desire, romanticism, icons, co-optation, consumerism
and green tourism'
– *Cynthia Enloe, author of 'Bananas, Beaches and Bases' (new edition)*

'In this landmark volume, world-class feminists undo Western thinking
on gender, development and modernity. Women's empowerment
over materialism, sociality over relentless progress, and sustainability
over biological invasion are some of the post-development alternatives
proposed. Indeed, the lively theory and vivid examples show that the
well-being of women in the South is tied up with the fate of the planet
itself. This indispensable resource will appeal to scholars
and activists in many fields.'
– *Aihwa Ong, author of 'Flexible Citizenship: the Cultural Logic of
Transnationality' and 'Buddha in Hiding: Refugees, Citizenship, and the New
America'*

'Here is a challenging set of inquiries about "development" from various
feminist perspectives, particularly the questions of progress and post-
development alternatives. This anthology is a noteworthy contribution
to current discussions about globalization, survival, the ecological crisis
and strategies for action.'
– *Lourdes Benería, Professor of City and Regional Planning
and Women's Studies Director, Cornell University*

Hb ISBN 978 1 85649 946 0
Pb ISBN 978 1 85649 947 7

# THE WOMEN, GENDER
# AND DEVELOPMENT READER

*Edited by Nalini Visvanathan (co-ordinator), Lynn Duggan,*
*Laurie Nisonoff and Nan Wiegersma*

Third World women were long the undervalued and ignored actors in
the development process but are now recognized as playing a critical
role. This book has been designed as a comprehensive reader presenting
the best of the now vast body of literature that has grown up alongside
this acknowledgement.

The book is divided into five parts, incorporating readings from the
leading experts and authorities in each field. The first part acts as an
introduction to the field, examining the key theoretical debates and
discourses surrounding women and development from a historical
perspective. Distinguished practitioners explore the ideas and
concepts fundamental for understanding the area: class, 'race' and
ethnicity, religion, reproduction, persistent inequalities, colonialism,
modernization, economic exclusion and patriarchy.

Part two goes on to look at the household as a unit of analysis,
exploring sexuality, single-parent families, agricultural production,
and environmental relationships, while the third part locates women
within the global economy, addressing issues such as industrialization,
multi-national companies, Free Trade Zones, the informal sector and
the feminization of labour. Part four views the social transformation
of women as a consequence of Structural Adjustment Policies and
intrusive state policies into women's health, reproductive rights and
sexuality. Next, the volume poses the fundamental questions around
women and ideology; do national liberation struggles conflict with
feminist movements? What is the impact of religious fundamentalism?
Are socialist development processes similar or dissimilar to capitalist
processes? How has the transition to capitalism affected women? The
final section of the book shows how women from the ground up are
organizing themselves for change.

Hb ISBN 978 1 85649 141 9
Pb ISBN 978 1 85649 142 6